Robert Prest was born in 1949 and ec
He obtained a flying scholarship and j<
basic training on Jet Provosts and adv
Hunters, he graduated from the Phanto
sion Unit) in 1971. His first operationa p
at Leuchars. He returned to Coningsby for the QWI (Qualified
Weapons Instructor) course, after which he completed 3 years on the
OCU staff, where his speciality was teaching Air Combat Tactics.
Following tours with 92 and 23 Squadrons, he left the RAF in 1980.
The next five years were spent flying Jaguars in Oman with SOAF
(Sultan of Oman's Air Force) and Nigeria (with British Aerospace
Jaguar Training team). That marked the end of his military flying.
Since then, he has pursued a civil aviation career with various airlines
in the Middle and Far East, flying a variety of Boeing and Airbus air-
craft, from the B737 and B767 to the A330/340 and B747, finally re-
tiring on the B777. In retirement, he still maintains a passion for
aviation, albeit in the slightly slower form of floatplanes.

F4 PHANTOM

Robert Prest

SILVERTAIL BOOKS • *London*

Contents

Foreword

As boy growing up in Cambridge I used to visit the central library with what now seems like swottish frequency. But I wasn't
studying for exams or coursework. Instead I was working my way
through the city's well-stocked shelves of aviation books. I discovered gems from writers like Bill Gunston (still a favourite), Arthur
Reed, Robert Jackson and Ralph Barker. And while I was aware of
Bob Prest's memoir *F-4 Phantom: A Pilot's Story*, I'm not sure I ever
read it. I think perhaps even then I suspected its appeal lay in the
strength of the writing rather than in the nuts and bolts of the information it would impart. Maximum speed, altitude, thrust in full reheat, or bomb loads didn't appear to be recorded. There were few
photographs.

It turns out, though, that I just wasn't ready for it.

Because when, thirty years later, I wanted to know what it *feels*
like to fly a F-4 on a lonely patrol out over the North Sea at night I
discovered that nothing else captured it quite like Bob Prest's book.
I was researching a book about HMS *Ark Royal* and her air group of
Phantoms and Buccaneers and, while Bob never flew his jet from the
deck of an aircraft carrier, once in the air his job was the same as his
naval counterparts. Based at RAF Leuchars in the 1970s, he, like
them, was charged with facing down threat from the Bears and
Bisons of the Soviet's long-range bomber force. But a brief summary
of what the book is about hardly does it justice. What's rare is the
quality of the writing. *F-4 Phantom* is distinguished by the kind of
precision and poetry that are more readily associated with bygone
classics like *Sagittarius Rising, Flight to Arras, The Last Enemy*.

Instead of the obvious romance of open cockpits, fabric and
propellors, Bob may have been writing about a twenty-five ton jet
war machine capable of flying at twice the speed of sound, but, like
Lewis, St Exupéry and Hillary, he was somehow able to bottle the

lightning and capture the magic of flying for readers. The result is a unique portrait of a pilot's life and a rich slice of RAF history: a special book that's as readable and rewarding now as it was when it was first published. A classic.

ROWLAND WHITE, 2017

1

First Glance

The newsmen come to tour the base today. The Station Commander briefs them and conducts them round the station. Their cameras and microphones, trailing flex, seek out the obvious and the heroic, channelling it down into tubes and valves to project across space and squeeze out once again into a million homes announcing the message 'Sleep well in your beds tonight, for while you sleep, your Air Force is awake guarding your castle ...'

Into the Alert hangar the cameras go, and the non-military mind of ITN *News-at-Ten* strives to make sense of the steel bulk that lurks in the shadows, solidly squat, its silence broken by the soft hum of the auxiliary power unit pumping amps into the sleeping circuits. The cameras will circle the monster, pause to peer into the maw of the intakes, scan the slab-sided walls of the fuselage, gaze into the black corrugated depths of the twin jetpipes before moving away into the crewroom to interview the more human elements of the machine.

There are two hangars housing two of these primeval looking beasts, but one room houses the four Lords of the Flies who sit in easy chairs lazily leafing through *Playboy* and *Penthouse*, studiously and politely answering the questions the amateurs pose on behalf of those hidden millions. To heighten their confidence still further, the Base Commander initiates an alert from the tower and the viewer at home will see those two monsters leap into burning life at the command of their space-suited masters. Within three minutes they will hear four sets of turbines begin to revolve, and almost immediately they will see two missile-carrying shapes hurrying in line astern down a blue-amber lit taxiway to line up echelon starboard on a diamond-studded launch pad, grey by day, black by night, before leaping off into the evening sky, each trailing a shock of flame as they lance heavenward to make war, leaving behind the familiar roll of godly thunder.

The Base Commander smiles, thanks the audience for their attention with a sincere warning about national security and departs, leaving the population contentedly secure as it switches over to *Coronation Street*, where life is just as remote as that of the Lords they have just witnessed climbing into the sky on a banner of flame. The safety of Britain is indeed in the hands of those two, but as for the rest of us, we reside in the bar talking in loud, uncoordinated voices, quaffing draught lager and throwing arrows at the board, never thinking of the time when we too might have to leap off into the cold night air to chase a mysterious target on a radar screen. Sleep in Peace.

2

....

In the Beginning

I wait three years before I fly the beast for the first time. But although the tunnel may be three years long, my patience is absolute because I have already waited to enter this world of aviation for two decades. To be sure, I have passed through the phases. I have built Airfix kits and balsa wood gliders. I have spent hours on the Common launching the models into the wind. I have skimped and saved, sixpence every week, to turn my room into a veritable aerodrome, littered at first with the camouflaged, propellered relics of World War Two, and later with the sleek, silvery jets.

One of the jets catches my fancy in a curious fashion, for it is not particularly sleek and the pieces glue to each other at angles that strike me as odd, even taking into account my boyish incompetence. I study the instructions hard but they confirm that I am not in error. The shape is as it should be, yet I scratch my head and look again at the name stencilled on the cardboard box. McDonnell Phantom.

Every spare minute of the waking day I spend poring over books on flight, aeroplanes, things mechanical. My library of books, magazines, scrapbooks full of news-cuttings, they grow till I have nowhere to put them all and they start to gather dust, but I refuse to part with them. The family look on with amused tolerance and wait for me to grow out of the phase, but while my fellow schoolboys do indeed tire and turn their attention to pop music, girls and earthy pursuits, I remain in my second childhood, retarded and refusing to acknowledge anything else but the supremacy of aviation. I have a few other eccentric compatriots, but their obsessions lie with ships, trains, fire-engines, all the stuff of which boyhood dreams are made.

I play truant from school to go and visit the Airport, standing in the biting wind up on the spectators' gallery for hours on end and simply watching the machines come and go. I ride miles on my bicycle to the air shows – Biggin Hill, Farnborough, Duxford – and I stare longingly at these heroes as they swagger out to their machines and roar off to dazzle us with their expertise. At one of these displays I meet the living copy of that curious model in my room. It is big, much bigger than I imagined possible for a fighter aeroplane, as I walk round the example standing in the static display and climb up the long ladder to peer at the baffling collection of switches and instruments in the large cockpit. It belongs to the Royal Navy, and later on the pilot bends it around the sky in a startling display of reverberating thunder, a brutish shape, angular camouflage wreathed in high performance condensation mist, afterburner tailpipes glowing orange, deafening, gone in a flash up, up into the deep blue. I stand with head craned back, staring up after it, long after it has gone and I resolve ...

The memory lingers faintly at the back of my mind, but the resolve is strong as I struggle through differential calculus and the Hundred Years' War, Macbeth and Ovid, the economic distribution of cattle in Argentina. But while one half of my mind does battle with binary equations, the other looks forward to Thursday afternoons with the Combined Cadet Force, where for the whole afternoon I can live aeroplanes with the RAF contingent. Gliding courses, flying scholarships, summer camps at RAF bases, they all serve to keep me sane as I do my 'time', complete my enforced confinement to the classroom, after which I am free to enter that three-year tunnel. I plunge into it without a moment's hesitation. I sweat and suffer the physical toil of Initial Training School, hot days on the drill square, the assault course, canoeing down rivers, climbing mountains, cold nights of escape and evasion in the fields and forests dodging the 'Rock Apes', the RAF Regiment troops. To be caught by them invites dire consequences and this proves a wonderful motivation to spur us on when fatigue begins to take a grip.

I slog through Basic Flying School, many hours of repetition as I practise, and practise yet again those early bread-and-butter manoeuvres to build the foundation of my trade. The Jet Provost Mk3 Basic Trainer. Jet. It is just as silky and smooth as I imagined it would be. The very word itself spells that out for me, an image of something free and fast-flowing. Jet.

In this machine I take to the air like a duck to water. I tell myself I was born to fly, it is my destiny, it is the will of God, and thus at one stroke I justify my whole existence to worried parents anxious for a better, more traditional return for their expensive investment in my education – 'Why don't you become a doctor, or a lawyer or join the Foreign Service? What do you want to become a *pilot* for? It's so dangerous!' It takes a long time before they are finally convinced that I am not about to abandon those childhood dreams and they finally resign themselves to my will.

Low-level navigation at 180 knots and my mind boggles as the world rockets past below. I quickly get lost while still only thirty miles out from base in the low-flying area and I think – How can Man live at such speeds. But slowly the pieces fall into place as I gain experience, taking my first faltering steps on that long road.

A machine comes on a practice diversion to our timid Training Command airfield tucked away in the Vale of York. We all tumble outside to watch it go round the pattern. It is only the second time I've seen it since that day at the air show, months ago. It cruises through the circuit, in and out, trailing long plumes of smoke from its engines. Our trainers are also in the air, but they are minute in comparison and they are silent compared to the muted thunder of this beast. Its great bulk is full of menace, threatening; indeed the trainers are forced to climb out of the way because it overhauls them rapidly in the pattern. It is a new machine in the Air Force inventory at this time and so Air Traffic give it priority over the lesser beings in the circuit, and now its pilot is obviously delighted at being able to show off his big, solid fighter machine to the curious, admiring audience gazing up from the ground. To me, it looks evil and brutal, a bull shark entering a pool full of minnows and pilot fish, a Dreadnought battle-cruiser surrounded by trawlers. It departs suddenly, in an appropriately spectacular fashion, accelerating vividly around the finals turn, blasting past over our heads with its tail on fire and then pulling up to punch a hole through the clouds, its bulk belying its speed. When it is gone, the trainers drop back into the pattern, fluttering down to buzz around the circuit, like little clockwork motors in comparison to the war machine that has just departed. This makes the ultimate impression on me and once again, I resolve ...

At Advanced Training, flying the Gnat – sports car of the air – I experience the first thrills of high performance flying, supersonic high altitude, subsonic low level. Hawker Siddeley Gnat of the Red Arrows, twinkling rolls (bugbear of student pilots striving for precision), scarlet flash hurtling down valleys and across lochs, sliding through impossibly narrow passes, pulling up over ridges, rolling over and dropping down into ravine, recover and away, joyous carefree days training to be fighter pilots, the young Tigers.

Graduate with wings and on to the Hunter at Tactical Weapons School. Hawker Hunter. To the man in the street, 1950s, Farnborough Air Show, hot summer days, Neville Duke and Hunter, sleek of frame, shiny silver and occasionally virgin white, here and gone in a Doppler wave of howling Avon (the famous 'Blue Note'), or perhaps just a pencil thin trail of white vapour bisecting the heaven, from one horizon through the zenith and on to the other, swift silent mysterious man-machine remotely godly way up there in the sky. Or maybe sixteen of the breed, black and 'Treble One', masters of the art of mass formation aerobatics wheeling in a diamond wedge, toylike, cohesive, graceful above the popcorn-munching crowds gazing up in admiration at those magnificent men in their magnificent machines.

To me, 1972, Hawker Siddeley Hunter, obsolescent, ergonomic nightmare of haphazard instrumentation, illogical positioning of booster pump switches, UHF radio set, G4 compass, inverter circuit breakers, temperamental starter motors, oil-and hydraulic-streaked dirty grey belly, bug spattered windscreen and flaking paintwork. Yet it is functional and purposeful, an ageing lady no longer beautiful but still unique, retaining its nostalgic charisma and reminiscing on past glories as steely new breeds thunder overhead, vaunting their afterburners and stealing all the limelight.

Nevertheless, here at Chivenor I am introduced to the first stages of applied flying, using my steed as a weapon of war rather than just a pure mount. I get a taste of what is to come; long days (and sometimes nights) of formation flying – high and low, air combat (the sport of kings), two-and four-ship strike, air-to-air and air-to-ground gunnery, bombing, rocketry, all the skills of the fighter pilot. It is blood, sweat and practice all the way, the tunnel is long, strewn with pitfalls, challenging, demanding and yet enjoyable as well. But there is a light, a 'dream' at the end of the tunnel, towards which I work with a single-minded purpose for those three long years through the thick and thin of review boards, 'chop rides' and comrades falling by the wayside. The standards are high and so therefore is the failure rate. I care not. I have known for a long time what I want and over those years of resolution I have been tantalised and tempted by the 'dream' – now at last the dream materialises. On 228 Phantom OCU I begin my long affair with the machine that has developed into another charismatic legend in its own time, the Phantom F4.

If the road before was hard, now it is sheer travail. Although I fly the beast for the first time, it is not new to me for I have spent many hours in the classroom learning the routeings of its hydraulic sinews and electric veins. The ground school lecturers have taken me beneath the duralumin and titanium skin to lay bare its metallic innards. They have rationalised the intricate collection of wire, pressed steel, carbon fibre, bakelite and vulcanised rubber that lies beneath that purposefully smooth exterior. They have attempted to explain the thoughts that ran through the minds of the McDonnell designers when they decided the wing tips should slope up 12 degrees, and the tailplane should angle down 23, that the spoilers and ailerons should move as they do, and the flaps and speedbrakes should droop to the position they do. I learn the purpose behind their madness. I have studied the aerodynamics behind the concept and they have expounded at some length about adverse yaw, boundary layer separation, post-stall departure, manoeuvre buffet and high-speed variation of aerodynamic centre, neutral point, stability index and C of G shift. I acquire a whole new vocabulary and my conversation is laced with jargon. I know, on paper at least, what to expect from this machine in the air, in each corner of the flight envelope. From the myriad graphs that profess to predict, I can sit down and determine in which region of flight it will be happiest, where flight will be smooth, stable and relaxed, and at the other extreme, where I will have to devote 100 per cent of my skills and concentration to prevent the machine from falling from the sky and killing me. The computers, mathematicians, aerodynamicists and test pilots created these theoretical and statistical nominals of performance, studied them and drew their operating parameters long before the first F4 left the ground at St Louis, Missouri. They fed the data into their simulator to produce a machine that flew like the real thing and yet never left the ground. So, sure enough, I too, like thousands of F4 pilots before me, follow their precedent and after those four weeks of theory in the classroom, I gather my kit and move across to the simulator, that boon or bugbear (depending on your point of view) of modern flying.

It is housed in a huge white corrugated building cast from iron, and I have to show my pass before the sergeant at the gate will press a button allowing the door to swing open to let me in. There are two simulators in this building and each costs as much, if not more than the real thing. In the next few months at this OCU, I will get to know them very well. But for now, I practise my drills and procedures. I start the engines, take off, perform supersonic runs, shoot innumerable instrument approaches on one engine and two. I experience fires, flameouts, hydraulic and electrical failures, trim runaways, pressurisation blowouts, engine and control malfunctions, and I emerge two hours later, a couple of pounds lighter in sweat but having put to synthetic practice all the theoretical knowledge gleaned in the classroom. It is all a build-up to the first time in the air, the third stage when I will get to know how the bird really performs, when I learn how I will get on with this machine that is to be my mount for the next few years. This is when I will formulate my own opinions about its little quirks and foibles, its deficiencies that others have complained about, or its finer points over which others have eulogised. In the end, in the long run, only I will be the judge.

Preparing for modern flight can be a lengthy business. For my one-hour flight, I will often spend two hours in preparation. I report to the crew locker room at 07.30, where I spend ten minutes struggling into the paraphernalia of jet flight. Over cotton vest and longjohns I don a G-suit, jungle green and festooned with laced webbing that secures the air bladders to my calves and thighs. I zip up the side fasteners, securing the whole garment and leaving the lower part of my body in the vice-like grip of artificial fibre. I am now better equipped to withstand the extra stresses of combat. Then comes the struggle of inserting my body into the rubberised immersion suit that will keep me alive for several hours in the sub-zero temperature of the midwinter North Sea – not the best of places for man, and although I curse and swear as I push the G-suit hose, my head and arms through their respective rubber-sealed holes, I know this suit can mean the difference between life and death. Two heavy waterproof zips, front and rear leave me feeling rigid and uncomfortable. I feel even more Michelin-like after wriggling into the skeletal harness. It too is shaded dull green. A 'Mae West' (better known as Lifejacket Mk2, fluorescent orange and ravelled up) is incorporated and with its straps and buckles, is of Houdini-like ingenuity. I lace up my black hide flying boots and don a pair of cream pigskin chamois gloves before finally picking up my white Mk3 helmet, with its PREST stencilled in black on the crown and dayglo cutouts of Phantoms silhouetted on the squadron crest.

I look in the mirror. The reflection that stares back at me is a bizarre one. I look just like the 1950 popular conception of 'the Thing That Came from Outer Space'. With helmet on, I move to the end of the room. The Godfrey Test Cabinet in the corner checks out my RT lead, miniature oxygen regulator and oxygen mask in a two-minute session of blinking lights, squeaking tones and winking dollseyes. I am ready.

Forty-five minutes later, the Duty Instructor finishes a lengthy dissertation on the format of the coming flight; I sign authorisation sheet, Royal Flight Order Books, consult wind velocity and temperature charts, note Diversion and Base weather, check Notams and Air Traffic warnings, receive final words from Ops Officer on serviceability state and configuration of our particular machine, and finally board the crew coach for a two-minute ride to the line hut, a quarter of a mile away.

The scent of Avtur hangs heavily in the autumn air as we stand for a moment and seek out our particular aircraft from amongst the serried rows of parked Phantoms glistening wetly, camouflaged grey in the cold sunlight after their all-night stand in the open. We enter the wooden line hut where a cheerful crew of NCOs waits on the other side of the long white counter separating aircrew from groundcrew. They are the Debrief Team, each expert in his own field, troubleshooters and analysts ready to diagnose instantly or to advise the doubtful aircrewman on the daily foibles of his sick bird.

To the Sergeant we turn to query the vagaries of Spey engines, to the Corporal we direct questions on AWG 12 radar, from the mouth of the Chief Tech come pearls of wisdom on INAS and its peculiarities of the day. We have to consult them several times as we leaf through the Form 700, the Radar Log and INAS Log. 'Two Red Star engines, flight idling not incorporated, Phantom STI deratings carried out, left engine bleed lights come on when flap is selected down, power controls modified to incorporate utility hydraulics, check hyd, caption comes on when undercarriage lowered …' I continue to read through four red and green pages of points to be noted regarding the aircraft and I inwardly receive and digest the information, so that should a caption illuminate, I will think twice and consult my mental pigeon-hole before shouting panic over the airwaves.

The Form 700 is a thick book and it enfolds the history of aircraft XT 893. I know how many hours the airframe has flown since it was delivered from McDonnells, how many hours to its next primary servicing, how often the engines have been started, how many take-offs and landings, pressurisations, engine starter changes there have been. From this document I can discover all the limitations, modifications, extensions to servicing dates that I require, but today I am mainly interested in how many thousands of pounds of fuel they have loaded on board, what stores I am carrying, whether oxygen, oil and hydraulic tanks have been replenished and whether the chute has been repacked. After which I turn to yet another section to see whether any malfunctions occurred on the previous mission, and more to the point, what was done about it. Only then, when I am completely satisfied, am I allowed to put my signature in the acceptance column which thus says that I, as captain, accept as fit to fly one £2.5 million Phantom F4 Fighter Bomber, property of HM Government, and which will cost the Air Force £1,000 for the next hour's flying. I sign.

We pick up our bonedomes and kneepads, note the aircraft slot number, check that a starter crew awaits us, and once again go outside.

The starter crew is indeed ready and waiting. At other stations, on older, more mundane machines, groundcrew life can appear bland and colourless. The efficiency is there, but now that the thrill is gone, he finds it difficult to tear himself away from the coffee-drinking, card-playing warmth of his crewroom and venture out into the cold for the boring task of seeing yet another student mission depart. But, at this station, on this aeroplane, things are different. To start with, not one but two crew chiefs await me, which is logical for it takes two to fly the machine. Moreover their responsibility on this ship is a diverse one, not simply to hand the straps to the pilot, but to carry out several pre- and post-start checks on the airframe. Now as they see us approaching one of them turns to the yellow Houchin generator parked beside the aircraft and stabs the starter button with his thumb. The diesel engine groans and coughs a couple of times and then wheezes into an uncertain life at first, but with gradually growing strength and authority as combustion warms its metal frame until it runs with an insistent and deafening roar.

A brief exchange of greetings takes place between the four of us before the navigator climbs the metal ladder clipped to the left intake while I stow my helmet on the ground and commence a quick walk round the aircraft. This walk round is a ritual that sometimes amuses me, for the habit is as old as flying itself. It takes a score of manhours' servicing for every manhour of flight, and yet I will insist on kicking the tyres, thumping drop tanks, peering up wheelbays at hydraulic lines, oleo gauges, pneumatic accumulator gauges, power control accumulator gauges, wing fold pins, flaps and speedbrakes, starter and auxiliary air doors. I gaze for seconds up the twin black maws of the jetpipes and run my eyes over their steely complexity; I stare up at the swept fin sixteen feet above me to ensure both pitot and bellows headcovers have been removed. I examine the great steel hook for cracks, leaks, loose screws, examine the stabilator tips for damage due to somebody's over-rotated take-off. I look for open panels, popped rivets, sheared fastenings, non-standard drips and leaks. I push, prod, poke and peer my way round till I am back at the foot of the ladder, and once again, after 300-odd times of doing the same sort of thing, I have found nothing amiss. The fact is, if the technicians with their hundreds of hours of detailed engineering training have gone right ahead and assembled a bolt the wrong way round, then I doubt very much whether I, in my two-minute walk, will be able to notice. But occasionally an eagle-eyed aviator notices a crack here, a screw loose there, a wrongly fitted fire wire here, and for his vigilance he is awarded a 'Good Show' in the Flight Safety mags. So indeed I try hard to ensure that all is as it should be, but for my pains all I have found is the occasional tyre needing a few more psi of air, or a union nut needing a few more ft/lbs of torque to seal the drip of oil from the starter bay. But I am happy that it should be that way, for the pilot's worst enemy is the incompetent 'Murphy' in the hangar. All else I can control, difficult interceptions, bad weather, a stiff formation ride, instrument rating tests, but I am at the mercy of that insufficiently torqued bolt on the jetpipe shroud that will work loose somewhere in the bowels of the aircraft, to release a blast of hot air at 600°C onto the waiting firewire lining the fuselage walls that will in turn cause a bright red 'FIRE' caption to illuminate (spuriously) in the cockpit, leaving me with the justifiable option to eject and abandon £2.5 million to a needless watery grave.

I pick my helmet up from the concrete floor and climb ten feet up to the cockpit. My navigator has already been in there, for the glow of warning lights bears witness to his passing. He has sat in my seat, rearranged a few switches in accordance with his checklist and then looked out at the crewchief standing by the throbbing Houchin. The crewchief has consulted his dials, and satisfied that 200 volts, 3-phase, 400 cycles AC is being generated, gives the navigator a thumbs up, the signal for the navigator to move two generator switches on the starboard front console from 'Off' to 'Ext On', an action that sucks those electrons through the thick black hose snaking from the Houchin up through a plug in the left intake and into the multiple mileage of wiring that make up the electrical busbars in the aircraft. To signify their approval of his action, gyros start up, warning relays click closed and needles on gauges come to quivering life. This little part of his duties done, the Nav moves to his home in the rear cockpit and busies himself with the mysterious happenings that go on there, unknown to me, as he prepares himself to fly.

Before I step down into my cockpit, I balance precariously with one foot on the ladder, the other on the wedge-shaped top of the intake ramp, holding onto the clamshell canopy for support, and I examine the top surfaces that have been hidden to me during my walk round on the ground. How can such a shape fly, I wonder. The wing-tips are cranked up, the stabilators sharply raked down, the fuselage slab-sided and studded with vent holes and auxiliary air intakes, the wing delta-shaped and absurdly thin for the task in hand – 'looks like they delivered it upside down' – 'a triumph of thrust over aerodynamics' – and yet if you don't look at it too closely …

Today you will not hear any Phantom pilot call his aeroplane beautiful, for beauty is the last emotion in the brain as 40,000 pounds of thrust catapults the reeling senses inexorably heavenward while heads, hands and feet struggle to maintain mastery over the forces unleashed. And yet if you don't look at it *too* closely, the F4 is indeed a beautiful if not a classic shape in the modern art form, brutally purposeful, functionally precise, solid and dynamic, it shares the same qualities as the other heavy Mach 2 brigade of fighters such as the Lightning, Voodoo, Thunderchief, Delta Dart – a breed that is as unique in form and lines as those previous classics, the Spitfire and Hunter. So that is why, in moments of peace, flying battle formation – sunset and contrails – on the way home, watching an F4 taxiing out to the runway, seeing them stretched in serried ranks along the line, then the thought that this is a beautiful machine is allowed to rise in my mind.

Strapping into an aeroplane can be a thing of pleasure, simplicity itself, or it can be a neck-breaking, finger-catching torture. Martin Baker has designed ejection seats for the Air Force ever since the concept of rapid departure from aircraft in flight was first considered. His seats range from the Mk1 to the Mk10. I sit on the Mk7a. The seat embodies the experience of twenty years of design. It is a pleasure to strap into this seat, as much so as it was a chore to attach oneself to, say, the seat in a Canberra T4. Gone are the festoons of parachute and harness straps and buckles with adjusting bands and loops littering the cockpit. On the F4 I already wear my harness before entering the aircraft. All I have to do is clip myself to the seat via two Koch fasteners at shoulder level and slot two lap straps and a negative G strap into the quick release box situated, midriff-high, on my combined harness. I then operate the locking mechanism and give a brief tug on each of the straps in turn to leave me mated to the seat, immovable Operate the locking mechanism (Go Forward lever) again and I can lean forward with the permission of the inertial reel shoulder straps unwinding inside the back of the seat and holding me through the yokes of the Koch buckles. All that remains is to fasten two leg restraining straps round my legs just below each knee and to clip the PSP dinghy lanyard to my harness; the process is complete in two minutes.

The final touch involves taking my helmet from the airman who has been standing on the ladder ready to offer any assistance required. In a final burst of activity I don the helmet, fasten the chamois chin strap, ease the side fasteners on the bonedome forward to make the fit even tighter, remove my visor dust cover and stow it in my kneepocket, plug my PEC connector onto the seat, plug the mic-tel lead of my helmet into the PEC portion, slot the oxygen mask hose over the outlet of the finely engineered miniature oxygen regulator clipped to my chest and select Oxygen On. A white dolls-eye indicates oxygen flowing, after which I press the P-type oxygen mask to my face and operate the over-centre lever to seal the rubber and bakelite to my face. Then I reach up and ensure I can reach the face screen ejection handle on my seat before giving a thumbs up to the crewman waiting. This is the signal for him to remove the two pins on the top of the seat and hand them to me to push into the holes provided on the left console to join the five others I have already removed and placed there. 'Face screenpin, seat pan, guillotine, banana sear link, canopy initiators (two of them), rocket motor ...' Rocket motor. This is the subtle difference between this seat and any other. Only a few minor details exist on the outside to tell the inexperienced eye that it is possible for me to operate this seat while sitting on the ground with zero velocity, and leave the aircraft at sixty-four feet per second under the influence of an ejection gun cartridge followed a fraction of a second later by an even greater surge of thrust as a six-foot lanyard attached to the seat triggers a pack of booster rockets that send me rushing in a smooth parabolic curve 300 feet into the air. There, in a three-second flurry of whirring barostats, triprods, release locks and drogue chutes I separate from my seat and float down to the ground beneath a multi-coloured twenty-four-foot silk canopy, and thirty seconds after initiating the ejection sequence I am picking myself up from the ground and dazedly wondering what went wrong as I contemplate the burning wreckage. It is a big seat in a big cockpit, surprisingly comfortable, which is good for later on I will have to spend up to ten hours at a stretch in that seat and it will not be the torture it could have been.

And so I start up, taxi, line up and take-off, and in the air, I float through the exercises, manoeuvres and procedures that I have practised many times on the ground, and because 'practice makes perfect' I slip easily into my role. The long days of training leave me well prepared for the adventures to come. My aircraft and I, we are together.

3

....

'Fourteen 104s Inbound'

'Four-three ... er ... we have a contact ... er ... bearing 060, eighty miles, suspected faker, request you ident, over'.

Exercise Strong Express, 07.00; I have been sitting on CAP for three hours circling the task force of ships progressing slowly southwards on the ocean below me.

'Roger Four-three leaving CAP to investigate, request exercise instructions.'

'Four-three exercise ident.'

'Rog ...!' The voice comes from deep in the bowels of United States carrier *John F. Kennedy,* flagship of the task force that is making its way south down the English Channel to rendezvous with another convoy of warships before the final battle. It is a big juicy target for any marauding Bear pilot and his Kangaroo missile. That is why I am here; to guard and protect. Our squadron will maintain a twenty-four-hour CAP for the three days it takes the fleet to transit our Air Defence territory. This is part and parcel of our main role, maritime air defence. Now those few words from the controller in the bowels of the *JFK,* that little green blip on his smokey radar tube, spells trouble approaching for the ships. For me it means an adrenalin-pumping surge of excitement, some welcome activity to allay the boredom of a seemingly endless trek round the CAP pattern with nothing but the glowing instruments to hold my attention. My navigator, sitting six feet behind me, stirs himself out of the stupor into which he has fallen and on my repeater scope in the front cockpit I can see his elevation strobes waving gently up and down as he commands the scanner in the nose to nod gently under the influence of the hydraulic servos, the thin pencil-like radar beam sweeping out over the miles and spreading to cover many thousands of feet of sky. Anything that flies into that beam we will see. He is searching in the pulse doppler mode, which gives us a supreme advantage, for that target could be lurking at fifty feet in the ground clutter, apparently safe from the prying eyes of radar, yet we would see him. The energy we are generating in one simple pulse, would that we could harness it, could provide power enough to light a small village.

'He bears 080 from you now, range fifty miles and closing. No IFF squawk observed, suspect hostile but we still want an ident.' The southern accent drawls across the airwaves into our aeroplane. I send back a laconic 'Rog' in reply. I have accelerated to combat speed, I have tuned my four Sparrow missiles, the four Sidewinder heat-seekers are glowing ready. All eight missiles are armed and ready to go, so the Missile Status panel tells me, and therefore my forefinger sticks prudently forward, clear of the red unguarded trigger on the moulded stick grip in my right hand. I am carrying dummy hybrid missiles, but I am practising for the real thing. I take no chances. My eyes are intent on the green B scope in front of me, following every movement of the sweep as it leaves its faint afterglow in its horizontal journey to and fro across the screen.

'Okay, I got contact'. His voice is soft and confident from the back. The el-strobes, their job done, are steady and I can see the little shadow that represents a target in PD search. A second later he has acquired it and immediately that magic brain, the fire control computer, generates the various signals and symbols to give us the information we will need to complete the intercept successfully. My eyes take it all in automatically in fractions of a second – the target, whatever it is, is flying at a height of 8,000 feet, he is closing head on with us at a combined velocity of 900 knots TAS, which gives him a ground speed of 500 knots.

A little dot weaving gently in the centre of the scope tells me I am on a collision course with him. The computer has even generated a marker to tell me when it estimates I will be in range to launch the Sparrow missiles at my unseen target. All I have to do is to fly that dot in the middle of the circle until the 'In Range' light illuminates. My right finger will then flex, and seconds later my aircraft will be lighter by one Sparrow which will have departed and homed on the target, its own little radar having locked on to guide it there, explosion, death; remote, unseen, unknown, emotionless modern warfare.

However, this particular bogey could be a friendly aircraft returning perhaps without a radio, and so I must identify before I kill. Therefore we position ourselves for an attack from the stern, sneaking round and behind without (hopefully) being seen. Westinghouse have simplified our task by providing us with this black magic radar. In its electronic innards are stored the complex means whereby we are able to baffle the enemy with our attack.

'Four-three to Buzzard Four Zulu, we have a contact bearing 070. We're not sure yet, but there may be more than one of the bogeys. We're closing to investigate.'

'Okay sir, your range from the ship this time is five zero miles.'

I suddenly notice we are in cloud. I glance at the altimeter, 6,000 feet. My navigator confirms my suspicions.

'Those mothers are heading down. Speed has also gone up.'

I acknowledge, check that my radio altimeter is switched on and reading, and ease gently downwards, still enveloped in the cloud. The target or targets are now displaced about five miles on our port and as they reach the 45-degree etching on the scope at seven miles, so we start a gentle turn to port, using 45 degrees of bank. We turn in behind the contacts at two miles and it is easy to see from the search picture that there are quite a few of them, maybe five or six … 2,000 feet, and I continue my slow descent. I notice my speed is up to 480 knots to stay with the bogeys. 1,000 feet … the radio altimeter and pressure altimeter agree roughly and satisfied that I am not about to fly into the sea I keep on going down. We are now thirty miles from the carrier force and closing rapidly. At 800 feet we suddenly burst into the clear air below and my eyes nearly pop out with surprise. Stretched out in front of me from far right to far left are F104s, exercise bogeys all at 300 feet and going hell for leather towards the ship. My surprise lasts a second before I hit the transmit button. Standard RT goes out of the window,

'Hey, we've got ten … no, twelve of them heading straight for you!' The controller wasted no time.

'Okay, hold them off, we'll send you everything we've got! All Buzzard aircraft vector 070 and buster, bogeys twelve-strong heading inbound …'

I only half hear this because I am busy fighting for my life. I have loosed off two Sparrows at two 104s that drifted into my gunsight before a startled squawk from the rear seat sends me into a 5-G break. These guys are no fools. They have stationed two of their number in three-mile trail and well spread to cater for just such an attack, and now these two are homing in fast and smoking. We have been so busy eyeing the main force ahead that we missed these two. My starboard break forces a massive fly through (the 104 turns even worse than the F4), he pulls high and then accelerates downwards and away. We reverse and look for the other. He is a little wiser. He has yo-yoed up into the cloud and now he drops back again and I can imagine him coaxing his gunsight down to bear on my tailpipe. I am having none of that and with full afterburners lit I crank hard into him, giving him an impossible angle off to hack. He too flies through and accelerates away towards the main force. For a few moments, he has successfully taken the heat off his comrades. However, my energy is still high too, having unloaded with full AB and so I have time to place the gunsight reticle on his glowing tailpipe and squeeze off a Sidewinder in his direction. Meanwhile the main battle has been progressing forward and as we set off in pursuit, we see fellow F4s appearing from every direction. The carrier has pulled all the other CAPs off their stations to meet the incoming raid. So now Phantoms wearing the colours of RAF, US Marines, US Navy, are all joined as one in hot pursuit of the enemy, all with 'burners blazing as we weave and duck, zoom and dive back down. We penetrate the carrier's Missile Engagement Zone and the controller is frantically calling on his fighters to haul off or suffer at the hands of his trigger-happy gun and missile crews, but this is peacetime, a war game, and so we ignore him. The Belgians (for that is who they are) are bent on laying their bombs on the carrier and we are bent on harassing them as long as possible to upset their aim, and so in one great gaggle we burn towards the carrier standing out fortress-like in the sea. We are at deck height, easing up slightly to avoid the parked aircraft and weaving madly either side of the aerial studded island. The last impression as we race over is of a huge deck littered with aircraft equipment and at sea of upturned faces gazing up at this aerial madness of a battle rushing past a few feet above their heads, deafening, thrilling.

On the other side, the enemy, their attack completed, all turn port and arc skywards in a left-handed zoom for the sanctuary of the clouds now at 10,000 feet above the carrier. We follow them up, twisting turning and harrying to the end, and now that the fight has moved away from the surface, it becomes truly three-dimensional and the collision hazard becomes a real one as aircraft intent on manoeuvring into someone's six o'clock flash past within feet of each other. And so slowly common sense and coolness prevail. We listen to the cries of the controller sending us back to our respective CAPs, and we leave the Starfighters to run for their distant home, disappearing in a gaggle over the horizon, the smoke trails from their J79s staining the skies long after they are gone.

Meanwhile we all queue up to refuel from the waiting tankers and get down to logging the kills and claims.

4

....

In the Midnight Hour

It is Sunday today and on Sundays the Air Force is off duty, stood down, its minions scattered across country with, as I well know, far from military thoughts occupying their attentions. Although I belong to the Air Force twenty-four hours a day, fifty-two weeks a year, the work for which I am paid uses up but a fraction of that time. I work five days a week, fly for maybe six hours in that week, and on the remaining two days of that week, if I am not on Alert or Exercise, I can be as unmilitary as I wish to be, within the bounds of reason. That is why I know they will come like the proverbial thief in the night, on a weekend while I am watching the midnight movie in some London flat many miles from my base and its hangared aircraft. While I am sitting heavy with dinner, drugged with wine and mesmerised by kaleidoscopic electronics on the screen before me, holding warm flesh in my arms, that is when they will come. Yes, I know that it will be when the clock in the square marches towards the sleepy midnight hours, its balance wheels dripping from the condensation formed by the steady drizzle of frontal low stratus, that will be when the electronics officer in his Bear at 40,000 feet will make the last adjustments to his guidance mechanism before sending the Kangaroo projectile on its short journey through the dank clouds to the earth.

I know this well because we have listened to the lectures on global strategy and tactical warfare. Erudite intelligence officers have expounded at self-important lengths on the channels the enemy mind tracks along. Instructors have outlined political theory, drawn historical precedents, analysed balance of forces and arrived at the same conclusions a caveman would have drawn after two minutes' neanderthal thought. Indeed the whole of my combat training is designed to sneak up on the other fellow undetected if possible, shoot him in the back and run away before he has time to retaliate. So I practise in foul weather, at night and on the occasional weekend because, say what you will, that is when I shall go. Yet in typically human fashion I know that it will not, cannot happen. So weekend follows weekend in secure untroubled bliss and as I sit, no such thought ripples the molecules of my mind, so I wonder if I will even have time to be surprised when that Kangaroo touches down and ignites just down the road in Piccadilly Circus.

I am sitting in the bar, sinking 'frosties' when the telephone rings. Someone picks it up, listens for a moment, replaces the receiver and then turns to inform me that I will be scrambling on northern patrol around midnight. That is in four hours' time. I leave the bar, return to my room, shower and sleep till the alarm clock tells me it is time to go down to the squadron. The Exercise is in its second week, but the fleet is still far to the north, warring off the Norwegian coast. I am to relieve one of our Phantoms on patrol and remain on station till I myself am relieved. I do not know it, but I am about to experience the longest trip I have ever flown in this machine. The plan is that I will scramble to rendezvous with a tanker off the coast of Scotland, and together we will progress north up towards the edge of the Arctic Circle. The briefing is over in minutes, I have done the same many times before, and at midnight I move the twin throttles through the gate, accelerate down the blackness of Leuchars runway and leap up into a warm, starlit September sky. I will not see that runway again for another six hours.

Border radar give me a vector towards the tanker and soon, at 30,000 feet I am in contact with him, both visually and on the radio. He is busy topping up his own tanks from a fellow fuel dispenser and I take up station a half-mile away to port and watch with interest this mating of the two great beasts in the night sky. From this range, they are nothing but a collection of red, green and white lights, a shade brighter than the surrounding specks of heavenly bodies inhabiting the domed vastness. I ease closer, to observe, and the forms take on a more solid outline. The coupling is complete within minutes and probe and drogue separate, the hose twitching with an orgasmic spasm.

The two tanker captains bid farewell and one turns and disappears quickly in the darkness behind, leaving the two of us to continue on our lonely way. On the left, Scotland is a vast expanse of shadows studded with the flashing diamonds of city lights – Aberdeen, and the dimmer emeralds of villages. Along the coast, an occasional ruby flares red, natural gas from the offshore oil rigs burning away in the atmosphere, torches in the night, seemingly very close and yet many miles away, according to Tacan and mapping radar. But such is the pace of jet flight that this panorama also disappears rapidly behind us and soon there is nothing but the sea, grey and gloomy beneath. This too lives a short existence as a belt of altostratus, flat white smoothness, extends to meet us. There is no moon tonight, but even so this whiteness below and the stars above mean the night is not totally black. I am warm and comfortable in my humming air-conditioned office, glowing suffused night-vision red, autopilot smoothness, calm efficiency.

The ghostly needles on the instruments are busy telling many stories to the interested audience in my head. I pick a few at random; one dial says that the plexiglass canopy is doing a good job of keeping a pressure bubble of air around me, protecting me from the alien environment waiting a few feet away. I am a fearful intruder because I know I cannot live outside in this six-mile high world. So I maintain a constant interest in that needle which says the pumps are holding that air bubble at a pressure of 8 pounds per square inch, and I am happy. Two other needles are telling me that the turbines in two Spey 201 Military tubofan engines buried in the belly of the aircraft thirty feet behind me in the darkness are rotating on their shafts at 92 per cent of their maximum allowable revolutions. Two further pointers immediately below these indicate that the gases leaving the combustion chambers are doing so at a comfortable, homely temperature of 586 degrees centigrade, and I am happy. Yet another instrument informs me that the liquid oxygen tank, located three feet below my ejection seat, is now holding 8 litres of the fluid and a blinking dollseye assures me that the liquid is indeed vapourising into gas in the stainless steel lines, filtering past my regulator through my mask and into my lungs so I might continue existing, and I am happy. The stories come from all around my little five-by-three office, and I am happy with the tale being told.

200 miles north of base, my centreline tank has emptied and really for want of something to do, rather than a dire need for fuel, I tell the Victor captain that I would like to top up. He too welcomes the little bit of activity to relieve the silent boredom, and his crew busy themselves lowering the hose drum unit from what used to be the bomb bay (the Victor has been converted from a bomber to the task of airborne petrol station). When the HDU is locked down, the eighty-foot length of refuelling hose is streamed out and he clears me in for contact, 'wet till full!'

Air-to-air refuelling is a tricky task at the best of times. The whole exercise appears improbable. How can anyone fly a probe into that bobbing foot-square target that is progressing through the air at 400 knots, at the mercy of all the hidden stratospheric currents, the whims of meteorology, the slightest twitch of man at the controls. I recall the words of an instructor long ago – 'It's like taking a running fuck at a rolling doughnut.' In the early convex days, I asked my fellow pilots 'How do you do it?'

'Well, you line up this light with that edge … put the basket at eye level but don't look at it … run the E2B compass up the hose … square up the wing markings with the edge of the pod light … come in with offset rudder and kick the probe in … I just do it, don't ask me how!' So I went up by day and practised and practised yet again. It was not impossible. In fact, as in everything else with flying, like riding a bicycle perhaps, it became more and more natural. But, if day tanking is hard work, then night tanking, like night formation, has got to be the be-all and end-all of sweat, labour, fear, tension, concentration and anxiety and desperation and resignation and coordination, at least so it seemed the first few times I tried it during my operational work-up days on the squadron. However, that particular bugbear lost its mystery too. Nevertheless, without a doubt for sheer physical and mental effort, for total unwavering and wholehearted devotion to the task in hand there is nothing else to beat it. This, of course, is if you wish to succeed. I could easily go in there relaxed, carefree, 'doped off', 'thumb in bum, mind in neutral', in which case I would die, and probably take a few poor unsuspecting tanker souls with me. No, I am interested in staying alive, but probably just as important, my professional pride dictates that I will try

24

to plug that probe into that tiny basket first time at every attempt, for that in black and white is the measure of my success, even more so than holes in the gunnery target.

Tonight I am lucky because the night is clear, the air is smooth and there is a definite horizon. On some nights I am forced to refuel in cloud, the drogue whipping around in the turbulent air. The tanker's wing is the only horizontal reference and the rotating Grimes light in its belly casts an eerie glow off the surrounding whiteness, causing my senses to reel with vertigo. On those nights I earn my pay.

I extend the probe, the whole aircraft vibrating as the phallic symbol emerges suddenly from its slot above the starboard intake, to stand ramrod stiff, whiteness quivering in the airflow. I trim the out-of-balance forces caused by the extra drag and slide up towards the great white belly of the Victor. The basket is invisible till I am ten yards away and then I pick up the little green bulbs set in the canvas periphery, outlining my target. I pick my line and move up slowly, steadily. I do not look at the basket as it passes by on its way towards the probe sitting four feet away from my right ear, and I hear and feel the reassuring 'clunk' as it makes contact and see the hose flex slightly as the probe slides home to be gripped by the locking device in the womb of the drogue. Green light on the pod flashes on and my own instrument panel lights wink on in agreement, to show that fuel is rushing at the rate of 4,000 pounds a minute into my depleted tanks. I hold formation with easy gentle movements. The tail of the Victor towers huge above me, its belly a mere fifteen feet from my head, the HDU itself about twenty-five feet away, everything frighteningly close and delicately poised to the untrained eye, but simple routine to me. I can imagine the eyes in the tanker peering down their periscope at my shadowy shape, ensuring that I don't get too close. That makes them nervous. (Tragic irony, as I write; this morning on the news I hear a Victor tanker refuelling two Buccaneers had a mishap and crashed in flames with the loss of four crew. Life continues regardless, and we go refuelling in the afternoon …) In this close union, intercourse at 30,000 feet, we float along, a source of mystery to the sailor staring up from his ship, an object of curiosity to the passenger idly glancing out of his airliner window, the most natural thing to the aircrew in the two metal monsters.

In no time we have had our fill and I draw back and disengage, a fine spray of fuel jetting forth as the connection is broken. I call that I am complete and resume station out of his port side. Because we must fly at the tanker's best speed, the trek to the fleet takes two hours and we finally gain contact with the ships somewhere to the north-west of Bodo in northern Norway. All is quiet. There have been no marauders since nightfall. It is now 02.00. The world is sleeping except for the vigilantes in the air and on the sea. Our controller tonight resides in a Dutch destroyer. His accent is difficult to decipher. We give the correct IFF squawk and authenticate his interrogation. Even so he has taken the precaution of sending the Phantom CAP to intercept us. Now, happy that we are who we say we are and not some hoaxing enemy bomber, he instructs the Phantom to continue on his southerly heading on the long haul back to Leuchars, Scotland. A fellow squadron pilot, he wishes me goodbye and happy hunting. We part from the tanker who goes to set up a racetrack centred on the ships, while I fly a circling patrol round the whole fleet. I settle down to the routine of Combat Air Patrol. Miles to go before I sleep ... Engines, weapon systems, life support systems, all check out okay. Tacan is locked solidly to a Norwegian station; radar sweeps; I continue to do my periodic checks ...

Checks. My life revolves around checks, for only checks keep me alive. The other day I was sitting in the crewroom idly leafing through one of the numerous Flight Safety magazines that are standard crewroom decoration, and my eyes landed on 'Accident of the Month' which told the sad tale of a Harrier pilot who had the misfortune to suffer from nozzle failure just after a VSTOL take-off, with subsequent loss of control. The pilot ejected at very low altitude with the aircraft in a vertical dive, well outside the parameters for the seat, and, needless to say, aircraft, ejection seat and pilot buried themselves deep into the Lincolnshire soil. The subsequent Board of Inquiry discovered that there was no way this pilot was going to survive that emergency simply because he had failed to carry out the most vital of checks, namely that of his ejector seat lifesaver.

The safety pins that are normally inserted in the various sears of the seat unit when the aircraft is on the ground must be removed before getting airborne. The Mk7A rocket seat possesses seven pins that are stowed in the pilot's cockpit. One of these pins disables the rocket part of the system. On this pilot's seat, the pin was found firmly in place – mistake number one. Mistake number two was his failure to remove the pin that makes safe the seat pan ejection handle and in the Harrier, unlike the F4, this is the only ejection handle, there being no upper face blind handle. Tests showed that the pilot had given two tugs on the handle before realising the seat pin was still in place. He removed this pin and dropped it on the cockpit floor (where it was subsequently found) and reinitiated the ejection sequence. But, having released the control column for the first ejection attempt (of necessity a two-handed effort), the aircraft had pitched nose down and in the delay that followed the second ejection attempt, the Harrier was well on its way towards the earth, and the seat (minus its rocket element) was given an impossible task.

I read this and thought incredulously of what must have been a suicidal mental approach to the job. And yet yesterday or the day before … I rush out to the aircraft, we are late, I do a rapid external check, clamber up the ladder and commence to strap in. Simultaneously I am switching on radios, pitot heaters, testing booster pumps, warning lights, selecting Oxygen On, navigation lights to flash, IFF and Tacan modes, all it seems in one breath so I can check in with a 'ready to start' call to my leader because it is 'punchy' and operational to get the formation airborne rapidly, and I am on 43 Fighter Squadron and we are all fighter pilots, aren't we? So that is why I do my checks as I strap in and give a thumbs up to the crewman while he removes the two pins from the top of the seat to join the two canopy initiator pins already waiting there. The next few minutes are one mad rush of RT checks, start engines, check generators, spread wings, check flaps, check flying controls, check trims, check speed brakes, check stab-augs, check gyros, checks, checks by the dozen and it's 'Taxi for Runway 27, QFE 30.35 inches', wave the chocks away, disconnect the groundcrew telelead and follow 200 yards behind leader on the mile-and-a-half trek to the threshold of 27.

Because of this we have time to take our time over the next set of checks, the most vital ones perhaps, and this is where I will live whereas that other pilot died, for my navigator reads it and cross-checks from his flipcards – 'Oxygen, Anti-ice, Trims, Horizons, Compasses, Fuel, Generator Warning Panel, Vent Knobs, Defog, Pitot Heat, Temperature Selector, IFF, Tacan, Circuit Breakers, Hydraulics and Pneumatics, Canopy, Harness and Leg Restraints, PSP Lanyard, Flying Controls, Pins … seven stowed …?' I look again at the corner where the pins are stowed. The red discs on the ends of the pins are covering three empty holes. I look down. Goddamn. Staring at me balefully, seat pan pin firmly in position, rocket pin solidly at home, guillotine pin nicely slotted in. Cold sweat. I say nothing to the navigator, but instead rapidly remove and stow the pins and confirm '7 pins stowed, ready for take-off'. But, in my mind's eye I have visions of a smoking crater and lying beside it a twisted seat with an undeployed 'chute and red pins glinting in the sunlight.

A blip materialises on my radar screen. An electronic pulse has seized on the metal, plucking it from the darkness. We report it. The controller admits he is baffled. It does not figure in any published flight plan. It is not sending out a recognisable identification. He instructs us to investigate. We all know what it probably is – some airliner off course, straying away from the beaten airways track, maybe a fault in its inertial system or a couple of degrees' error in heading undetected by the crew. We don't care; it is there and it is something to do to stop us dozing off in the soporific atmosphere – all quiet on the Northern Front – we home towards the contact and carry out a standard vis-ident approach, stealing up from low in the stern. As we turn in, I look out, eyes straining to penetrate the blackness. There is a patch of sky that is uncharacteristically devoid of stars, a patch that is nevertheless shifting slowly. We close in the turn, and suddenly we can see the rows of lighted portholes running along the sides of the patch. We delay our report for a while and close right up beneath the shape. At this range, it spreads hugely, blanking out half the Milky Way Galaxy. Four long, wispy condensation trails stream from the great engines, the wing tip navigation lights spread from horizon to horizon. It sits solidly, effortlessly, a colossus apparently unmoving, Juggernaut in the Sky. It is a 747 Jumbo, possibly en route to the States from Tokyo via the Polar route? Who knows … who cares? We sit and admire its massiveness

for a while and I smile as I imagine the bustling humanity existing inside, sleeping, eating, drinking, watching the in-flight movies,
trim hostesses tramping the aisles with their trays. I think of the
flight crew sitting quietly bored atop that great fuselage, making
their airways report, filling in the flight log; a moving microcosm of
humanity, a city in the sky, and all blissfully unaware of the Black
Widow, the Black Mamba, the Black Panther, the Tiger Shark lurking a few feet away in the darkness behind watching silently with
glowing eyes, evil dealer of death and destruction, alien war machine ...

I back off and turn away, leaving them to go their peaceful way
while I take my dark beast elsewhere. I have no quarrel with you,
big brother. The last I see of them, they have merged into the velvet
blackness to become yet another star amidst the thousands, a rapidly
dwindling speck of light defying the eye to keep track. Yes, four in
the morning is the world of the jet. They appear, sudden, out of the
sky, and just as they come, they go, truly nations of the air.

I ponder over this analysis. 'A nation' says my dictionary 'is a
people either of diverse races or of common descent who inhabit a
territory bounded by defined limits'. In the air a 747 Jumbo jet is a
nation, because by definition no 'territory' has more clearly defined
'limits'. Within that massive stressed skin there lies a government
with the power elite of president and ministers – the captain and
fellow officers with their ranks and responsibilities. It has its own
social hierarchy of first and economy class, together with the ser-
vants who wait upon them. The nation has its own laws and rules,
its own community facilities and services, and even its money has
its own duty-free value. Its history, however, is a short-lived one.
The nation that flies from Tokyo to New York lasts only nine hours
and forty minutes.

Mind drifts. It is 04.00, I am not in the cockpit of a Phantom
jet orbiting in the middle of nowhere, I am lying in bed, in a darkened room ten ... fifteen years ago, and I am awake in the limbo
land of half sleep, in the twilight zone between dreams and reality.
I lie relaxed, unmoving, my thoughts are of flight and other things
yet to be experienced. Overhead the jet birds, flaps down, float into
Heathrow, tubular steel dropping bat-like down from the heavens
with muted thunder and flashing lights – fantastic monsters trem-

bling earthbound.

My mind projects and I am with them, drifting through the fresh, chilly, early dawn air, over the sleeping houses and waking petrol stations, across brightly lit highways, symmetrical chains that stretch on all sides, a fairyland of illumination as the jet from another world courses over, remote.

The night air is blue-black, but as I look I see the blueness is studded – reds, greens, purples, multi-coloured diamonds set into beckoning runway, approach, taxiway, tarmac, beacons, a kaleidoscope to which is added the amber cockpit lights, with the white-shirted captain rubbing his brow, weariness and 'miles to go before I sleep'. His hand moves and the aircraft's belly opens to disgorge an eight-wheeled bogie unit that presses into the hard airstream with hydraulic thumps. Another movement allows the wing to dislocate itself further as slats and full flap grind to the limits of their travel. Now all is ready, with 80 per cent set, established on the 3-degree slope, and the letdown is steady but sure for there is no wavering from the glide-path. Flashing green light on the panel attracts the eye. The 'inner marker', sitting lonely in a field below, has signalled 'the end is near'.

And so over the approach lights, past the hangar complex, level attitude across the threshold, throttles drawn back and the fabulous cylinder, primeval machine, elevates its nose into the dawn air and rumbles gently onto a dewy runway, smoothly.

Reverse thrust and groaning brakes curb the beast. Heathrow … Frankfurt … Rome … Hong Kong … a new world for a while. The landing lamps cut across the reddish-green turf as whispering compressors with juddering brakes urge metal and men along a flare-marked path to the glass terminal where sleepy-eyed slaves wait to refresh and refill the silver machine. Like germs we have floated through the airstream, a metal world flung 30,000 feet into the air. Thus we have straddled continents, and now we rest for a while, for indeed there is nothing like jet flight.

I return to the CAP pattern with my thoughts. I deliver the Phantom back to its appointed slot in the sky and with a few deft movements, trim it into the groove, engage autopilot and sit back satisfied. I am absorbed with the intricacy of flying, intrigued by the finesse, amazed by the delicacy of touch as I manoeuvre my aircraft. Of late, with growing experience on the machine, my performance in flying the GCA instrument approach has improved more than somewhat. Now, I nail the speed to within a few knots of 'On-Speed', nor does it vary all the way down the slope. The rate of descent pegs at around 750 feet a minute down, and only wavers slowly up and down as I subconsciously react to estimated changes in the ideal glidepath line drawn in my brain. The attitude indicator sticks at 8 to 9 degrees nose up, trim 2½ degrees, RPM 86 per cent per side, and when the man on the ground is finished with heading corrections, I freeze my hands which in turn (if the air is smooth) freezes those needles to their designated spots, and it is then, when I see everything in ordered perfection, progressing in dynamic harmony of man-machine, it is then that I wonder

> What a piece of work is Man?
> How noble in reason, how infinite in faculties.
> In form and movement how express and admirable,
> In action how like an angel,
> In apprehension how like a God.
> The beauty of the world, the paragon of animals.

I mull over those lines of ancient verse for a while. My navigator and I, we are both silent, for there is nothing to talk about. We have been on CAP for over an hour and we will be here for a further two before the next aircraft arrives to relieve us. Our bird is flying well, all systems functioning smoothly. On short busy flights of, say, one hour or so, where I am constantly moving throttles and controls, my machine will sometimes complain with an odd rumble here, a thump there, rushes of air from the pressurisation system, jerks and twitches from the autopilot. But, on multi-hour missions, I notice there is a cut-off period around the three-hour airborne point. After that time, the whole aircraft is in a definite groove. The engines hum smoothly on their bearings at a constant RPM. The radar is happily looking after itself in three-bar auto-acquisition scan. The needles on the instrument gauges are all steady at their appointed places, in the green sector, were there such markings. My body has grown used to its somewhat hard seat. I feel as if my aircraft and

I together could remain up here forever; harmony that makes me think of the words on a record in my room miles away …

'You are as much a part of me, as me'.

I break my search now and again to go to the tanker to top up my fuel reserves. At these times I am a complete slave to a digital instrument glowing red at the top right-hand corner of the instrument panel. I am a shameless respecter of this blandly round-faced dial, because I do whatever it says. Pilots may treat with disdain the laws of man and even those of God, but without fail they all pay the greatest respect to the fuel gauge. Its own laws are quite straightforward. They state quite simply that if I do not refuel or land soon my engines will stop and I will be forced to parachute out into the cold night air. In a relaxed state we may be, but the engines are still gulping Avtur at the rate of one hundred pounds or twelve gallons a minute. Yet this is nothing compared to the huge thirst those combustion chambers would develop if I suddenly decided to engage maximum reheat and maintain it. My tanks would be drained dry in about five minutes, all 2,500 gallons' worth. The flight manual is rather understating things when it says 'The use of reheat should be judicious'.

Refuelling is complete in a few minutes and I return to CAP, satiated. I am flying an American aeroplane and because of that my vocabulary of flight jargon is full of Americanese. The Britisher tries hard to resist it, but there is no way we can avoid falling into the habit. So, in fact, I don't often call them reheats, no, they are afterburners. It is not a tailplane but a stabilator. I use my speedbrakes not airbrakes. The instrument in front of me is not an artificial horizon but an ADI, Attitude Display Indicator. The one below it is not a compass but an HSI, Horizontal Situation Indicator. I call 'finals gear down' not 'undercarriage', and when you consider that I do not have an autopilot but an Automatic Flight Control System, then you will begin to understand why I am forced to speak in abbreviations. To the uninitiated, the Phantom pilot in conversation about his aircraft could just as well be speaking Serbo-Croat for all the sense it makes. But when I debrief my line chief on a fault, I don't have time to explain that the Aileron Rudder Interconnect Circuit Breakers are causing yaw transients in the Automatic Flight Control Stability Augmentation System, which in turn is feeding back to the Inertial Navigation and Attack System. Instead I abbreviate, which is one step nearer to telepathy. In our circle, in our 'club', we are crystal clear to one another and this language appears the most reasonable and logical in the world.

The Dutch controller pulls me off CAP to investigate a slow-moving contact near the surface. I leave my CAP height of 15,000 feet and descend. At 8,000 feet I plunge into the layer of alto-stratus that has been lying below us all night. It is just like sinking into a bowl of cotton wool, the deeper I go the darker it gets. I fly instruments. We lose contact with the ship at around 5,000 feet, understandable as we are over 130 miles from him at this point. I flick a switch that commands up a navigation computer range and bearing from base. At this point in time, it tells me in glowing red numerals, we are 1,000 miles north-east of Leuchars airbase, Scotland. I suddenly feel very lonely and hope those engines continue to do their good work of keeping me in the air. Should I go down into those icy seas below tonight, the chances of rescue before I froze to death would be zero.

The cloud is not very thick and we are in the clear again at 2,000 feet. We are in radar contact with the aircraft, and as usual, must identify first. Unfortunately this particular fellow is flying at 180 knots and going round in circles. Obviously some type of maritime patrol aircraft, but which? Nimrod? Atlantic? Orion? Neptune? Maritime names for maritime aircraft. I am curious about who is sharing my lonely world and so I close up for (hopefully) a visual. Easier said than done. He is at around 800 feet, probably in a sub-hunting pattern, so I must try to ident him from above. I have throttled back and we are hanging in the air at 200 knots with flaps down. The Phantom does not fly very well at these speeds, especially with the weight of fuel we have on board. My hands are full maintaining control of the beast and I am having to fly half on instruments and half visual to see what is outside, a technique not advised at the best of times. I fleetingly recall the number of lost control accidents that have happened in just such circumstances, but almost immediately draw the curtains over that part of my mind. It is very dark beneath the cloud, but I can see his navigation lights blinking brightly red. I am weaving to stay behind him and on the outside of his right-hand orbit. My eyes strain to pick out the number of engines, whether there is an MAD boom, the shape of the fuselage ... but there is no way. All I can be certain of is that it is too darkly camouflaged to be a Nimrod. However, it could be any one of the others, with the odds on a Breguet Atlantic because of its slow speed, that is the best we can do – an educated guess; as it turns out we will eventually discover that our guess was a correct one.

Night low-level vis-idents are strictly for the owls. However, I understand they are developing new low light night telescopes, but that is cold comfort to me right here and now. I haul off and leave him to continue his own business while I climb away to report back.

Steady on heading and climbing back through the cloud, the accumulated tension of the past five minutes slowly diminishing, I am suddenly hit by an attack of vertigo, insidiously betraying my sense of direction, bringing on that curious unworldly sensation. I steel myself, but before the attack can get a real hold on me, we pop out of the cloud into the clear starlit air, the sirens disappear and the world instantly slots back to normal, the gyros in my head re-erected. I breathe a sigh of relief.

Disorientation – as much an accepted part of flying as any other hazard that is to be expected and guarded against in my profession. They have lectured *ad infinitum*, shown films, written essays in Flight Safety magazines, they have preached, prophesied and postulated. I know the symptoms, the remedies, the causes and the cures inside out. Yet when it hits me, it never fails to bring an uncanny chill to my toes, because I know it has killed so many in the old days of ignorance, and even in these modern times those not practised in the precise skill of flying instruments.

Take a night last week, black, moonless, stratocumulus from 5,000 up to 30,000 feet, nicely encompassing the parameters of the briefed target envelope for the night's interceptions. We line up echelon port on the runway. I switch my taxi light off, the signal for lead to call 'take-off'. He goes, 'burners blazing in the still night air. I wait thirty seconds and then blast off after him, up and out into the sky. Turning starboard, the lights of Dundee are spread below, but soon we penetrate into the cotton-wool mist, not the definite cloud of cu-nim, but the hazy, all-enveloping uncertainty of stratus where the world is a goldfish bowl and only the glowing red cockpit exists, linked to the earth by the radio transmissions from the ground and between aircraft. Engines hum quietly and only the needles and dials smoothly revolving, rotating, oscillating, indicate that I am anything but dynamic. I look out and see nothing; nothing moves; we are stationary, and yet moving at 400 Kcas across the North Sea. Intercepts commence and almost immediately the radar fails, the transmitter is refusing to push out pulses, we must depend on ground control.

'Two-five, Gadget bent, request Alpha control.'

'Roger, target thirty miles, bearing 250 displaced eight miles on your port, come left 10 degrees'. Now I am a tool, a slave to his commands, and we bank and wheel, accelerate and climb on his instructions. I am locked onto the instruments, 30,000 feet and we are half in, half out of the clouds, in a turn, milky, hazy sky, and I make the mistake of glancing outside. Immediately the world rotates about me, there is no horizon, stars are below, black earth, sky, sea, cloud above me, I am inverted, I am climbing vertically, I am in a steeply banked turn in the opposite direction, all is confusion, unreal, ethereal, the canals in my ears are lost, but training takes command. I have been warned of it, I expected it, it is here and I know what to do. I lock onto the instruments. The ADI tells me that I am not, in fact, plummeting earthwards, but straight and level, speed is not on the verge of a stall, but rather steady at 0.9 Mach, the HSI too is steady, everything is in harmony and I know it is true despite the canals in my ears telling my brain that we are performing loops, rolls and inverted turns. The adrenalin flows and I am excited, silent, but also half smiling because it is exactly as advertised and I am performing exactly as advertised, hands rock steady on the controls. I refuse to engage autopilot and take the easy way out. Instead I fly the Phantom manually and I ignore the false sensations while noting them in an almost objective manner because it has happened before and will happen again, I know it. So pretty soon, slowly, surely everything settles into its proper position, as if I had been spinning round and now standing still, watch the world fall into its appointed place of up and down, and I breathe again and smile inwardly. Yes, disorientation really is an accepted part of flying.

I report our find to the controller who gives a brief acknowledgement and is silent. There also is another soul who is wondering what he is doing playing war games at four in the morning. The tanker captain calls that he must now return to his base and would I refuel now please. I go to him, plug in and suck till I am full to the brim once more, and bid him farewell. When he goes I really am alone. The likelihood of a raid by Orange (enemy) forces at this time of the morning is truly remote. Even the marauding low-level artists, the Buccaneers, pick reasonable night hours for their ship strikes. This usually involves getting the job done and landing back at base before the bar closes, a sensible objective!

On the way back to CAP the Master Caution caption illuminates. I look down at the main warning panel. The 'Stat Corr Off' caption is glowing balefully amber. All this means is that the instruments are not receiving static correction, no sweat at these speeds and heights. It will only bother me if I am travelling very fast and very low, or about to land, when all my pressure instruments will misread by a certain amount. I wait a few seconds and then recycle a switch on the left engine panel, the light goes out and the pressure instruments give a little twitch of satisfaction before settling down, happy again. I idly wonder what caused it to trip off. There is a computer in the bowels of the aircraft called the Central Air Data Computer whose sole job is to work out static correction and feed it to various waiting workers in the aircraft. One of its thousands of tiny components must have decided to go on strike for a few seconds. My action with the switch whipped it back into line.

Computers are the shop stewards in this aeroplane, they run everything. A computer meters the fuel to the engines, catering for the many environmental changes the engine is forced to suffer during normal operations. Another computer programmes the ramps on either side of the intakes to open as I go faster to keep the airflow to the compressors subsonic. My old friend the weapon-aiming computer deals with the impossible ballistic calculations for missiles and guns. The navigational computer tells me where I am, where I have been, and where I am going, instantly. Whenever I fly this aeroplane, then I realise that computers really are a man's best friend.

At 04.30 hours John turns up to relieve me. We detect him and his tanker just going through the 'gate'. Our controller releases us from CAP. We bid him a tired farewell and set course, heading 210 degrees. The two inbound aircraft remain on our nose all the way down, and I see their lights flashing fifteen miles away. We rush towards each other and pass head on with them 3,000 feet above. I wish John better luck than we have had and continue south. It is a one-and-a-half-hour transit back to base and the weariness is really beginning to hit me. My eyelids are growing heavy and I have to give myself periodic doses of 100 per cent oxygen to revive my wilting spirits. I listen idly to John going through the formalities of establishing his CAP with the controller before they too fade away into the ether, victims of distance. For the next thirty minutes we will be in the middle of no-man's-land, as far as UHF is concerned, in radio contact with no-one. Should a disaster befall us now, we would disappear without a trace, a mystery forever. But I am too tired to worry about that.

Instead I notice that the sky in the east is lightening, the stars are clicking out one by one, and the sky is taking on a dirty white-washed tinge. We race south with the dawn approaching, although it is still too dark to turn off the cockpit lights. The coast of Scotland is painting strongly on the radar, and out of the blue, just as strongly, the voice of Border Radar bursts into my helmet. He has been calling us for a while, apparently. I pass him our flight level, heading, position and arrival estimate. We are under control again.

I start my let down when the Tacan needle says seventy miles to go. The sun is just beginning to peep above the horizon, but my descent pushes it back out of sight, although its reddish glow remains staining the sky. The engines grumble briefly as I disturb them from the 89 per cent RPM at which they have been slumbering for the past hour, and reset them at 75 per cent for the cruise descent. Now I have something to do, I feel somewhat fresher, rubbing the sleep from my eyes, disengaging autopilot, tightening the straps that I loosened off during the transit.

'Border, Four-three leaving 280 for 50, request handover to Leuchars.'

'Roger, set QFE 28.25 inches, clear descend, arranging the handover now.'

Speed pegs at 350 knots, speedbrakes pop out, airframe vibrates gently, I alter course a few degrees to intercept the 090 radial. Let-down checks are completed in seconds. The dawn is definitely with us now and the air here is cloudless. The sea below has the dirty grey hue flecked with creamy whitecaps, colours characteristic of early morning awakening. Border gives us a Leuchars frequency to chop to, and we thank him and go. The Leuchars controller sounds just as tired as we do.

'Leuchars director, Four-three levelling at 5,000 feet on the QFE, thirty miles out this time on the centreline for a GCA pick up.'

'Rog Four-three, we have you radar contact, clear to descend to 3,000 feet on the QFE, Leuchars is Blue on Runway 27, all aids serviceable.'

I ease the stick forward and continue down to 3,000 feet, back with the stick and we are level, speedbrakes are still out and so speed decays slowly to 250 knots, compressors still whispering at 75 per cent.

'Four-three, you're cleared down to 1,500 feet, call level with checks complete, in good radar contact twenty miles from touchdown.'

Stick forward again, vertical speed indicator swings lazily down and pegs at 2,000 fpm down. My left thumb jabs the speedbrake switch in, vibration stops, we are sliding through the air, quiet. 1,600 feet says the altimeter, a fraction of back pressure and the descent stops at 1,450 feet. A little rearward tweak sends the needle back to its correct spot at 1,500 feet above the sea. Speed sinks below 250 knots, gear lever down, rumble, thump, 'three wheels', 200 knots, full flap, fuel weight 5,000 pounds, 'On Speed 140 knots', I must fly down the slope at On Speed plus ten, 150 knots. The needle swings inexorably down and only when it approaches 160 knots do I move the throttles forward, and the engines take on a more urgent note. Speed pegs at 155. I leave it there for the time being ...

'Four-three level 1,500 feet with checks complete.'

'Roger, DOA for this approach is seventy feet. What is your decision height and intentions?'

'320 feet to land.'

'Roger, change to stud five for talkdown.'

Click, counter whirrs over and steadies with five showing in the window.

'Talkdown, Four-three how do you read me?'

'Loud and clear Four-three, seven miles from touchdown, check gear down and locked, do not acknowledge further instructions. Wind for your landing is 230, 10 knots. Commencing descent in two miles.'

Once I am in the hands of a good GCA talkdown, I may as well be on the ground, it is as sure as that. On the other hand, a bad talkdown can be one of the most frustrating experiences in existence.

'Approaching the glidepath, prepare to lose height, slightly right of the runway, come left 2 degrees onto 268.' I use a little rudder to take out the small correction. I anticipate the approaching descent point by throttling back 3 per cent on the engines, speed drops to 146, but I don't care for it will increase as I start my slide downwards, reducing the horizontal component of my velocity vector. I can see the base from this range, the runway jutting in from the beach, the surrounding countryside a soft shade of blue, six am blue. Nothing appears to be stirring.

'Four-three, you're five miles from touchdown, begin descent now as for a 3-degree glidepath and come left 1 degree onto 267.' Stick forward, check, VSI registers 1,000 fpm down, too much, check back again, needle retreats to 800 fpm and sulks there, light wind today so we'll stick with that and see how it goes; speed has dropped to 144 ... up with the throttles, needle reads 148, throttle back, speed holds at 148, 149, that'll do.

'Settled down on the glidepath Four-three, good rate of descent, you're on the centreline, four miles from touchdown.' 800 fpm seems to be good enough; I pray for days like this for instrument rating rides, smooth calm air that flatters my instrument flying. With few corrections to make, my job is made infinitely easier.

'Three miles from touchdown, come right 1 degree onto 268, on the glidepath, good rate of descent, final check of wheels, flaps, pressures for your landing.'

'All checked good for landing, Four-three.'

'Roger, two miles from touchdown, on centreline, on glidepath.' Leuchars runway, 7,500 feet by 150 feet, beckons, grey asphalt, glistening wet with dew, VASI's red-white telling me I am indeed on the glidepath, approach T-bar lighting marching up the beach across the scrubland of airfield boundary up to the black and white piano keys on the threshold coming towards me ...

'Four-three approaching decision height, look ahead and take over visually for your landing, I will continue to pass advisory information, you are on the centreline, glidepath is good ... three-quarters of a mile from touchdown ... half a mile ... approaching radar touchdown ... NOW!' He can see it as accurately as that on his scope, for the 'now' comes a second before my wheels kiss the hard concrete at 140 knots, the On Speed 'doughnut' (the only concession to head-up display the Phantom indulges in) shining steadily in front of me. The drag 'chute pops and we trundle to the end and turn off.

'Thank you talkdown, Four-three clearing to stud one.'

I have been airborne six hours and five minutes. The weariness suddenly floods over me again in great waves, and it is with a great effort I complete the after-landing checks and taxi back to dispersal where the patient groundcrew wait to prepare our bird for its next flight later in the day. On the chocks, throttles round the horn, the steel compressors grind round the last few revolutions before sighing to a halt, ticking and cracking gently with dissipating heat and rapidly cooling metal. Stiff climb down the ladder past the men working in well-practised silence, squadron operations, Air Defence Mission Report; one airliner, one maritime-type; log five hours and thirty-five minutes of night, thirty minutes of day, with twenty minutes' actual instrument flying time. Back to a still sleeping Mess, bedroom, bed, sleep – deep, heavy oblivion.

5

....

Forty-Three Squadron, Fighting Cocks

Air Combat, the sport of kings. Detachment to Malta and intensive flying phase, twenty-eight sorties a day. 'Okay,' Boss says, 'take tanks off ships, let's go do ACM!' Here I get my first early taste of Phantom combat. Surely this is what being a fighter pilot is all about, me against him, one brain against another, one set of muscles against another, he who flies the smoothest, the meanest, the most cunning, most aggressive, most tactical fight within the legal limits wins, it is as simple as that. So all eyes brighten, secret pet theories germinate. We will start off with one versus one. We fire up the birds and all day long leap into a superb cloudless sky to trail thunder across the Mediterranean Sea.

'On east, outward split for combat ... Go!' Fifteen miles and turn inwards. Inside my aircraft, two pairs of eyes scan carefully the piece of sky in which we expect him to appear. Today we are not using radar. Aerial lookout is a matter of practice and indeed my eyes sometimes take on the steely, faraway glint much beloved of fiction writers as I focus into the distance, and sometimes I amaze even myself with the acuity with which I detect distant minute objects.

In the crystal clear air I spot him, very low, very fast, curving up into a Sidewinder attack towards my blind quarter. The game is on. The stage is set, and like medieval combatants we set up our opening moves as carefully as any Grand Master switching Pawn to Queen's Bishop Two. My left hand pushes the throttles through the gate into the far left-hand corner. As the surge of 'burner lightup cuts in, I crank on right rudder and roll down into him. My aim is to achieve a minimum displacement pass to prevent his gaining an immediate advantage as we commit into our hard turns. I am also going nose low to ensure a maximum build-up of energy. Thus we pass head on at a closing velocity of 1,000 knots and combat is joined.

He approaches me as a small, smoking speck to start with, the both of us pointed directly at each other on a collision course, his machine growing ever larger in my windscreen till it seems we must surely hit. But at the last moment, the instinct of self-preservation takes command and with a little twitch on the control column, I flash over the top of his canopy, clear by a thousand feet, a miss as good as a mile. I now have all the energy in the world stored in my metal body which is good, because in the F4 speed is energy, is performance, and thus a 6-G pull sends me racing skywards in a tremendous zooming arc. The F4 has not got the best turning performance of Western fighters, but using the right tactics, and in the right hands, even in a close turning fight it is a deadly machine. My plan is to remain in the vertical and use the phenomenon of radial G to give me the edge. Upside down and pitching over nose down, I can use my ailerons to change direction in an effortless instant, and so cut corners that would be impossible were I at the bottom of the circle.

However, even so there is a limited number of opening gambits available as options in Phantom combat. Hence we have both pitched up into similar enormous vertical 'yo-yos' and we pass inverted, head on again at the top of the loop and start on down once again on opposite sides of the barrel. He disappears aft outside the limits of my vision, and I warn the navigator to screw himself round to look rearwards and report the 'enemy's' actions, a difficult task under 6 Gs. The aircraft is transitioning from Mach 1 plus at the bottom of the egg-shaped offset loop to under 200 knots at the top, from 10,000 feet up to 40,000, the physical laws of kinetic and potential energy are having a field day in this three-dimensional dance.

The game has moved into the development stage as we both try varying tactics and strategy to gain the advantage. My prime aim is to get him to lose sight of me, because we all know that in combat, he who loses sight, loses, period. That is why I try to direct my Saturn Five zooms towards the great white orb of the sun where I hang and poise momentarily before reversing my turn (if he is not threatening) to re-emerge from an unexpected angle. I go through the repertoire, trying reverse yo-yos, lag rolls, slice turns, rollaways, oblique loops and all the other curious manoeuvres peculiar to jet combat, yet it is all a game of chess because as I throw a move, so he counters, forcing me to counter his counter. I try more of the tricks taught to me at Phantom conversion school. Because he is a Phantom, I can afford to slow down and try to outfly him (a fatal move against low wing-loaded types) but anything goes in F4 v F4. Hence I can gamble on flying slowly yet as smoothly as possible, extracting every inch of performance without straying into the speed and energy sapping high drag regimes, aiming to force him out in front of me. I am conserving my performance by staying below nineteen units angle of attack, at every opportunity releasing to ten units to pick up those vital extra knots (when I have slowed down *too* much) that make all the difference between winning and losing (Air Combat gets so personal!).

The fight progresses. He tries to force me to fly through with a hard reversal, but this is an old trick and I pull up high, exchanging valuable speed for height, and yo-yo into the vertical plane. He follows, turning hard all the while and I am forced to turn with him, barreling into one huge vertical 'scissors', as I look directly down on him through the top of my canopy. We are both operating the controls instinctively, one manoeuvre blending into another with an almost graceful precision.

The aerial ballet continues, for such it is because at times for a few seconds I become objective, calm, peaceful even, as I stare out at my adversary. His machine is like a fish, floating silently in the currents of the deep, gently quivering in slow-motion, twisting-and-turning elegance, puffy wisps of cumulus disintegrating round it gently like some marine foliage. And now it becomes gull-like, reversing and winging over, swooping in sudden plunges in the liquid atmosphere, seemingly delicate and frail as it glints in the sunlight. At one moment arcing against the deep background blue of the sea and the next, arrowing straight up into the white heavens, scorched with sun, to hang and hover before slowly plummeting down again, wings shimmering with condensation. Condensation ... that is the clue.

Dreamlike it may be looking down, but the reality in my own

cockpit as I pull ever harder and commit back into the fight tells me the actual story of what is going on in that silver-grey toy wheeling before me. The engines at full afterburners are roaring in my ears, my eyes are foggy, senses reeling and blood pounding, all because the little clock marked 'G' on the instrument panel is steady at the figure 6. My arms ache, my neck muscles strain to hold up a head that is weighing six times its normal weight. My legs tense, assisted by the crushing, vice like grip of the G-suit to prevent the blood draining into those legs from my upper body and causing my eyes to go even foggier. As it is, I am still seeing stars, little flecks of black light that float across my vision. My breath in my own ears and my navigator's breathing over the intercom, both are harsh and heavy. We speak in grunts, forcing diaphragms to flex under the forces of gravity (hydraulic power is a wonderful thing). Right now this is war, and as I look out at that apparently serene object waltzing through the sky, I know the two bodies there are suffering the same torture, the same stresses, the same strain. They are sweating, groaning and cursing, necks twisting and eyes searching and their clock is probably reading 7 Gs. They are not at peace at all.

I sense that I am beginning to win because now, somehow, I have managed to work my way into his rear quarters. Now the ball is in my court for I must inevitably have an easier time when I am looking forward. He has to look back and fight as well, and every pilot knows he cannot fly his aircraft to the optimum under those conditions. My opponent is still turning hard, however, because I am still outside the ideal recommended cone for firing my Sidewinder, but I know it is only a matter of time. We have been fighting for three minutes – a long time in 1 v 1 combat – but I have the time and the fuel, as a quick glance at the gauge tells me, to continue playing my stalking game, because the cold certainty of victory has started washing over me in cooling waves and life is all of a sudden rosier.

He is beginning to lose sight of me for seconds at a time, perhaps tiring of the high G struggle as well. I can tell when that happens because I see his turn easing off for a moment, enabling me to bite off a few more degrees of angle off his tail. At last comes the major error I have been waiting for. He loses sight of me under his tail and reverses his turn, attempting a barrel roll counter – fatal. I recheck Sidewinder selected, Master Arm still on, Coolant on, and pull into the uncomfortable twenty-three unit plus region with the aircraft buffeting and shuddering as I strive to control the heavy wing rock – symptomatic of approaching stall and disaster – with large inputs of rudder. I do not care, because I must kill, and kill quickly before the slot disappears and he recommences his hard pull into me, forcing me to disengage and reposition. Instead, with those extra units, I bring the pipper on the gunsight (check thirty-five mils set) to bear on his jetpipe, still glowing white-orange with 'burner, beautiful. Acquisition Sidewinder growls with delighted anticipation. I squeeze the trigger and ... silence. The 'Winder is 'gone'. Five seconds later, had I fired the real thing, I would see a white puff as the explosive charge sent the metallic expanding rod slicing through his rear fuselage, severing hydraulic lines, control runs, electrical connections, and maybe then I would circle round the burning wreckage floating down, followed by two white parachutes of fallen foes.

But this is not war, this is peace. Instead I call 'Fox 2!' I win, you lose and combat is terminated. Then we either set up again, each determined to do better, sure, certain this time he will win, or else we call it a day and rush home short on fuel to smoke onto the strip, into the crewroom, coffee and argue over who did what, maybe look at films to confirm kills, and if you were vanquished, to secretly choke over it while sitting with a fixed grin – 'Waxed again!' Yes, Air Combat is the sport of kings.

In the left-hand corner of my cockpit is a set of twin throttles. It is amazing the soul, the life that exists within these two inoffensive looking pieces of metal. I only have to push these throttles as far forward as they will go in order to arc steadily, but surely in a vapour-trailed sundance climb, 30,000 feet in fifty-eight seconds, or to trail my silent thunder through the midnight blue stratosphere at two and a half times the speed of sound itself, or else to race my shadow across the green trees at 800 miles an hour, 200 feet above those branches, or even to fly non-stop from the UK to Singapore in fourteen hours.

With those two gunmetal grey levers in my left hand, I am able to unleash a fury of forces such as to send the senses reeling, batter machinery with unwelcome stresses and create a hazy turbulence in the heavens. With the moulded grips in my fingers, I am master of my own little destiny, the short-lived existence that is one flight, a compressed world that rotates from lift-off to touch-down and then waits inactively dormant till the next mission.

The two short angled stumps of steel move along twin grooves in the console, these metallic slits guarded by a flexible barrier of fine brushed bristle hairs that part to allow the passage of the levers and almost immediately hurry closed in their wake, denying entrance to the ever-present foreign object, cause of disaster. As I move these throttles, so I command laws of dynamics, mechanical regulations and rules of physics to fall into their allotted place to drive me ever faster, ever higher, ever tighter, indeed ever slower in my never end-ing search for performance. With one movement I can arrest the downward trend of airspeed after sucking my pattern right out onto the backside of the drag curve pitching in for the break. With an-other movement I can nail my machine right on the 'bug' in the instrument pattern. With a further movement I can dismiss with dis-dain the insidious wind shear at runway threshold in the last fifty feet as dangling oleos and expectant tyres reach for their concrete sanctuary, jumping at the last moment over the grass undershoot.

Further forward movement meets a resistance, a gate, a barrier to further progress. I worry not. Sideways pressure on those knurled grips overcomes a stiff spring, the levers slide outboard with a soft spongy click, geometric locks rearrange themselves, and all of a sudden those throttles, the engines, the aircraft, myself, we, are in another world, another dimension, another existence. Ahead of these levers stretches a new plane in which to run. Here the fields are greener, the trees grow taller, the rivers run with a greater ur-gency, the winds of change blow with hurricane force, and the sun that shines from this heaven is incandescent white with a terrible heat. The energy of life flows with a long thrusting motion unheard, unseen in that other world on the other side of that spring-loaded gate. Values are doubled, but then so is the price, paid in fuel, be-cause although birth has been given to a new era of travel, the generation has not been without much effort.

Yet we travel often in this land. I go there on every take-off. My hand commands it into existence every time I see an enemy ar-rowing towards my tail bent on destruction. The throttles must live there for a while to ensure their security in the more mundane world of 'cold power'. I send the throttles there on final approach when one engine decides it is tired of living and blows up in a shower of sparking compressors and white hot turbine blades spinning out of existence. I move the throttles there when I am at low level, over the sea, chasing Buccaneers in to the fleet and I must shoot fast, and I must get in range to do so. In the land of 'heat, hundreds of knots appear from nowhere in seconds, blasting aside mere forces of drag and density in a mad rush of acceleration, thirty-two feet per second squared, and tumbling physiological gyros. The onward rush is merciless and disregarding, it is brutish and uncaring, there is no subtlety or finesse, grace is sacrificed on the altar of the God of Power and only when the 'In Range' light has illuminated and my right forefinger has flexed on the trigger, only then do I draw those throttles back into the land of normality, the land of reality, to which I return in a bruising, breathtaking, shoulder-strap aching jolt of deceleration as the Gods retire once more into the hidden depths of machinery to lie sleeping until called for again. The land of the Afterburner is truly a wonderful place to be.

Last week, John ('Desert Rat'), on scramble to CAP, blasts down the runway, gets airborne and at a hundred feet snaps left into a maximum-rate afterburner turn off Runway 27 heading for CAP 1 and disappears behind the hills, smoking. A real Tiger departure. Unfortunately, he couldn't have picked a better audience – the Boss and the Station Commander standing outside the squadron, watching open-mouthed.

'It was him, was it? Tell him to see me when he lands – with hat on!' Trouble with the Boss. It comes to all of us. I just can't seem to avoid it. As a 'first tourist', I have no comeback, no excuse, yet it follows me around like some mystical albatross.

Yesterday, I climbed up through the cloud and murk to RV with the tanker. I spent one hour happily 'dry prodding' with an ease and relaxation born of not having an OCA or other 'wheel' breathing down my neck from the other aeroplane. So, full and fat with fuel, the Dynamic Duo decide to head for happy old hunting ground, RAF Valley, land of steel, to check the place out. I have not been there since training days. High level transit and its time to descend.

'Cloud base 1,500 feet visibility six kilometres', so okay, no sweat. I begin to wonder when, on the GCA – 'on centreline, on glidepath' – I am still solidly cloud cloaked at 800 feet. Still, am I or am I not a fighter pilot? Mind now switches to single purpose that I requested five minutes ago – 'one circuit and flyby' – so I go to local frequency and crank into the downwind turn.

I begin to wonder even more when over the sea my port wing is scraping the bottom of the cloud at 500 feet. Easing off the bank to gather wits means I fly wide downwind, lose the runway in the mist and rain and have to go round again. Call it a day and climb out? No way! How can a steely Phantom operator call it a day after such a screw up, especially as I know there will be an audience of gawking students watching below (I used to do it). So round we go again, tighter this time. The bird is heavy with tanker fuel and full military power won't peg that speed. It is buffeting like an old bus, so into 'burner, fly through the centreline, crank it tighter ... reverse ... onto runway heading ... drop down a little lower, level wings ... aim for the control tower and the little group of watching ants ... demon acceleration and Valley is gone in a surge of speed, rain, cloud and wet Gnats and Lightnings on the pan ... 'You are cleared for low level circuits!' before we punch back into the murk and out into the civilised blue above with sighs of relief that we had no time for in the brief five-minute heat of the moment.

So, high level transit, Practice Pan, single engine recovery, over-shoot into low level circuit (as if I hadn't had enough) and land. NRL meets me ...

'See the Boss pronto – with hat on!'

Oh, oh, and sure enough its the same routine. Last time it was OC RAF Leuchars I picked to watch my 'display'. This time its OC Flying Wing, Valley ... 'sitting down to lunch in the married patch when I heard this deafening roar and looked out to see a 43 Squadron Phantom with its burners blazing at a hundred feet(!). I mean that sort of thing is just ... Not on, old boy! Sort that young whippersnapper out.' So I get the rocket. My ear gets chewed out and I am sentenced, with a parting warning 'There won't be a third time!' I really must get rid of that old albatross.

Sometimes I am amazed at how little work I do for the amount the government decides to pay me. Take today for example. This week, my flight – A Flight – has the misfortune (depending on your point of view) of carrying out our flying task at night. Next week, we will swop with B Flight and do days. Anyway, this means I am not required to be in at the squadron till 17.45 in the afternoon. Therefore, I spend the whole day lazing around, reading newspapers, eating meals, playing sounds. I wash my car, go for a drive into town, visit the Post Office, return and write a few more lines in this manual, stare out of the window into space. Come duty time, I put on a flying suit and wander down to the squadron to find ... no aeroplanes. B Flight have done a good job of putting them all U/S. So I have a coffee, dutifully attend Met briefing, check the following day's programme and am told by Flight Commander to 'stack'. The time is 18.00. I have been on duty fifteen minutes. So I return to my room, shower, change and head for the bar where I ensconce myself for the rest of the evening. There I marvel at the generosity of the Treasury, and I wonder why everyone isn't a pilot.

It is true to say that I have quite a lot of free time as a 'JP' on the squadron, but it is also true that I am on duty twenty-four hours of the day, every day of the year, which is why the Air Force can recall me from leave at any time, drag me out of my warm bed at three in the morning to go and chase Russians or spend exhausting weeks flying on war exercises.

Meanwhile, I sit in my room, legs crossed in armchair, and I contemplate my flight crew bag. It takes my memory back to one I saw not so long ago in the house of an airline captain. This man was a commander of Boeing 707s and as I looked at his flight bag, I was struck by the professionalism that item of leather and silver epitomised. It was shiny ebony black with a flip-over lid and though I did not open it, I could imagine the mine of information it housed, whether 707 Manual or TAPs for Rome, Fiumicino, flight schedules or navigational computers. So as I looked at this bag, sitting there in the middle of his sitting room (plush, carpeted, functionally comfortable airline issue) and then redirected my gaze to its owner stretched quietly confident in an easy chair, I thought how well the two matched, both quietly uncommunicative, but indicating to those who know the nature of their profession.

Now, 3,000 miles away, I have a similar bag. Mine is Air Force grey and instead of a 707 Manual I have one bearing the title *Phantom FGR Mk 2 Aircrew Manual AP 101B* stamped on all sides with 'Restricted' in black. Beside it lies another manual no airline pilot will ever see; *Phantom FGR Mk 3 Weapon System*. Both books are a foot square and of Bible-like thickness. Both are blue in colour, one dark, the other a shade lighter, and both sit purposefully in that bag, beside my easy chair where I sit quietly, confidently contemplating my own profession.

In addition to my manuals, I have a thick checklist that contains procedures for normal operations and, in a red-bordered section, tells me what I should do if any of a hundred odd things malfunction in my aircraft. Then, I too have a folder containing my TAPs for all military airfields I am likely to visit, while beside that is stowed a box containing navigational equipment. To complete the contents of this particular bag there are two brown Air Force issue file covers enfolding précis of air and ground subjects from OCU training days, handling notes, radar intercept geometries, routine operating procedures. I carry this bag everywhere with me while I am in uniform. It is an extension of my arm, for although most of its contents are committed to memory, that memory must be constantly refreshed, updated and revised, and if there is anything I do not know, I only have to look in that bag and the answer is there. That is why I look at that bag with its books all lying beside me, with such a strange feeling of being a small part of a technology and profession that I think can be second to none.

Yesterday I was on Alert, Q1 on the IAF roster. Bill was my navigator for the flight. I came on duty at nine in the morning, signed out a 'noddy guide' booklet, collected my kit and climbed into the Land Rover. We drove across the airfield, about half a mile to the Q sheds, the twin corrugated steel hangarettes that house the two Alert ships. There, I took over my particular aircraft from the preceding crew, John and Doug. I checked the 700, signed it, walked out to the aeroplane and stowed my harness and helmet strategically ready for instant use. The crewchief cranked up the Houchin while I climbed the ladder and sitting in the cockpit, threw the generator switches to 'External On' and watched the instruments come to life. I then proceeded to do a normal prestart check, leaving each switch in the position it would be should I intend to start in the next minute in a hurry. With all complete and to my satisfaction, I killed the power, climbed out of the aeroplane into the Land Rover and back to the squadron where I set myself before our newly acquired colour television set and watched the Olympics.

IAF is like playing the gaming machine in the Mess Bar – luck with a capital L. Some of the pilots have been on the squadron a year and a half without having seen a Russian. Other guys get scrambled to intercept intruders practically every time they are on Alert. Our hopes are raised briefly at 11.00 when some activity starts up, but this quickly dies down as the bogey turns back north-east, is intercepted by Norwegian F 104s, and identified as a Cub (a Russian transport). Only if he had penetrated UK NATO airspace (and this extends out beyond Iceland) would I have been scrambled to investigate. So I sit and read my noddy guides, recognition journals, flip cards, watch television, eat lunch and dinner, drink coffee, chew biscuits and generally slip into the torpid languor that is invariably part and parcel of holding Alert.

At midnight, with TV exhausted, I retire to bed where I sleepily crash out and dream of being scrambled, and dreams become reality for at 03.30 the metronomic telebrief speaks out. 'This is Buchan for Wing Ops and IAF, we have one Zombie in Mike Lima November Lima, strength two, heading south-west, has just faded, last height 25,000 feet, speed 420 knots. We expect to scramble you to meet them in twenty minutes.' Eyelids jerk open, brain re-engages and mind functions as I struggle into flying suit and boots, wake the groundcrew and douse face in icy water.

'Mission 02 expect to scramble on the hour.' This from Buchan – 04.00. What a time to go flying, for God's sake. Q2 is aroused and I don my harness and climb up into the cockpit, lit in fluorescent red, where Bill and I strap in, power on, thumb on RT button. 'Mission 02 on five minutes' cockpit readiness,' and then wait. I wait while, at four in the morning, Buchan SOC and Strike Command HQ plot likely tracks and penetration times and ponder on decisions till finally, on the hour, 'This is Buchan for IAF, vector 350, make optimum Angels, call Buchan fighter stud seven-three, scramble, scramble, acknowledge.' As Bill acknowledges, I am already twirling my forefinger in a quick little circle that tells the waiting groundcrew I am ready to start, and as he gives me his thumbs up I select both engine master switches on and subconsciously note the drop in the clattering roar of the Houchin as the extra load of the booster pumps starting up drains a little more of its energy. Then I select the left engine start switch 'On' and as the gas turbine starter churns the great steel blades of the Spey through 5 per cent revolutions, I select the starboard start switch 'On', and from there on the automatic sequencers take over and all I have to do as the revolutions build up is monitor the fire lights, TGTs, nozzles, fuel flows, oil pressures, anti-ice, engine bleeds, starter auto cut-out at 38 per cent time to 47 per cent, min engine idling speed, static corr caption off, generators on line with Bus Tie captions out. I am ready to go. A waving motion signals for disconnection of the Houchin, removal of the four Sidewinder missile caps, arming of the four Sparrow missiles and removal of the chocks.

On stud one I call for taxi and the marshaller signals me to move forward out of the narrow confines of the shed. 'Runway 09, wind 240 at 10 knots, tailwind component within limits.' Outside the shed I spread and lock the wings and gingerly pick my way round the unfamiliar taxiway lighting (this is my first night scramble), as Bill chants out the litany of pre-take-off checks. The runway is a mere 200 yards away so there is not much time, but all the checks are completed by the time I roll onto the black strip stretching away into the darkness, the twin rows of runway lighting delineating my take-off path; indeed I do not stop, and with a last check of flaps at half, stab-augs on, anti-skid on and all warning lights out, three minutes after starting up, my left hand moves the two throttles to the first stop, pauses and then rocks them outboard and forward a further three inches. I feel the now familiar surge as the afterburners light up to send me leaping forward with a renewed urgency that puts me at 160 knots lift-off speed in no time at all, and I know that outside I am leaving a fantastic twin trail of diamond studded yellow flame thirty feet long washing on the tarmac as the aircraft rotates, nav lights flashing, venting gases and fuel from dump valves and above all else leaving that rolling thunder, reverberating and crackling in great cascading waves, that heralds the departure of an afterburning jet. Long after I am gone, the sound lingers in the still air and as far afield as St Andrews town, bodies are waking and wondering.

One would think that confronting a Russian for the first time in the air would be a sobering experience. Far from it. Engaged in a cold war we may be, but up there is the clear air, we are both airmen doing that which we love best. I learnt this today on my first successful live scramble.

'Wing Ops, alert one Phantom ... climb ... heading ... call Buchan stud ... SCRAMBLE!' Airborne and heading north, 0.8 Mach, Flight Level 310, everything calm. We continue past Kinloss, past the Orkneys, past the Faeroes till we are 480 miles north of base. Having completed a stern attack through the cloud in the search mode, we pop up to see the sight that I have been waiting to see all these years.

It glows silvery white in the hot, metallic blue sunlight, a long, slender cigar of a shape. The wings are also long and sharp, swept back at an impossible angle, and on them, like great molluscs, are the four giant Kuznetsov turboprops. They too are silver, except around the sooty grey exhaust ports from which are trailing great long condensation plumes. Each engine has two sets of four-bladed propellers that revolve in contra-rotation and I can see each blade as the silvery discs stroboscope in the sunlight. The mighty red star on fin and wings is a stark contrast on that metallic background. It is a Russian bomber, a Tupolev Tu 16, NATO codename 'Bear'. Recce quote: 'The stars of the Tupolev constellation are only to be seen in the Northern hemisphere'. The group is made up of the Bear and Badger family, a breed with a widespread and bewildering pedigree. The passenger-carrying civilian versions are almost identical in form and shape, but these military cousins are more likely to lob long range missiles onto fat carrier targets. This one is of the 'Foxtrot' class and it belongs to the Soviet Long Range Maritime Air Force attached to the Northern Fleet in Murmansk. Many intelligence and recognition briefings have ensured that I deduce all this the instant I catch sight of it. I even know that, as an ASW machine, it is on its way to exercise with a Soviet submarine operating just off the coast of Iceland, which is not so far from where we are right now. But these thoughts do not concern me at the moment. I am more interested in examining this living replica of 'them' and 'us', and so warfare is the last thought in our minds as I close up on his port wing, the internationally recognised interception signal, and Bill gets to work clicking away with his camera.

From this close range, I can see the faces peering through the portholes at us. Other members of the crew cluster round the larger windows and they too are armed with cameras. (As our pictures will be in the corridors of MOD tonight, so too will the ones they take of us be in the Kremlin. Our respective intelligence agencies will then pore over them, looking for new modifications, with which to update their files. It's a never-ending quest to stay one jump ahead.)

I ease even closer, nearer than my standard 200 yards, until I can see the captain's face quite clearly. He sits high in his seat in the huge cockpit, wearing a leather flying jacket and the curiously old fashioned cloth flying helmets beloved by the Russians. He smiles at me and gives a wave. I wave back. I remember the tale of one pilot who eased in closer to see what one of the Russian crewmen was holding up against the window. It turned out to be the centre-fold from *Playboy* magazine.

At this close range, I notice a strange and persistent vibration penetrating through my aircraft. I have been told of this phenomenon. They are harmonics originating in those turboprops, one of the most powerful engines in the world. I can actually *hear* them.

For five minutes we manoeuvre around it, taking notes and photographs for the men in Whitehall before Polestar, the GCI agency asks us to go and investigate his mate who has been following twenty miles behind. He too is a Bear F, but we spend only a few minutes with him before we have to break off and head for home. There are no tankers around. It is only as we turn away that I notice the movement of the 23-millimetre radar-laid tail guns that have been following us all the while. Then I am suddenly very much aware of the eight live missiles hanging underneath my belly and wings, all primed for action. One flick of the Master Arm Switch and I would have been in a fair position to start World War Three.

A few weeks later I set my traps again and this time catch eight Bears. It is the culmination of a week-long exercise by the Russians that has forced us to cease all normal flying and put every aircraft into the air on interception missions. The Russians are very bold in their exercise and a Bison manages to fly all the way down to the Wash with Lightnings and Phantoms in close escort. Our squadron aircraft meet up with Badgers, as well as Moss and May Early Warning and reconnaissance machines. This continues by day and night and some of them aren't too friendly.

Our American exchange officer is creeping up behind a Badger reconnaissance bomber in the pitch darkness when he is blinded by a high powered searchlight blasting out from the rear turret. He is forced to disengage and back off and wait for five minutes while his night vision slowly restores itself. Another pilot makes a night interception on a Badger who obviously detects him on his tail warning radar and promptly switches all of his lights off and throws the big machine into a tight corkscrew, descending down through the clouds to low level over the sea where he melts away into the shadows.

Our friends, the Americans, with F4s based at Keflavik, Iceland, also join in the chase, and at one stage a Bear has four Phantoms sitting on his wing, two British and two American.

To add to our problems, Scotland is socked out with weather and throughout the week the base is amber/red, the cloudbase hovering between 200 and 300 feet, the visibility not getting much above a mile. Our squadron aircraft are scattered around England on diversions to Leeming, Coningsby, and Valley. From there, they may turn round and launch off on yet another intercept.

On this particular day, the weather is 'Red' as I launch off at 05.00 to rendezvous with the tanker. The Norwegians have reported a mass force coming round North Cape. I hold CAP for three hours before they turn up, two groups of four in about five-mile trail. We decide later that it must have been an OCU tour of the three NATO Atlantic Air Defence Regions – the Norwegian, British and American, but on the radar screen it looked like the war had started.

Today, for some reason, we are by ourselves, so we have the task of photographing all eight of them. We have a field day of types as we identify the basic trainer Bear A; the reconnaissance Bear D; the photographic Bear E; the ASW Bear F. We are soon out of film, so we return to the tanker and top up our tanks and head for home, leaving the force sailing on towards Iceland and an American reception. We learn later that they all disappear into the Atlantic, and six hours later, four of them reappear on the way back to the Kola

Peninsula. As for the other four, Our Man in Havana reports that they have landed there. Later during the week, we lie in wait for them and catch them as they transit back to their base in Russia.

What they get up to during their six-hour blank period over the Atlantic is a mystery to me, but it's a fair bet they are keeping close tabs on the ever-present NATO naval fleets and updating their attack profiles and procedures against the American continent.

I make an approach to the airfield and fail to see the runway at my decision height. I decide to have one more try before diverting to Valley, the nominated alternate airfield for the day. We are making our approaches to Runway 27 which has a tailwind component. There is no way I can land on 09 because Balmullo Hill two miles from the runway threshold gives a decision height of 640 feet on the runway, as opposed to the 230 feet on Runway 27 with its approach over the sea. The cloudbase is fluctuating between 150 and 250 feet this morning. It has been raining, so the runway is wet. I am still heavy with fuel, so as I begin the descent down the glidepath I lower my hook and inform the controller that if I make it, I will be taking the approach end hook wire, rather than risk bursting a tyre under heavy braking on the slippery runway and going off at the end, with a wind behind me pushing me on instead of slowing me down.

It is a steady GCA and at 300 feet we break through the ragged cloudbase and I see the ground below. A moment later, at 250 feet, I see the red T-bar lights on the approach to the threshold and from there on it is plain sailing as I thump onto the ground straight into a savage but exhilaratingly smooth deceleration in the RHAG.

Since then, I have seen many Russians, and as usual it has developed into inevitable routine. My navigator, Bill, seems to attract Bears like a magnet. Whenever he is on IAF duty, he gets scrambled. The new pilots clamour to hold Alert duty with him, because the Bears seem to home onto him like a helicopter onto a Sarbe beacon! But after the climactic eight in one day there is a lull in the proceedings. Only the (apparently) scheduled monthly run to Cuba remains to hold our interest. Only on the next major NATO exercise, 'Strong Express', will the Russians come out again in force. The only other occasion is when one of their nuclear submarines breaks down and they provide an umbrella while it is towed slowly back to safety. But now I am advancing in seniority on the squadron, I am invariably Q2, which means I don't get the scrambles. It is time to let the JP newcomers have a go at Bear baiting.

6

....

Missile Practice Camp

Every year, the Squadron takes-off down to RAF Valley for MPC. There we are supposed to prove to ourselves the credibility of these streamlined sharks we carry under our bellies. At around £20,000 a time the opportunity to launch one of these missiles understandably doesn't come too often – about once a tour per pilot generally. This time, they have allocated two Sparrows and two Sidewinders for us to let off; I am to fire a 'Winder against a radio-controlled Jundivik target.

On Sunday we crank up five clean-wing F4s, get airborne and rush down to Valley where we smash into the circuit and land. There is no time to be wasted. On Monday I fly chase for John. He launches his missile, a good one. We return and land. Then it is my turn. Time for a quick coffee. I am leading, so I hastily re-brief my chaseman, review the profile we are to follow. Outside the groundcrew slave away filling my ship with fuel, switching the Bullpup photographic pod, loading and arming the Sidewinder. We are ready, sign up and walk out. As I strap in and carry out my checks, I mentally run through once again the attack profile. It is a low-level simulated combat engagement firing. The target will cross three miles ahead on a 90-degree TCA, spot me and then go into a turn towards me. My navigator and I must find him, lock on, track and fire.

Four turbines crank up, Houchins are disconnected, 'taxi clearance', and we trundle on stiffly sprung oleos to the threshold of Runway 32, 7,500 by 150 feet of asphalt. 'Line up and take-off ...' cleared, echelon starboard, check Number Two is slotted in and ready, tap helmet, nod once, brake release, surge forward, twin

RPM and TGTs register ... nod again, select full afterburner, nozzles flick open on light-up, runway rushes past with increased fury yet in my cockpit all is calm. Throttle back to half nozzle, he is staying nicely on my wing, airborne, gear, flaps, cut 'burners and at 500 feet it's a bank sharply left heading for Bardsey Island, the range holding point. 1,000 feet and I level, Number Two floating hazy against a blue sea, silver Lightning photo chase already arcing up to join us. The pace quickens – drop Number Two off at Bardsey, on into the range and Aberporth immediately vectors us onto the first heading for the run.

'Starboard 270, minus five minutes, attack run commences one minute, starboard 360 ... starboard 190, four minutes ...'

'Roger.' I check Sidewinder selected, coolant on, aural tone set at twelve o'clock, 35 mils dialled on gunsight, Master Arm safe, caption glows green, the missile is ready, my forefinger extends stiffly clear of the trigger.

'Minus three minutes, adjust to datum.' Throttles to max mil, accelerate, 550 knots on the clock, let down gently to 500 feet, it is very noisy, I can hardly hear myself think. How's the Lightning doing? 'He's right on' says Bill, '800 yards behind and slightly to port.'

'Minus two minutes, target twenty miles, 30 degrees right.'

'Rog.' Bill searches, finds, locks 'contact'. My eyes strain, I see nothing, Master Arm 'On' and an amber 'Ready' light joins the 'SW' green.

'Minus one, port 175.' Gloves move, at this speed reaction is instantaneous, one-two on heading. I climb slightly to get a better view, 'Thirty seconds', still no visual, I begin to sweat, but he is still locked up on radar, tracking purposefully across the nominal 90-degree TCA curve on the B Scope.

'Minus 5 ... 4 ... 3 ... 2 ... 1 ... PUNCH, clear to fire!'

'Roger, clear to fire,' and I spot him, minute, dayglo orange and yellow, crossing the nose slightly above, the flare on the tail bursting into life.

'I got him!' exultant, and it all happens in a rush; Bullpup camera on, ching, 60-degree bank, pull, 2G ... 3 ... pipper creeps up to target, now turning, relax the G slightly and then tighten, pipper hovers fair and square, I can hear a buzzing in my earphones, the 'Winder has locked on to the infra-red flare, it is raring to go. I have no eyes for the radar, I just concentrate on tracking that little object across the hazy summer Welsh skies. We close and Bill is busy watching the ranges; we want to fire at 1,500 yards, he times his call to perfection ...

'Firing,' 1,880 'firing,' 1,700 'NOW!' 1,600 yards, my finger flexes automatically, there is a bang, a whoosh, a white foaming streak of light rushes out to port, curves in towards the target and rockets past, the flash warhead detonating just behind the Jindivik, inflicting (as we were to discover) mortal damage. It is all over in three seconds. For me it is a cry of 'Store away', roll the wings level and pull up out of the debris, rolling away and then looking down to see the Lightning flashing past as it finishes tracking the missile to detonation point. Then it's Master Arm 'Off' and call 'switches safe'.

Anti-climax, yet also amazement, wonder at the performance of that machine, the unerring homing to the heat source, the remorseless closure and the finality of that explosion. Nothing can escape once you have manoeuvred into that deadly tail cone and fired. So we RTB, race into the circuit trailing our customary thunder, break and ease onto the runway, tyres smoking, 'chutes streaming, taxi in, canopy open, cool breeze on sweaty faces and MPC staff at the foot of the ladder; news ... we have destroyed the Jindivik, the first Sidewinder to have done so at MPC, and I marvel even more for we do not carry live warheads on these firings. So for a DH, the fates had decreed a fantastic coincidence of paths to enhance the already amazing accuracy of the weapon in order that Sidewinder and Jindivik meet in the same fatal piece of sky; indeed on the films we see that which was impossible to note in the air, the moment of impact with the pieces shedding from the rear of the target resulting in the subsequent total loss of control (shortly after our departure) by ground control operators. That night, Bill and I drink many beers.

08.30 on a typical Monday morning and I am on my way to my office to work. I rose from my bed at seven, showered, shaved and had a leisurely breakfast in the Mess dining room before sitting down for ten minutes to peruse the day's news in the papers. In that respect, up to eight-thirty my life was no different from billions of others in the world. However, from that point in time onwards, my path diverges markedly from that of my Civil Service or industrial colleagues.

The journey to my office occupies only five minutes of my time. I travel not pressed up in a hot, steamy tube train, or crushed in a crowded, smelly bus, but free and easy by foot. The air that I breathe on that short trip is not choked with exhaust fumes and factory waste, instead I take in country smells of the earth, the scent of blooming roses mixing with a faint tinge of Avtur borne on a light breeze wafting from the flightline to the west. At eight-thirty, I hear not the din of horns and engines or the rumble of rush-hour traffic pouring into the great city, but the chatter of distant birds tail-chasing in the spring air.

The country yokel or village doctor sees, smells, experiences just as much, if not more, and indeed in that respect we are together. But by 09.00 I am sitting in my office, and I begin to smile as I go about my work.

My office measures five feet by three. Its walls are decorated with many glass-faced dials and gauges. I stow my business papers not on a mahogany desk, but on a formed plastic coaming. In my right hand I hold not a pen with which to chastise erring departmental heads, but a black, rigid foot-long stick with silver studs and red buttons on the tip. With this stick I can make my office dance and gyrate, tumble and revolve, plunge and soar.

My telephone sits not on a desk, but in my white hardened helmet. The fingers of my left hand do not drum impatiently on said wooden desk; instead they hold two short steel stumps that run in grooves. My left hand is responsible for catapulting my office through space at twice the speed of sound. My seat is not plush leather and swivelling, it is hard and steely with festoons of straps, buckles and tubing holding me in a firm umbilical grip. My secretary sits in another office, but this office follows six feet behind me and goes wherever I go. His fate is in my hands.

But the best part of my office is the view from the window. When I turn to look outside I don't see Battersea Power Station or Richmond Sewers, I don't see the gasworks or the brewery or traffic-choked streets. At nine on Monday morning I see a sparkling yellow orb of a sun set in a dazzling sky. In the same sky as the sun is a moon still refusing to fade away after its night-time activity. I see a green sea stretching to one horizon and a chequered brown earth stretching to another. The only streets I see up here from my office window are formed by little white clusters of clouds dotting the air all around.

There are other people in their offices up here in this workshop in space, and I communicate with them through my telephone as we conduct our business together. Indeed, we come together to confer and we move intricately about each other, solving the daily problems that we have been tasked with, and when that is finished, we play.

With the help of that stick in my right hand and the twin stumps in my left, I can think my office through the atmosphere. I can perform my sundance, paying homage to the God of Flight, tilting and falling before floating upwards again, the sun and earth, sea and sky smoothly revolving and merging into one seemingly mad kaleidoscope of colours and shapes as we carry out our ritualistic manoeuvres. At such times in our work-play, we are like so many sharks cruising in the crystal ocean of air, miles above the earth, undoubtedly black dots to the curious clerk gazing wistfully from his open window in his office shackled to traffic-jammed Oxford Street.

And when I am steady, I ponder, who in his right senses, at nine on a spring Monday morning – who ... which person on this planet earth would rather be anywhere else but here, in this office, in the sky?

But then, maybe I'm biased ...

Although my prime role is to keep the skies clear of marauders, I also have to refresh myself on the other skills that are part of the fighter pilot's trade, so every so often the armourers load SU 23A gun pods on the centreline station and feed belts of 20-millimetre ammunition into the chambers. We then go off to the ranges and either 'move mud' or attempt to put holes in a flag towed by a Canberra. Prior to the phase, the squadron QWIs spend hours briefing us on sighting theory, Air-to-Ground theory, ballistics, LCOSS handling and the dozens of other subjects the powers-that-be have decided we must be lectured on before embarking on any weaponry phase. Afterwards, to stop us falling asleep in the briefing room, the flight commanders take us out into the hangar and we assist the groundcrew in harmonising the gunsights. My aircraft is K-Kilo, and with the aid of a huge, hieroglyphics-covered board, I spend a lot of time over this task. There are enough variables in gunnery as it is, many outside my control. Harmonisation is under my control, however, which is why I strive to ensure that at least it will be one variable less to worry about.

This morning I am Number 4 in a four-ship simulated strike mission. We will hit two targets in the low-flying area before climbing out high-level to rendezvous with a tanker on Towline 3 off the east coast, going from there to Druridge Bay range where there should be a banner-towing Canberra waiting for us. There we will spend forty-five minutes practising air-to-air gunnery. As Number 4, I have the easiest task of anyone. I simply follow the rest. My main job, in fact, is to keep my eyes open and make sure we are not bounced. The squadron is not providing a bounce today, but nevertheless the low-flying area is full of steely eyed killers all set to have a go at four Phantoms passing by. We will be prey to Harriers, Buccaneers, Gnats, Hunters, USAF machines and other F4s during our travels. Our aim will be to see them first and either run out unseen or, if necessary, stay and fight and shoot them down first.

Black Leader (OC A Flight) drones on, covering routes, frequencies, formations and positioning, tactics, attack profiles, alternative sorties, target briefings, weather, low-level restrictions, warnings, range orders, camera settings, sight pictures ... we will be ticking off a lot of crosses on the stats board on this mission and so the briefing is of necessity a long one, even though we have all done it before. At last he finishes. A few questions from the floor to clear up a few ambiguous points and then we escape with relief to gulp fresh air. Today we carry ammunition sufficient only for the air-to-air phase and so we will not be using any air-to-ground ranges. Our simulated targets will be bridges, radar masts and the like.

We line up as a four on the runway, and right on the hour, the first pair roll. My leader, Black 3, waits ten seconds, glances at me and seeing my thumbs up, nods his head sharply. Brakes release. He nods his head again and I select afterburners. My attention is divided between holding formation on him and checking that my take-off path ahead is clear and that I am not drifting off the runway. He unsticks, an ungainly extension of oleos and spinning wheels, and I follow an instant later, bouncing slightly in the hot air. Hands grope blindly for the undercarriage and flap levers before returning to the throttles. I must hold it smooth and steady – you never know who watches these take-offs, and fellow pilots can be so critical – till 500 feet when I have been briefed to go out into battle formation. The navigator calls the height and a rapid movement with the stick sends me darting out and away to a position a quarter of a mile away and swept back about 60 degrees. Today we have briefed to fly the first two legs in a standard low-level battle, rather than missile spread or escort 'card' formation. Black Lead has already turned onto the first heading for the low-level entry point and we remain at full throttle till we catch up and can then reduce to our nominal low-level speed of 420 knots.

We enter the low-flying area and ease gently down to our transit height of 250 feet. At this height and speed, the earth moves inexorably past, not in a blur or flash as the movies would sometimes have us believe, but rather in a well controlled creamy motion of landscape unfolding. Trees, pylons, rivers, railways, roadways, farms, hamlets, telephone boxes, trucks, grazing sheep, fell walkers all move past in a steady, never ending stream of colours – browns, greens, greys, whites, yellows, an infinite motley of shades. In our progress we leap with ease over ravines, we forge across great stretches of river and lake, we leapfrog hills and straddle ridges in the onward rush. It is true to say that low-level flying, especially in a multi-plane formation, is one of the great experiences of life. Our four shadows race across the earth, here and gone instantly, we are dynamic, we cannot be stopped, our four camouflaged bulks hurtling purposefully across the countryside, bouncing in unison in the turbulent air.

Occasionally our wings dip and we wheel and turn, crisscrossing intricately to maintain formation integrity as we turn onto a new heading where once more we settle down to our ruler-straight course. Lead and Number 3 are responsible for navigation. Black 2 and I are busy polishing eyeballs, checking our six for the bounce. None comes. Approaching hilly country, the clouds thicken slightly to cover the hill tops. Lead elects to take us through the valleys.

He calls us into 'low arrow' formation. We close up into a compact mass, almost close formation, but tightly swept back. Now he can wind down the valleys, round the tight turns and reversals and it is up to us to 'hang in'. Really it's a case of hang in or get scraped off on the hillside flashing past not so many feet from our wingtips. So I jockey with throttle and stick, rudder and speedbrake to hold a good safe position. As Number 4, I have a hard time because all the errors, slight time lapses and microscopic delays are magnified by the time they get back to me, and I am going from idle to full power and see-sawing backwards and forwards as we penetrate down a curving ravine. I am thankful and sweating when we emerge into relatively flat terrain on the other side and resume once more a spread battle formation. The first target approaches and Lead briefs us over the air. This is to be a simulated guns attack on a radar site on the coast. Number 3 moves the two of us over to the starboard to ensure we will be on the correct side for the pull up. I have no idea where we are, although my man in the back professes to have some vague clue. He tells me that we are on the IP to target run. Sure enough, thirty seconds later, Black Lead calls 'pulling up', his aircraft arcs suddenly skywards and then tips over to the left. A second later Number 2 follows, immediately followed by 3. I make a last check of switches, ensuring Master Arm is 'Off' and still wire-locked because I have a live gun on board. Instead I switch the Telford camera on. This will record the accuracy or otherwise of my pass.

It is time to pull up – danger time, when I leave the close comfort of the ground and expose myself to gunners, missile batteries and defending fighters. I must spend as little time up there as possible so I waste no time. 2-G pull and we are up at 2,000 feet in a left banked turn. I use the other three aircraft of Black formation to lead me in to the target. Lead is already pulling off his target and banking sharp right, Number 2 is just coming up to firing point and 3 is halfway down the dive. I see the targets – five small, white radar dishes pointing skywards, a disused site. My target is the one on the extreme right. The panorama is just like the target photo Nav leader flashed up during the briefing. I tip in and plant the pipper firmly on the white blob and accelerate down the 10-degree dive. The blob grows larger and yet almost in slow motion, because I have time to notice odd details; the broken piece of fencing round the perimeter of the site, the weed-encrusted footpath, the rusty steel poles supporting the guys. I know this site has been derelict for some time, but even so just as I reach my firing point, I catch a glimpse of an upturned white face peering from a wooden door in the building at the base of my particular scanner. Whoever he is he must be wondering what had hit him this bright and sunny day with four howling monsters plummetting out of the sky towards him ... Then my subconscious tells me I am in range, my eye has estimated that the target is filling the correct number of mils in my gunsight, the range analogue bar round the edge of the sight is saying '500 yards' – my right thumb hits the pickle button, causing an event mark to appear on the film for later assessment, and because I know all about target fixation and its fatal dangers, my right hand selects 4G on the control column and I am out of the dive.

'Four out!', I call as I slam the stick hard right and dive down into the valley we have previously briefed will be our escape route. I have already picked up the other three racing away, hugging the trees, and I set off in hot pursuit. In long line astern we run out till we round a bend in the valley, at which point Lead calls us to reform wide battle as he sets course for the next target, a set of bridges one hundred miles away.

I wipe the sweat from my eyes and take up position again, at the same time giving Black Lead a 'Bingo' fuel call. We have twelve minutes of relative relaxation before the next hectic strike. Concentration is 100 per cent because in this environment I cannot afford to make a mistake. That old adage 'to err is human' can be quoted and used as an excuse from one day to the next, but in my profession, unlike many others, the making of a serious mistake all too often results in rather unpleasant circumstances. My whole training, my whole aeronautical upbringing, indeed the whole outlook of the Air Force is geared to the elimination of all mistakes, whether in the routine day-to-day operation of my machine or in the tactical manoeuvres of warfare. Either way, the penalties for any serious errors can be literally fatal. My good friend Chris, high speed low-level in his FGR 2 Phantom in the hills, snow showers, lowering cloud, and the leader calls 'pulling up'. The SOP is to select full AB, rotate to 30 degrees nose up on the ADI and get the hell out of it. The leader made it; Chris did not. He and his aircraft joined the endless list of unfortunates who have impacted while low flying. The primary error lies in allowing oneself to be drawn into the mesmeric, Medusa-like snare of weather dodging in hilly country beyond reasonable limits. We all press on down the valleys and squeeze through pillarbox gaps between hill and cloud, and maybe we sweat a little and secretly think there, but for the grace of God, go I. One hopes that good judgement coupled with that inherent instinct for self-preservation will cause one to pull out long before it becomes a case of dicing with death. It has often been said that there are old pilots and there are bold pilots, but no old bold pilots. Perhaps that is the hallmark of the true professional, one who goes as near to the limits as possible, but always as safely as possible because he has weighed all the pros and cons and made a rational decision to go so far and no further. I quote 'A superior pilot may be defined as one who stays out of trouble by using his superior judgement to avoid situations which might require the use of his superior skill.' So now I appreciate the necessity to temper my flying with a touch of fear (survival instinct), because I have been told there is no such thing as a fearless performer in any 'dangerous' sport. 'Accepting and respecting the dangers is perhaps the first and more important role for fledgling aces. A fearless racing driver won't last long; an over-cautious one is wasting his time. Let enthusiasm be tempered by fear, the safety valve for all hazardous pursuits ...' That was a motor racing ace, but I sometimes think of these words when I am flying as I consider the dangers – what if an engine fails on take-off, a double hydraulic failure on finals, ADI failure in cloud, failure of some vital component? Yes, I think about them, but I do not worry about them, instead I resolve to improve my chances. At night I position the wander light to shine on the standby ADI should the main one fail, I switch on the radio altimeter to monitor and cross check the readings of the main one (far too many people have misread their altimeters and plunged into the sea or ground at night). Before every take-off, I mentally review my abort procedures. I check and double check every action possible because I know 'to err is human' and leaving everything to luck will only hold good for so long. It is all part of that myth of 'professionalism'. Therefore, I practise and strive for perfection because tied in with that instinct for survival is that other adage that is bandied around 'If a job is worth doing its worth doing well' (hackneyed, but true nevertheless).

I am happy that I have known these things ever since I started flying, but sometimes I think flying really is a state of mind. There is no difference between the pilot hurtling through the stratosphere at Mach 1 and the street-sweeper ambling pedantically through Regent's Park. Both are human beings with performances that suffer at the whims and moods of particular circumstances. These circumstances are as infinite as space itself because they are governed by both physical and mental laws, subjective and objective, and both are so interconnected that they affect each other's performance.

Yesterday, for example, I took-off and found my way down to the gunnery range and for twenty minutes I hurled my aircraft at the Saab strafe targets. Looking through my gunsight I directed, in the space of twenty minutes, 150 rounds of Her Majesty's 20-millimetre lead and copper at those canvas panels and departed at the end somewhat disgruntled, because only 10 per cent of those rounds had arrived at the appointed meeting place. Today I go across and this time nearly 40 per cent of those rounds thud home to signal an electronic score up in the range officer's hut. The difference? With my inexperience being the common denominator yesterday there blew a 25-knot wind at a 40-degree angle to my track which thus put in motion a whole new set of variables to upset the already complex ballistic and sighting problems involved in successful air-to-ground gunnery. Today, however, the air was still, the pattern was smooth, my pipper stayed where I put it on the bullseye of the target, man, machine and elements worked in smooth unison. The whole trip is smooth and satisfying for today, inexplicably, I am in a state of mind where I can do no wrong, yet I am fooling myself, for the well-being is due to the easy conditions producing a good sortie. But yesterday the opposite was the case, so to be sure, nothing succeeds like success and like Napoleon surrounding himself with lucky generals, I wish to surround myself with lucky days so that success can breed success. It is true that luck in flying should play a very minimal part indeed, and my aim is to eliminate the element that chance plays in my flying fate, but this element, although reduceable to microscopic proportions by supertraining and application, all too often proves to be the guardian of that twilit zone dividing success and disaster.

'By the IP ... Hack!' Black Leader calls. Target two is approaching in three minutes. A double set of bridges, the brief calls for a laydown attack using retard bombs. Black 3 has already started slowing down and I move up into close formation on him. He will now fly our two aircraft as one. On his call, I will press my button and our four (simulated) 1,000-pound bombs will drop in unison to straddle the target. As each bomb is forced explosively from the ejector racks, drogue devices will spring out into the airstream to retard the weapon, enabling us to make our escape unscathed. Delay fuses will then cause it to explode at the appropriate time. However, anyone following closely behind the releasing aircraft is likely to get blown up, which is why my leader and I now drop back to three-mile trail. We do not wish to be blown up. The pull-up point approaches. Aviation Man has spent decades studying the best method of attacking a ground target from the air. It is safe and comforting to strike at high speed, level with the treetops, but the ballistic computations are formidable. The blitzkrieg approach of the Stuka demanded a high-angle dive-bomb attack, plummeting steeply from the sky, accurate enough, but also at the mercy of every gunner for miles around. Today we choose something in between, a compromise. Lead calls the pull-up and we see his pair lift suddenly into the air in front of us. The turn onto attack heading is only 40 or so degrees. We will be bombing down the line of bridges. However, my concentration is devoted wholly to flying on the other aircraft in our pair. The air is still bumpy here and I am having to fight to stay in. He has eased it up to 500 feet on the run in to make life easier for me. Today we will not be performing any acrobatics or crossovers on the turn in to the target. Should I lose out and drift further away than about 300 yards on these manoeuvres, my leader would be forced to abort the pass or else wipe out his lagging Number 2 with his retard bombs. Today it is relatively 'no sweat' as he calls pulling-up. I stay with him as we are up and wingover gently. Out of the corner of my eye I can see the double line of bridges spanning the river, but it is his problem to resolve the sighting and get us pointing at the right-hand stretch. He calls the countdown, and on the 'pickle' call I squeeze the little red button on the top of the stick.

'Bombs away', and we run out straight ahead.

Bombs. Nuclear, neutron or whatever, one thing is certain and this is that I can make life a misery for troops warring on the ground. In our little four-ship unit, we carry seeds of destruction, the capability of wreaking more havoc than a whole wing of wartime B17s. So I am able to drop from the heavens, airborne cavalry abandoning its task of defending airspace to assist beleaguered comrades on the ground. With my 20-millimetre bullets spraying remorselessly ahead, I command the enemy to hide in their foxholes where they must cower in the dirt before the onslaught. But woe betide me if one of their own missiles should strike, forcing me to parachute down into their midst. Their long knives will be sharp and waiting ...

On today's mission, we are not expecting an attack, we have no 'bounce' programmed to harass us along the route. Not so on other days. I picture another sortie in my mind ...

Below us flows not the hard green earth, but an equally hard blue sea. We are spaced out in 'escort' formation. Ahead of me by two miles is Merv, who is Yellow Leader. To his left, about one mile spread, a hazy blob to me is Roger, Yellow 2. I am Yellow 3. On my left about a mile and a half away is Mike, my wingman, Yellow 4.

Our four sets of throttles are producing 90 per cent of total revolutions. Four airspeed indicators are hovering at the 480-knot mark. Altimeter needles – both radio and pressure – are waving gently round the 200-foot etching. Inertial navigation bearing pointers are steady on two-zero-zero degrees true heading. The destination inserted into those pots, when translated into coordinates on a map, reads 'Wattisham Airfield, Suffolk, England', home of our sister Phantom UK Fighter Squadrons.

Today, Yellow formation have turned into a section of simulated low-level raiders racing across the Channel to lay sticks of HE bombs across the expanses of RAF Wattisham and the aircraft parked thereon. The UK is at simulated war. We are expecting attack. Interceptors, Lightnings, Phantoms, F104s and Mirages are on deployment as well as Hunters on local airfield defence, all will be trolling up and down on various CAPs. Their radar beams, those that have them, are already sweeping out and searching for the raids they know are coming in. We, in Yellow formation, know they are there, waiting for us. Now we are set as we start the final part of the profile, the 200-mile high-speed dash in to the target. I ponder on the significance of my being here in this alien role of strike bomber. In the Air Defence world, we look upon ourselves as the true fighter pilots, engaging in the clean chivalrous sport of aerial combat. Our machines are traditionally lightly laden, free to twist and turn, agile and nimble. When I ask my engines to give me Performance, I expect to get it – fast. Not so the 'mud mover', who must pay the penalty for hauling his bombs around the sky. But I am sometimes asked to escort him into enemy territory, so I fly his missions and I experience his problems. I also gain a double bonus because from the other side of the fence I can examine Air Defence tactics with different eyes and so spot potential flaws or cracks in the armour as other fighters attempt to disrupt our flight.

The inertial counters are giving 110 miles to run to target, ninety-five miles to 'enemy coast', and my eyeballs are busy swivelling, checking across to clear Number 4's six o'clock. He should be doing the same thing for me, clearing my blind area behind me. Nothing seen as yet. Today, the dice is loaded in our favour. The cloud base is around 2,000 feet. Anyone popping out will be silhouetted nicely against the ragged grey background. It is true to say that we have a unfair advantage with our detailed knowledge of what are our own tactics. I find that I am putting myself in the shoes of a prospective attacker, deciding how I would perform the intercept and then in turn plotting my own counters to any such moves. It is a never-ending game, a circle of perpetual motion. In fact, I am half hoping that we do get intercepted and shot down without seeing the attacker before its too late. After all, they are fellow Air Defenders. On the other hand, professional pride also dictates that today, Yellow formation in this temporary change of role will penetrate to the target unscathed. With the fire-power and weapons systems we carry on board, it will be very difficult for anyone to attack our four-ship team and escape without being seen.

The reports start coming in.

'Yellow 2 to Lead, we're getting a radar paint bearing 270 degrees coming towards.'

'Okay, Padlock!' Lead has instructed him to watch the bogey.

'Yellow 4, we're getting a warning in the left aft quadrant All eyes automatically swivel to that sector. A passive warning receiver signal indicates someone is getting close, I search hard but see nothing out there. I report '3 to Lead, no visual threat out there this time.'

'Okay, Yellow 4 keep an eye on it.' Number 4 monitors his instruments, looking for the indications and responses that will direct his eyes onto the bogie.

'Yellow 2, that contact now bears 250 degrees, range twenty-five heading 030 degrees, 10,000 feet.'

'Yeah, Yellow 4, got a CW lock indication in that quadrant.'

'Roger, Lead pushing it up to 520.'

My navigator is getting intermittent paints on the bogey as I advance the throttles an inch or so and our progress takes on a renewed urgency. The formation has instinctively sunk lower, closer to the surface, as we seek to hide ourselves behind the waves, lost in the sea clutter to the prying eyes of GCI and Interceptor radars alike. However, with the higher power settings, our aircraft are producing heavy smoke trails, ruler straight giveaways to anybody seeking to pick us out against the blue-grey background of the sea.

I ease my machine farther out to the right, away from the dead line astern position from the Leader. To hit his jetwash at this height and speed would make my eyes water. Now the panorama does unfold at a much greater pace at such ultra-low levels and higher than normal velocity.

Oil rigs, trawlers, liners and freighters rush towards us and flash past as we subconsciously ease up over the masts or weave round the larger vessels and rigs, but our eyes are busy scanning. Four pairs of pilot eyes search the sky, four pairs of navigator eyes search the scopes.

'Yellow 4 – strong contact, two o'clock position.'

'Yellow 2 – bogey now bearing 280 degrees, 3,000 feet, he's on us!'

'Okay, Lead to 3 on the visual, I'll be breaking starboard into him for a standard split by my element. You stand by with your element to cover our tails.'

'Rog,' I acknowledge. There's no need for him to spell it out again as the tactics are clear in my mind, but I can understand the fever pitch of anticipation that is gripping us. I allow 4 and myself to drop back even further behind the other pair. It makes it difficult to keep sight of them ahead, but it also decreases the chances of the enemy fighter gaining a visual pick up on us following behind, unless of course it is us that he has locked onto. But, the odds are that he has locked onto the lead pair and such is to be the case.

'30 right, ten miles … 40 right now … going off the edge at seven miles, 2,000 feet high on us …'

Yellow Lead and I see the fighter at the same time – a silvery Lightning in a starboard turn, belly up to me and obviously carrying out an attack on Lead. I had expected a Phantom.

'Yellow Lead here, I've got the bogey out right three o'clock, five miles turning in on me.'

'3's visual – thirty seconds to the kill if he keeps turning, stand by to break starboard, Lead … Okay, GO!'

My weapons are armed and the Sidewinder is selected on Station, the aural tone humming gently in my earphones as the background radiation from the sea filters through its seeker system. The bogey is halfway round the turn and approaching my one o'clock sector when I call the Leader to break.

It is a set-piece manoeuvre. The lead aircraft pulls hard into the bogey, generating an ever increasing angle off and destroying whatever tracking solution the enemy might have gained and also giving any potential missile launch the maximum problem as far as missile seeker head tracking rates and manoeuvre capability is concerned. The Air Force recruiting posters love to stress the importance of teamwork and it is at times like this that I appreciate afresh the apparent lack of effort and the economy of movement to be seen in the working of a smoothly coordinated team. The compact mass of our formation rearranges itself fluidly as our four aircraft slide through the sky, each motion counterbalanced by another, an apparently haphazard shuffling of positions with only the trained eye being able to note a method to the madness. It is a demon trap that we set together and then wait for the prey to grab the bait! The experienced attacker, once he sees his initial pass disrupted, engages his reheats, unloads the aircraft and accelerates down to zero feet and exits stage left at sonic speeds to look for less troublesome targets or to call in reinforcements.

Our man today does none of these things. As the Lead pair go into their defensive manoeuvres, and as my finger starts to flex on the trigger, alarm bells must be ringing in his cockpit because the Lightning suddenly abandons its starboard turn and drops its left wing just in time to see the rear two aircraft of Yellow formation closing fast for the kill.

'3 to Lead, he's switched to us. You're clear to reverse and truck on!'

The heat is off him and he must continue with the primary task of getting the bombs to the target. I see him reverse his turn and unload away, 'burners blazing bright orange, a shimmering bundle of energy. I see no sign of Yellow 2. All this happens in no more than a few seconds, yet the Lightning is approaching fast. The angle at which he is crossing my track indicates that, in fact, it is my wing-man he has spotted and not me. I reach down to the missile status panel and switch the selector to Sparrow III, at the same time calling to my back-seater.

'Go Boresight! I'm going to take him head on!'

The target is framed in my glowing gunsight and almost instantly it seems the symbols spring up to indicate a successful radar lock.

'Okay, you're cleared to fire,' he yells from the back. I go ahead and fire, although at such close range, the chances of a missile completing its arming and fusing functions before it has passed the rapidly closing target are degraded, but at least that white plume of smoke plunging towards him would get his attention and cause him to think again before pressing home his attack. We will claim that one as a possible.

The Lightning rushes down my left side, a great silver, slab-sided shark of a shape, almost co-altitude 200 feet above the waves. He yo-yos upwards in a hard right turn. An instant debate flashes through my mind – stay and fight or run? As simulated bombers, we would have to jettison bombs into the sea to fight on equal terms, in which case his mission would have been accomplished in preventing us from putting the load on the target. On the other hand, a straight run out might put him right in the middle of his missile firing bracket.

The problem is solved for me. I am just about to call Yellow 4 into a cross-turn counter when the Lightning disappears into the cloud bank above. He has underestimated the lowish cloud base. It will take him a long time to get back down and re-acquire us.

'Yellow 3 to 4, let's run out. Thirty port – GO!'

Mike knows exactly what to do with full AB engaged and the aircraft 'unloaded' we are at 650 knots in no time and back at sea level. This coupled with a 30-degree heading jink means that that is the last we see of the enemy.

'3 to Lead, we've lost the bogey. Go Air-to-Air Tacan.'

The counters on my HSI click over obediently and when they steady up the figure 7 is showing.

'Okay, we got a good lock. I think we're six miles in your seven o'clock.'

'Roger, I'm slowing down to 400 and coming left 60 for the join up. Call when you get tally on us.'

Number 4 and I are still down at very low level and pushing 500 knots plus, so I see the other two members of the formation quite early, standing out above the horizon at almost 500 feet, four miles away.

'We got you; reverse starboard 210 degrees and we'll be in.'

Thirty seconds later the formation is regrouped and the INAS is telling us we have fifty miles to run to the target.

We get a few radar contacts and intermittent PWR pick-ups, but nothing appears to lock onto us. We are through the main belt of CAPs. The next opposition will be found around the coast on local airfield defence. As the coast approaches we have to climb up to 1,000 feet to avoid annoying the local populace on the beaches, but once inland we drop down to operational height for the final ten-mile run in to the target.

Because this is peace-time and rules and regulations still apply, Lead has to call up Wattisham Tower for clearance to attack the airfield. This call is the signal for them to set off their 'Air Raid Warning-Red!' sirens, alert SAM batteries and vector the local airfield CAP on to us. An unfortunate artificiality as far as the attackers are concerned. I have found this one-minute call very useful for putting me in behind Mirages, F5s, Jaguars and Buccaneers inbound to attack airfields I have been defending.

'Yellow formation, you're cleared in for airfield attack, circuit clear.'

(*Briefing:* 'Okay, you're all familiar with Wattisham Airfield. We'll be carrying out a straight forward laydown attack, maintaining our transit formation throughout. We will not be performing any split heading coordinated runs, except that I want the rear element to take appropriate lateral and vertical spacing for debris avoidance. The attack vector will be on runway heading. Lead and 3 will take the radar heads and domes sited on the north side of the field; 2 and 4 take out the pans and dispersals on the south side. Attack speed will be standard, height the same. Work out your own sight settings. Wind is down the runway, 15 knots. Everyone call 'Off' the targets. I'll be carrying out a right turn after the strike and clearing to the north. Everyone join up in loose battle, 3 and 4 watch the crossover …')

The first sign I see of the local airfield CAP is a brilliant white flash out of the corner of my eye, up to the right as he selects the afterburners in. I call the bogey, a Phantom of 56 Squadron, to Yellow Lead, but he is busy fining down his navigation for the last thirty-second run in to the target. However, the bogey is of no immediate threat to him, but he is a sitting duck for me as he has not seen the rear two aircraft at all. I simply tweak the nose up a few degrees to lay the sight on, the Sidewinder growls on the two big reheat plumes and I squeeze the trigger – 'Fox 2 on that bogey!' I inform Lead.

'Roger, ten seconds to strike,' he replies.

The defender, in the absence of a real Sidewinder smoking up his jet pipe is very much alive as he slots in behind the Leader, and no doubt starts to reel off streams of missiles. He is still unaware of my presence half a mile and fifty-odd feet below and behind him. Indeed his proximity is beginning to worry me as he drifts closer and I am thinking that perhaps I will have to abort my pass when he suddenly hauls off and away to the left. A second later, grey asphalt flashes past below me, a runway, followed by three dirty grey latticed 'golf balls' (the protective domes for the radar heads) looming out of the gathering dark haze. I have little time left to boot the sight on and squeeze the pickle button before we are through, the trees of the woods behind streaming just below the wingtips.

The first two aircraft are already pitching skywards and banking to the right as I glance left and see my wingmen racing past the control tower at first-floor level. There is no time to contemplate the commotion our presence must be making before the airfield perimeter rockets past below and I ease the stick back a fraction to send my machine zooming up in a climbing right-hand arc.

'2 out ... 3 out ... 4 out ...'.

'Roger, check switches safe. Wattisham, thank you. Yellow's climbing outbound, going to en route frequency, good day!'

Back to the present and the relative calm of today's mission and I think – mud-moving strike missions are all very well in peacetime,but come the war with real hard-nosed SAMs, triple-A ground fire and enemy fighters by the hordes, I know where I'd rather be.

The seven-minute transit to the coast is uneventful, which is just as well because we are getting rather short on fuel. Coasting out, the formation pulls up and the ground drops away into insignificant doll-like detail, finally to be replaced by sea. Northern radar gives us a vector to the tanker and soon we are alongside, astern hoses, plugged in, sucking, 7,000 pounds of Avtur, sufficient to see us through our allotted time on the air-to-air range fifty miles to the south.

As I sit there refuelling, I think what a pretty picture it makes, the four of us and the tanker, all bobbing up and down gently in the smooth air. Today I am at ease, but it is not always so.

One thing I find hard to understand is the fashion in which my concentration sometimes lapses the minute I think I am under scrutiny. Now air-to-air refuelling normally gives me no trouble whatsoever. A first-time plug-in is the normal rule, occasionally I succumb and have to take another prod, but I am happy in my mind with the techniques and procedures. My peripheral vision is tuned to the picture I expect to see when that basket is hovering in the correct position in relation to that probe. Out of the corner of my eye, I can sense it is there, correct, and as I edge forward I expect, as a matter of course, to feel the clunk of penetration and see the hose twitch and flex as it is wound in on the hose drum unit. Yes, normally it is subconsciously easy.

But the other day it all fell apart. We gathered four aeroplanes and launched skywards to practise close formation in preparation for Battle of Britain Saturday ...

I don't feel too good from the start; maybe my metabolism is inexplicably low in one of the downward troughs of normal everyday life. I am not in the groove. The feeling compounds itself when during the preliminary PIs we get shot down not only when acting as target, but also as fighter! Whereas the other day I saw them at twelve miles, today I am blind because I see nothing at all even with the radar locked up and ranging thirty left at two miles. When that happens, I know all is not quite there, and the seeds of doubt are sowed, cancer-like in my mind.

We go and rendezvous with the tanker; the Boss and John line up behind the hoses and plug away for ten minutes, first time in every time while Phil and I hold off to port and watch. Then it is my turn, and automatically, unreasonably, I become conscious of six pairs of eyes watching me, riveting their gaze on my performance. Automatically my mind, instead of fixing itself on the task in hand, a task that requires complete and utterly unswerving dedication, concentration supreme, instead of keeping my mind on the job, instead part of my concentration drifts to the Boss and John, successfully complete, sitting ten yards on my starboard wingtip gazing at me. I close up and miss. I draw back and stab again and this time penetrate – not good, but not bad. I suck 4,000 pounds from the Victor's bowels. Now for dry prodding. Phil has got in first time (he is a smooth pilot) and is waiting for me. I position, hold it steady and move forward and … miss.

'Ten o'clock over the top!' Bill says from the rear. Beads of sweat break out. I draw back again and stab forward, with a slight air of desperation, and again I miss. It is like a nightmare, it is like being back in the days of tanker convex, but magnified. I am on stage to a large audience, tanker crew and the other three aircraft of Chequers Black formation. My failure is plain for all to see. Desperately (fatal) I lunge forward again and miss yet again. I am making the big mistake of not taking it slowly and easily. I am in a haste to perform, I am not concentrating, I am relying on luck, not the customary skill and judgement. I am ignoring all the basic tenets of refuelling. I am not stabilising behind the drogue, I am not holding a constant attitude, I am not holding the correct alignment of pod light and pylon, I am not positioning the basket behind the E2B compass, I am not flying smoothly, accurately, conservatively. In fact, I am screwing up in a big way.

Finally common sense prevails. I draw right back and call Phil to go ahead and take his prod while I gather my wits. I take a deep breath of 100 per cent oxygen, heart rate slows down, nerves soothe and calm, hands steady, steely glint returns to eye, cold calculating determination overrules previous self-consciousness. I am ready. Victor Captain adds insult to injury – '03 are you happy to try in the turn?', curt 'affirmative', tanker banks into left turn. I slide up and to the right behind it, approach the drogue smoothly, slowly and hook up straight away in the turn. No problem. He rolls out and I take my next two dry prods one after the other, in and out. I am back in the groove. I should never have been out of it. So I am bitter and curse my stupidity, for my professionalism has been clouded in the eyes of my colleagues.

The Canberra is already on tow as we enter the range. Black Lead detaches Number 2 to descend to sea level. He will act as range-sweeper reporting on any shipping straying into the path of the formation. We do not wish to pepper any passing matelot with empty shell cases, or live 20-mil rounds for that matter. The sweeper will fly at low level in front of the rest of us and call us to cease firing should he see anything. The remaining three of us form up in long line astern in the descent to 10,000 feet, run up to the tug from line astern and break over the fluttering flag up into the pattern. As I start my break, Black Lead is already tipping in for his first dry cine pass. From here on we must work as a smoothly coordinated team, keeping the action flowing if we are to maintain the rhythm as we have only thirty minutes left now, and that is tight with four of us to fire.

Air-to-air gunnery can be a frustrating sport. At this time on the Phantom force we are still relative novices at the game. Aviation Man's other major task in life has been to discover how he can guarantee that 100 per cent of his bullets arrive at the same point in space and time as his intended target. Whether he flies Sopwith Camels or F4 Phantoms, the problems remain unchanged. The QWIs have told us the secret of good gunnery scores. They are simply a function of smooth coordinated flying, careful tracking of the target and a short gentle squeezing of the trigger, at least that was the theory. Pilots had their own favourite secret keys to success, keys that did not figure in any weapons manual. The old hands talked of using rudder, sliding pippers, tracer-type hoses, high-G angle-off shots, all *verboten* if the weaponeers were to be believed. I am new and I have to do it by the book. I have little experience. I get low scores.

The flag is thirty feet long and six feet wide, quite a big target you may think. It is towed at 180 knots, 900 feet behind the tug aircraft. Our firing range is from 400 down to 300 yards. We are not allowed to fire inside 15-degree angle-off or else the Canberra pilot gets upset (he is flying straight and level. The Americans fire on a turning Dart target). The firing pass is made from a perch a few thousand feet above the flag. A good pass begins right from here. Events happen fast. I roll in, call 'In Hot'. Reverse, set the throttles and squeeze the red button to achieve a radar lock on the flag if the navigator has not already done so. Range information immediately appears on my gunsight. I hold a switch outboard of the left throttle forward with my little finger to 'cage' the gunsight till I have closed in range. Navigator calls a check on speed and I concentrate on tracking the target in the gunsight, coarse tracking at first and then fining it down as I close to firing range. At 1,000 yards I release the switch and the gunsight bobs down slightly and shivers gently as the gyros and amplifiers work out the dozen odd calculations necessary before the pipper can predict where my bullets will strike. While these calculations are progressing, I must hold the aircraft in a smooth stable flight path. Any twitches or inadvertent application of extra G than the two I already have on will cause the computer to throw up its hands and start a fresh set of calculations (albeit instantly). The flag grows larger and larger, its tail end fluttering wildly. There is a great black circle painted in the middle of its whiteness and that is my aiming spot. I check finally – Master Arm On, centre station selected and glowing, Telford camera on, air-to-air guns selected, and we are at firing range, my 2-mil pipper filling a third of the flag's width. My forefinger flexes, there is a dull whooooooooooooo ... as the SU 23 Gatling gun winds itself up to its maximum rotation speed and spits out ammunition at the rate of 6,000 rounds a minute.

I track while I am firing, even though it is a short burst, approximately one quarter of a second, and then I am into the break to avoid hitting the flag. Rudder, back pressure and the Phantom rolls soggily, buffeting – we are still heavy with fuel and so it is not handling at its best. We hit the tug's slipstream as the flag flashes past below us and then I reverse, call 'out' and start the climb back to the perch, at the same time checking the Master Arm back to Safe, camera off and pulling the nose up to avoid a head on collision with Black 3 who is halfway down his dive. A good pass, I think. If my harmonisation was up to scratch, if my sight was predicting the correct amount of lead, if my aircraft did not hide any undetected slip or skid, if my tracking was indeed 'right on' at the *moment critique* of trigger squeeze, then I think I got quite a few hits on the pass. Moreover, I am firing red-painted ammo, so I should be able to see on my next few passes whether I was successful or not. Red, in air-to-air seems to be a lucky colour. The SU 23A is an accurate gun. At the ranges we are firing, there is a very small spread in the bullet group – fine for air-to-air, but not so good for air-to-mud.

So the sport continues for the next twenty minutes before I am sent off to do my stint as sweeper. Black 2 fires out at last. We all re-form in battle four, drop back to sea level and stream across the sea towards base, where we rush into the circuit for a four-ship break to land.

The debrief will take many hours, for after the verbal debrief strike films will be assessed. The Canberra follows back to our base at a much more leisurely pace, drops the flag beside the runway and then returns to his own airfield. Gloom and glory commences as hits are counted (we each have a different colour of ammunition – the greens and blues will spend a long time arguing which hole belongs to whom) then it's back to the cine room to look at air-to-air film and decide why we did so well (or so badly). By evening it is all finally ended with a wash-up where everybody puts their oar in, for better or worse. The formation will then retire to the bar where the arguments will continue over the foaming 'frosties'.

Happy, carefree days on a fighter squadron.

7

....

Display Flying

Many is the time I have sat on the ground at air shows or whatever and gazed up at Red Arrows, Gemini, Macaws, Diables Rouges, Pelicans, Simon's Circus, Blue Angels, Thunderbirds, all wheeling and rolling and revolving in tightly knit precision across the summer sky and I often wondered – what is the skill involved in manoeuvring a few feet from another aeroplane as the world tilts uncaringly about you? Well, this year Stu (champion of the JPs) puts it to the Boss – the junior element for this year's Battle of Britain four-ship formation team. Boss reluctantly agrees 'Why not ... But if after the first wingover I'm on my own, then I'll have to look elsewhere!' Fair enough. The days of practice are long and traumatic, and it is hard work, but come the day, we know everything will be all right, it always is.

Saturday morning dawns, cloudy but clear. A sea of multinational flying suits spreads as visiting display teams arrive. Every sortie is preceded by a briefing. Battle of Britain briefing is the biggest and best of them all. The display pilots all gather in Wing Briefing Room and the day starts with words from the Metman and a time hack. I am Number 3, so I can afford to let a lot of the routine procedural chat float over my head. I find a dark corner and ease my body into a chair. I listen. For the next hour, Display Coordinator drones on about procedures, rules, regulations, timings, frequencies, all mainly for the benefit of the visitors. Leuchars Wing have heard it all before. Now pilots put in bids for revisions to the schedules and arguments develop with Lightnings running short on fuel, Spitfires requesting curved approaches, VC10s demanding ten-mile finals and Chipmunks getting in the way. Display Coordinator is a diplomat (that's why he was picked for the job) and an hour later ruffled feathers have been smoothed and everyone is reasonably happy. Station Master stands up and implores all to keep it safe, no hiding behind the trees please, gentlemen. He makes a special plea – do not start engines while the C-in-C is taking the salute from the massed pipe band.

At last, we all stream out thankfully into the cold fresh air. The crowds of rubberneckers have already gathered, sideshows, stalls and joyrides are doing a roaring trade. I smile. I remember many, many such hours of rubbernecking, a member of the selfsame crowd, an outsider. However, now I move with ease and confidence through the crowds. I sport a lightweight green flying suit. Underneath, all I wear is a G-suit – I will need it – otherwise torso is bare. Flying formation is hot work, and I will be hot, I know it. The final touch is the black and white chequered silk squadron scarves we all wear tied nonchalantly round our necks, the ends floating in the breeze. We are the inheritors of the Battle of Britain tradition, modern descendants of those fighter pilots of a bygone age whose memory we are now commemorating.

The Land Rover transports us out to the aircraft parked at the end of the runway. Time for a quick pose for photographs of this year's team before the hour arrives to climb aboard, strap in and wait for the ball to roll. Our leader, the Boss, is overall formation leader. He has sixteen aeroplanes to control this year, not a particularly large group as formations go. I remember seeing thirty-six aircraft all lined up at the same time at Tactical Weapons School. Today, his formation consists of four Phantoms from 43 Squadron, four Lightnings from 23 Squadron and eight Phantoms courtesy of 892 Naval Squadron. I am Deputy Lead of this mass. The thought briefly crosses my mind and is instantly dismissed. All will be well.

Timing is critical for the whole show and so right on the button we crank engines. Mercifully, all start first time. There are no major snags. I have a static correction problem, but decide to take it. Pretty soon, the whole formation has checked in and we are taxiing, 100 yards apart, for two miles round the airfield to the threshold of 09 Runway.

Looking back from my aircraft, I see a long, long line of aeroplanes and it is a sight to behold, so many steel turbines churning the summer afternoon air. The Gods smile on us for all of a sudden the sky has cleared and it is 8/8 blue. The Boss taxis onto the runway, John, Number 2, is beside him, I move right up into the gap between them till I can almost reach out and touch either aeroplane. Phil tucks in on the other side. 892 forms up on the ORP in a big eight-ship echelon while 23 forms a four behind us. We sit and wait for the go. To my left is the crowd line and it is a solid unbroken sea of faces stretching halfway down the borders of the runway. One minute to go. Boss gives the signal and our four sets of canopies come down as one and seal with a clunk. The roar of engines becomes a muffled hum. Last check round the cockpit and all is well, final check of trims, flaps, stab-augs, warning lights, all is Go.

'Leuchars combine for take-off', we are cleared, wind is light south-westerly. Lead calls 'rolling, rolling ... Now.' Brakes release and we are off. I have 80 per cent power on, holding the brakes. Boss's aircraft moves away in a cloud of heat haze and turbine smoke, the dark jet pipes flicker and glow orange white as the afterburners light up. Five seconds, John's aircraft gives a lurch and rolls away. My machine shudders and rocks under the combined blast of their two jetwashes. My stopwatch is ticking away the seconds. Outside I know the crowds are joyfully suffering the phenomenal noise that is battering at eardrums and vibrating ribcages. Leuchars Wing is on the roll.

Bill counts down, 'five ... four ... three ... two ... one ... Now', my feet release the brakes, my left hand advances the throttles through the gate to their stops, right hand draws the stick back into my stomach. Eyes monitor the twin RPM gauges winding up to 97 per cent power and TGTs hovering around their red-marked limits. Ahead of me, the Boss's aircraft is already airborne and John is just unsticking. I pity the Number 16 man today for the air will be well and truly tortured and chewed, and his run will be long. But for me the air is still relatively calm, eighty knots, one hundred knots, one hundred and forty ... the nose rises sharply. I check forward, one hundred and sixty knots, we are airborne, gear up, flaps, the ground disappears rapidly, the beach flashes past beneath and then sea. I leave the 'burners in as I search for and pick up the smoke trails of Lead and Number 2 ahead and above me. I cancel the 'burners and use a quick dab of speedbrakes to slide into a loose echelon position on the port side of Black Lead's aeroplane. A few seconds later, Number 4 appears and eases into a loose slot position and we all ride along bobbing gently in the smooth air. All is now calm and peace, we are 'hanging loose'.

In my mirror I see several smoke trails. Everyone is safely airborne and checking in with their callsigns. Boss calls for a big check in and all sixteen rattle in, Chequers Black, Eagle Red and Navy Blue callsigns filling the airwaves. So far so good. We are already at Bell Rock and into our holding pattern, a great thirty-mile racetrack that enables all to join up in the sixteen-ship diamond for the flypast. On our left are four Navy ships, another four to the right and finally the Lightnings in the slot. After the second orbit, everyone has settled down and it is time for the run in. Boss turns the formation onto 270 degrees and descends the unwieldy mass to one thousand feet. He calls, 'By the IP chaps, tighten up!' That is the signal to 'clamp'. I wriggle my toes and take a fresh grip on the pole before easing in till I am half a wingspan from the other aircraft. John and I have spent many hours trying to find a common suitable reference point and now we strive to hold it. To my left, the Navy are sitting too low. Boss rebukes the element lead and he moves it up a shade. Thirty seconds' – I start to tense and have to make a conscious effort to relax. Movement now is measured in inches. From the corner of my eye, I see the airfield and crowd drawing nearer, passing below us. Muscles are rigid as I hold it perfectly still, painfully steady, breathing, heart, nerves all frozen, we are catatonic as the tableau glides swiftly across the stage and from the ground it looks good, before we are gone in a doppler wave of sound receding. In the cockpit I have come alive again, we are through and clear of the field, limbs relax, sweat is wiped from dripping brows and we move out a couple of feet. I can hear the Lightnings breaking off to commence their show and the Navy have also peeled off and are heading in a big gaggle to their holding point on the coast before returning to carry out their mysterious Type Bravo attack on the field.

Chequers Black is now established in a wide downwind leg. We have four minutes before we are 'on'. The Boss is slowing down from 400 knots to 250. He calls gear down and then flaps, holding the speed at 180 knots. We still fly it loose. Round the corner onto finals, I can see the Lightnings carrying out their final bomb-burst manoeuvre. It really is a beautiful day, I think idly, the sea is blue, the fields are green, I can see for miles and miles and there is no other place in the world I'd rather be right now. 700 feet, altimeter says, and the Boss calls, 'Okay, move it in!' This is it, all the practice of the past two weeks is about to culminate in the next three minutes. I will be on stage in front of an audience of thousands and quite simply, I do not wish to screw up. I clamp into position again. Phil looks good below me, steady, and John looks the same. It is time to 'hang in there'.

Overhead, throttles seesawing, Lead calls 'overshooting' – power on, simultaneously reach for gear and flaps lever, smash them up, back to throttles, formation bobs through the trim change, pulling up for wingover left and he calls 'Burners ... go', four sets of throttles move forward through the detents. He pulls it high and then rolls to the left. I slide in and follow it easily round the turn. All I have to do now is hang on. He calls 'flying it down towards the crowd'. I am not interested. All that concerns me is keeping that stabilator tip lined up with the other and trying to keep the engine blow hole lined up with the trailing edge navigation light. He calls 'tightening', and the G comes on. I drop slightly, but dare not relax the pull or I will drop out, shame. My aim is to hold a constant pressure so the 'yugs' will not show to those on the ground, civilians and critical aircrew alike.

Boss calls again 'reversing for 360'. The world tilts and in one smooth motion the panorama behind his aircraft changes from blue sky to the patchwork quilt of the airfield as he reverses into the long right-hand 360-degree turn. I relax for a micro-second and gaze down at the airfield, crowds and static aircraft all laid out below me, but my momentary lapse in concentration means I slip out a little. A warning cry from the back seat 'hang in there!', and I give a quick panic-stricken boot of rudder and slide back into position. I am sure I am crushing the stick to powder, my feet are tense on the rudders, once again I feel my breathing and cardiac processes have long since ceased, but I am flying a steady path and everything will be sacrificed to that goal. The turn seems to have lasted forever. At some stage, he calls 'tightening' and the' little clock marked G winds up to 3 ... 3½ ... 4 as he strives to hack the pattern, but I notice not a thing. All I see at one point is John's aircraft develop a sudden monumental 'yug' and pitch rapidly about its central axis, a unique sight. His is an uncomfortable position to fly, because looking up at the sky, he has no real references concerning the progress of events apart from the startling and unwelcome appearance of Big Ball Sun straight in the eyes. Life at this moment for him is interminable.

Nevertheless, the 360 comes to an end and lead reverses to port, straightens and calls 'pulling up for wingover left and change into line astern'. For a few seconds we have the luxurious and ridiculously simple task of flying formation on an aircraft that isn't tossing and turning, but the pleasure is short-lived. We arc upwards followed by a steep bank to the left as he calls 'line astern ... go'. This is my signal to move. I throttle back and transfer my gaze down to Number 4 who has been sitting pretty in the slot all this time. I have no wish to collide with him – he has a wife and new child to go home to – so I move with care. I am not a Red Arrow ace able to change positions in the twinkling of an eye. On the other hand there is no time to waste. John and I move back as one, sliding back and down, at the same time continuing the wingover left, a three-dimensional movement par excellence. I slide underneath Phil's belly and then push the throttles forward to slot my nose in beneath his jet pipe. Behind me John has done the same for his call of 'Two in!' comes very quickly. Now I can ease the crick in my neck from looking to the right all the time. Instead I peer forward and up underneath the canopy arch. The Phantom looks huge, belly dirty grey, streaked with hydraulics, and covered with numerous numbered access panels. Life's objective now is to keep the jetpipes and two wing tanks framed in my forward windscreen. That is the correct position.

The Boss flies it down to 500 feet and levels. As he does so, a small 'yug' develops which whiplashes down the line and I mentally apologise to the fourth man in the line as I fight to damp out the oscillations. But we are steady quickly and the run in front of the crowd for the final manoeuvre is smooth, steady and evenly spaced. In these final stages, concentration is 100 per cent, the sweat pouring into my eyes and down my cheeks and chin, but I cannot put hand to face. Rather, hold it steady, hold it smooth, hang in a few seconds more ... till the words I long for crackle across the RT wavelenths.

'Chequers Black, stand by to break!' and the Number 4 man in the line chips in 'breaking, breaking, go ... and now ... and now ... and now!' At one-second intervals, we snap on the bank and pull upwards in a fan break till we are strung out in a line astern horizontal tailchase. The left turn must now continue through 270 degrees till we are pointing straight at the crowd. Ahead I see the tailpipes of the lead two aircraft flicker as their afterburners are lit. We are at 1,500 feet and its 'burners in, 5-G round the corner and dive down to level at 500 feet ... 400 feet ... 300 feet, stepped slightly to the right of the aircraft in front and so in a tight starboard echelon Chequers Black sweeps across the field, acceleration phenomenal, ASI climbing instantly to 600 knots, mach .96 (the Boss has warned 'no supersonics – windows and eardrums are expensive'), and in one long man-made thunder, condensation clouds steaming in a wreath around the Phantoms, so we burn across the crowd in one thrilling race and disappear into the heavens, leaving behind faces upturned in awe at this demonstration of sheer power and performance.

8

....

QWI

Now I train to be an Air Defence Qualified Weapons Instructor. I move down to the OCU once again to become a student, long days and nights and weekends of cold sweat, cold towel, cold swot. I've got to get down …

Graduation day, and gone are the carefree Junior Pilot days. I am vested with authority, I deliver lectures, write procedures, amend tactics. I give unit briefings, attend conferences and meetings, I join directing staff at weapon meets, I judge and assess performance. I am an instructor at the OCU and some of my students are former instructors of mine from past training schools. Life is ironic.

On the OCU, as an instructor it is part and parcel of my job to fly in the rear seat of the Phantom. Normally a regime that is the haven of navigators, whose concern is mainly to shoot intercepts, pilots are nevertheless sometimes forced to occupy their slot for the purposes of checking out other pilots. For the QFI, his task is to teach the newcomer to the Phantom force the delicate art of flying the beast in a safe, if not accurate manner. Similarly, for the FWIs ground attacking (or, should I say, mud moving) it is to ensure the tyro bomber pilot is not about to fly himself into the ground attempting good strafe scores or DHs in the retard bombing pattern. For me, an ADWI, my main interest is to ensure that the would-be fighter pilot will be able to manoeuvre his aircraft in combat without the risk of straying outside the performance envelopes and either overstressing and breaking up the aeroplane or, just as effective as far as the enemy is concerned, losing control and spinning in off a high-G barrel reversal.

Flying back seat in the F4 is an interesting experience. There are specially modified aircraft which enable us to do the task (some unfortunate IPs in some aircraft, like the Buccaneer for instance, have no such luck). These aircraft have a removable stick installed in the rear cockpit. In addition, there are a set of throttles (military power range only), RPM gauges, VSI, undercarriage and flaps indications and (very important) a set of angle of attack chevrons.

A week after joining the OCU, I am detailed for my first back seat checkout with the squadron QFI. As I strap in, the first thing of interest to note is that forward vision is almost nil. The instrument panel (about a foot from my eyes, as opposed to two to three feet in the front) extends almost up to the roof line. Projecting on either side is the mass of equipment associated with the front ejection seat. I discover that there is a limited forward view by peering down through two tunnels on either side of the central mass, tunnels that for some fortuitous reason have nothing filling them. In this fashion, I can see the extreme edges of wherever I am going. On the runway this means that when I am lined up I can see about half of the total width before me.

I take this in as I finish strapping in, at the same time noting something else. Looking down through this tunnel and through the side of the front canopy, the world is distorted. The plexiglass was never designed to be looked through at that angle. So surrounding concrete takes on a distinctly warped air. I make a mental note not to rely on that picture for my final landing cues.

I make the final connections, the ground crew stows the pins, disappears and leaves me to take further stock of my surroundings. Sitting in the front cockpit of the Phantom, the cockpit sidewalls where aircraft body meets canopy slope quite markedly down towards the nose and front windscreen arch. In the rear, this view is even more accentuated and this is not helped by the almost claustrophobic air of sitting in what I imagine a midget submarine conning tower must be like. The cockpit sidewalls reach up very high, the instrument panel is at eye-level and I notice now that the instruments aren't laid out in the standard T fashion, but are instead strewn around in an apparently haphazard fashion that involves not only rapid eye movement for an adequate scan but also changes of focus as well. It is like watching two tennis matches simultaneously, one near, the other far.

I busy myself aligning the INAS and storing destinations. The engines are started in the front, an almost noiseless procedure to me in the back with my canopy sealed down. Only the RPM gauges winding up to idling at 55 per cent tell me the two Speys are churning away behind me. I listen to the afterstart routine, while at the same time switching on the radar and sending it through its built-in test (BIT) sequence. The Squadron Leader in the front seat completes his control checks and hands over to me for a ritual peculiar to the two-stick F4. Because the stick is removable and because the laws of Murphy state that if its humanly possible, someone will connect the control wires the wrong way round, there is a requirement that the line chief comes out to perform an independent check. There has to be a check anyway because from the back, as from the front, it is impossible to see the ailerons, spoilers, rudders, flaps and suchlike control surfaces in operation, hence the need to make sure that what I do with the stick in the cockpit agrees with what the surfaces are doing outside. The line chief plugs in to the intercom system:

'Ready for independents, sir?'

'Rog' I reply, 'stick back ...'

'Tailplane leading edge nose down'.

'Stick forward ...'

'Leading edge nose up'.

'Stick left ...'

'Left spoiler up, right aileron down, slight left rudder.'

'Stick right ...'

'Right spoiler, left aileron, slight right rudder.'

'Rudder right ...' Check '... and left ...' Check. 'Okay Chief, check the trims please ...' I move the two-axis trim button fully to the left and right and he ensures that the ailerons move in sympathy. In the front, I have a gauge to tell me the position of the aileron trim. No such luck in the back. He talks me into a neutral position. I thank him, dismiss him and hand back control to the man in the front, who goes ahead and raises the flaps and completes the afterstart checks. The radar has finished testing itself and seems happy to go.

'Taxi 26 right, QFE 1020', and we move down the taxiway on the two-mile journey to the take-off point. Pre take-off checks, runway checks, line up, brakes on – 'You have control' he says. I stow the flip cards, crane down to look through the right-hand tunnel (which I have already decided will be the most comfortable to use). My hands move the throttles to 80 per cent, feet release the brakes and we start to roll. Max military power. I am keeping straight by ensuring the right-hand edge of the runway does not approach any closer from its present position.

''Burners please', the extra thrust cuts in and in a few seconds we are at 140 knots, the nosewheel is lifting, I am checking forward to hold the attitude at something that feels right and before I know whether it is or not, we are airborne and I am transferring my gaze to the miniature ADI and trying to decide which etching on the ball signifies the 10-degree climb angle.

'Gear and flaps' I call to the front-seater and he obliges. 350 knots is on us very soon, the 'burners come out, we change to approach frequency and I settle down to fly instruments. Cloud envelops the aircraft while I lower my seat to a more comfortable height and take stock of events. The engines hum quietly, there is faint background chatter on the RT, the pressurisation hisses gently to itself, the airflow on the skin outside also hisses, but at a slightly different frequency.

The first thing that strikes me – I could be flying a Chipmunk, or a Cessna 150. I could be in a VC10 or a Belfast. I could be in the Jet Provost Link Trainer of so many years ago, for all I am doing is sitting in a square box with a stick in my right hand and throttles in my left with a set of instruments in front of me. It takes a conscious effort to look outside and when I do, there are no visual references (we are still in milky haze stratus) so the outside world does not intrude. Instead, all I have to do is make a series of combination movements with the stick and throttles till the instruments in front of me revolve and whirl and gyrate into the ordered pattern that I desire. So I juggle and experiment till the airspeed is pegged at 400 Kcas, the altimeter is winding steadily through 14,000 thousand feet, the ADI is registering a 9-degree climb, the compass is steady at 100 degrees and the engine RPM gauges read 97 per cent each.

My body experiences no dynamic sensations whatsoever, I am not in a missile hurtling upwards through the stratosphere, I am not in a Phantom fighter penetrating upwards at eight-tenths the speed of sound. I am instead sitting in a comfortable air-conditioned box carrying out an exercise in coordination, pure and simple. Only my experience on this particular aircraft enables me to do the job faster, more accurately and more economically than Joe Soap from down the road. I think – this isn't flying, this is machine management.

That is the effect of flying pure instruments from the back seat and due to the lack of external visual cues, even on good, gin-clear days, I find that more often than not I am committed to using those instruments to aid my judgement. However, instrument flying has always been a means to an end. Only the IRE indulges in this esoteric sport as an art in itself. For me, the instruments are simply there to help me get back on the ground when the air is cloudy with mist and rain, or to help me in the job I am doing now, namely flying the aircraft from the strangeness of the rear seat. No, my purpose in being up here is to get used to handling the aircraft in a visual environment, in the world of air combat manoeuvring, kill or be killed.

I notice that we have popped out of the cloud layer at 15,000 feet. I level off and head on further eastwards till the Tacan needle reads 080 degrees fifty miles from base. Here the air is clear, the cloud layer four-eighths broken 6,000 feet below us and another layer of alto-stratus starting about 5,000 feet above, ample space for the exercise I am about to carry out. Rigging checks, security checks, fuel and pigeons check and for the next half hour we twist and turn, dive and climb, mixtures of sky, sun-whirling horizons, afterburners and G, buffet, nineteen units angle of attack, rudder reversals, rolls. Unload, accelerate, pull up, pitch back, six … seven G, minimum time turn reversals, G-suit crushing my legs, foggy grey vision, feet braced against the rudder pedals as the machine shakes, buffets, rocks and lurches in tune with my hands heaving and pushing on the pole and my feet kicking the rudders first one way and then the other.

In combat, the Phantom is a strange aeroplane. As I pull tighter and tighter, as the angle of attack needle climbs higher and higher, the familiar rules of aerodynamics take a sudden turn. In this state if I try to turn the aircraft using normal aileron movements, it refuses to roll, indeed it turns the other way, sometimes in a vicious fashion that rapidly develops into a 'departure' which is usually followed by a spin if I maintain my ham-fisted actions. Instead if I want to turn safely and efficiently, I must leave the stick central and turn, roll, reverse with the rudders. 'When it buffets, use your boots', the words of my first Phantom instructor always float through my mind at these times and I do the right thing instinctively.

Now from the back seat, I am rediscovering new things like the position of the nose as it arcs round the horizon. I have no AOA gauge in the back (only the indexers which are inoperative anyway with the wheels up), so I must develop a feel for that nineteen unit area where the Phantom is turning at its best. I loop and roll my way through aerobatics, getting used to doing things without a horizon in front of me, for referring positions halfway through a slow roll for instance. It is hard work, but I am expected to do it competently. I am an instructor. I will be teaching those who have never done this before in this aircraft. I will have to recognise their strong points and their weak points. I will have to know when they are not manoeuvring at max performance and demonstrate just how to do so. More important, I must recognise when they are approaching the ragged edges of the envelope where aerodynamics enter a new, dangerous realm, the realm of lost control and I must draw them back from this edge before they plunge over into the abyss.

And so the fuel gauge in the front cockpit winds rapidly down under the influence of prolonged afterburner activity, and as we start to recover, my head is slightly dizzy.

'Vector 260 degrees, descend to 5,000 feet with QFE 1021, stop mode three squawk and call base on stud three.' Midland Radar has disowned us. Speed brakes, idle/idle, 350 knots, plunge earthwards, field approach checks and level – 'Coningsby, 21 at 5,000 feet passing Teapot this time for GCA' – descend to 1,800 feet, cockpit checks advise complete, call radar talkdown stud five … I wend my way down a routine GCA glideslope. Already in the short hour I have been airborne, the movements required have become utterly familiar. I look up at decision height, crane forward to find my little hole on the right, and with a little direction from the front regarding my line up, I fly down to the runway and at some stage when my subconscious says the picture all round looks right, I tweak the stick back and we touch lightly.

Full power, airborne, gear, flaps, stud one – '21 rolled from radar entering the visual pattern', and so for the remaining ten minutes of the sortie I 'bash the circuit', normal ones, flapless ones, single engine rollers, overshoots. Finally we touch for the last time, 'chute streams, landing roll out, turn off at the end, canopy open to let in cool breeze sweet as wine washing away sweat, neck slightly stiff from all the bending forward and the unusual sitting angle in the back. Shut down, bus back to the crew room, coffee. Debrief consists of a laconic 'No problem, was it?' I agree and go and change out of my flying gear.

Some days are made for flying. Just as some days I would rather sit tight, warm and comfortable in the crew room swapping 'war stories', so also there are days when it is positively sacrilegious to remain rooted to the ground. They used to call it 'Flight Commander's weather' because on such days the voles appear out of their admin holes, brush the dust off their bonedomes and cluster around the Ops Room making the Programming Officer's life a misery as they seek to insert themselves somewhere in the day's flying programme for a little quiet SCT. On such days, we rush airborne with carefree abandon. Met brief is a mere formality for it is eight-eighths blue with some scattered cumulus just to make his presence not totally useless. Visibility is thirty kilometres plus, wind is light and variable, anticyclonic.

In the air, after take-off, the world does suddenly take on the appearance of a Geography, Natural History and Current Affairs lesson all rolled into one. Rolling out on my climbout heading, with autopilot selected in, engines trimmed out at 94 per cent and humming quietly, the rush and flurry of take-off and channel changing complete, I have time for a few minutes to look outside at the panorama unfolding beneath me as I move at 400 knots towards the coast.

Lincolnshire is always thought flat, dull and uninteresting, but on days like today I see things afresh, rediscover new angles and aspects of objects I once thought familiar. Tattershall Bridge floats gently past behind me. I have driven over it many times before, but today it is a new object. The river winds metallic silver under its ancient arches, the dull grey of the road twists and turns up to the bridge, across and away, geometric motion I never really appreciate from ground level. Woodhall Spa Airfield, weed infested runways and all comes and goes, a disused railway line that I never even knew existed runs ruler-like across the landscape, to disappear in the distance. To the north-east, I can see the tall spires of the power stations issuing puffy clouds of smoke along the banks of the River Humber and, beyond them, the sprawling industrial centre of Hull.

England really is a patchwork quilt and the fields of corn, golden and cropped, lie side by side with their greener neighbours where cows and horses leisurely graze. The Tacan miles tick away and in a few minutes we are crossing the coast. On my left, two miles away, my Number 2 hangs gently in the sunlight, flying a neat battle position, dartlike, trailing a faint banner of smoke from his engines. My thumb hits the transmit button:

'Midland Radar, Charlie 02, 03 coasting out, we'd like to turn left onto 060, passing Flight Level 150 for 210, Victor Mike Charlie.'

A laconic 'Roger, you're cleared' comes from the poor soul sitting in his darkened room underground in the Area Radar Control Centre. I am sorry for him, staring into his smoky green tube at the blips and etchings on his scope while here I am looking at the real thing. Skegness holiday town is to my starboard, a collection of greyish houses arranged in neat segments bisected geometrically by the road system. Another group of buildings verging on the beach I know to be Butlin's Holiday Camp. Its two swimming pools are crowded with bathers, from this height black and ant-like hordes with their bikinis, ice cream and suntan oil. The beach itself is not particularly attractive, a dirty yellow in colour stretching into the distance. I can see from Theddlethorpe range on my left down to the Wainfleet and Holbeach range complex on the shores of the Wash to my right. From 20,000 feet, the Wash itself with all its creeks and inlets lies nakedly exposed, the perfect map for any teacher willing to transport his class thousands of feet into the air, but the map disappears as we turn north-east.

21,000 feet approaches and I make a small adjustment to the twin throttles and to the autopilot and we are level, cruising northwards at .85 Mach. 'Fuel is feeding okay, my oxygen is good – nine litres and flowing, cabin altitude is 9,000 feet, RPM, TGTs, fuel flow, nozzles all look good, circuit breakers all in.' This little ritual complete, I redirect my gaze to the panorama beneath me. The sea just off the cost is dirty grey in colour, polluted by the tons of silt carried seawards by inland rivers. But, as we progress and the shoreline recedes into the hazy distance, the sea takes on a multitude of differing shades and hues. Firstly, with not a breath of wind to disturb it, the surface is smooth and waveless, and from this height etched with little rippled corrugations. The colour changes from grey to blue and then green and then to a combination of the two, aquamarine emerald. The sun highlights the submarine structure and here and there the shallows make their presence known by subtly altering the shades of blue and green, creating a dappled effect. Moreover, little specks of cumulus have formed in the noonday heat and these cast a multitude of shadows, deceptive, to mingle with the other colours and shades serene in the sunlight. Now and again a ship appears, furrowing purposefully towards the shore, its wake stretching for many miles behind it, straight as a die, but from this altitude ship and wake are a mere two inches long. Again there are the many trawlers and fishing smacks sitting motionless, apparently inactive, truly 'painted ships upon a painted ocean'. Occasionally, the presence of man is illustrated even more forcefully by the rigs, searching for North Sea oil, great metal platforms standing on matchlike stilts with drills that plunge all the way to the sea bed and below. They too appear silent, slumbering in the soporific air except for one where I spot a helicopter hovering like a dragonfly over the platform, its blades strobing in the sunlight.

But now, with the Tacan saying base is 240 degrees, 120 miles, there is nothing to be seen but the huge, huge expanse of sea, from horizon to horizon, 360 degrees, and I am overwhelmed by the sense of immenseness. However, I have little time left to wonder as Midland calls – '02, 03 call Neatishead on Fighter Stud 41', and my mind clicks over to the more serious business of getting down to some intercepts and suchlike war games.

On the OCU I may instruct, but I also learn as well. I learn about Air Combat. Air Combat is the name of the game. I have been playing at it before, but now I really get into it. I follow in the footsteps of Boelcke and Immelman, Ball and McCudden, Mannock and von Richthofen. My mentors are Tuck and Johnson, Bader and Beurling, Lacey, Steinhoff, Galland. My studies are of the tactics of the

Somme offensive, the Battle of Britain, MiG Alley – Korea, Thud Ridge – Hanoi and the Golan Heights. Our crewroom chat is of people and machines, hands waving the air in the fashion common to all fighter pilots as manoeuvres are described, dissected, defended, destroyed in critical argument. Volumes of literature lie on the tables in our office. Their titles speak for themselves – *US Navy Tactics Manual; Central Trials and Tactics Organization Manual; Fighter Weapons Newsletter; Air Combat Manoeuvres; High AOA Manoeuvring.* The pages speak of reverse yo-yos, barrel roll attacks, high yo-yo and counter, offset loop, lag pursuit roll, high energy zoom. The diagrams are laced intricately (Phantom in white, MiG 21 in black) indicating flow lines. Their titles read – offensive split, defensive split, separation manoeuvre, the pitch back, combat extension options, ident shooter, vertical vis-ident. I study and digest the mass of information, trying to sift the wheat from the chaff and yet realising that many thousands of minds have over the years combined to produce this, the current state of the art. Right now, we are at the current peak of knowledge in this sphere, the result of research and recording of the campaigns of bygone (and present day) heroes, their rules of thumb ('Beware the Hun in the sun'), those ancient noddy's guides ('Good gunnery is the key to success'), the unwritten laws ('Never reverse your turn in combat'). 'Hell, the last time I reversed was in basic training!'

But whereas the fighter pilot of old carried out his manoeuvring by the seat of his proverbial pants without really understanding why he was achieving the results that he did, today my generation has analysed those once intangible elements of success. The whys and wherefores have been computerised and laid down in black and white. Now my text book speaks of energy manoeuvrability, specific excess power, optimum climb gradient curves, buffet boundaries, performance envelopes, acceleration graphs, maximum turn rate gradients, energy overlays. In the vault there is a document to which I go and refer in my quest for knowledge. This book, several inches thick, contains page after page of graphs, energy manoeuvre overlays of any other fighter I might conceivably come up against in combat. Superimposed in a darker shade of red are the overlays for my particular aircraft, the F4 Phantom. At a glance, I can tell instantly where the enemy has the edge over me in turn performance, zoom capability, sustained acceleration and all the other qualities that go to make up the air combat arena. I must study and memorise the general contours of these graphs, invent my own rules of thumb to serve me in battle. Hence I investigate the envelope available to me. I know the altitude and speed bands where I can force the enemy to flee rather than face a fight. I also know where it would be imprudent, if not dangerous, to stray. The ultimate, I think to myself, is to have these graphs readily available in a computer in the cockpit and selectable on the instant of entry into combat, with a readout of instructions. However, such is Man that he has already done this, and gone a stage further. The latest lightweight fighters designed specifically to excel in the world of air combat are programmed to provide the optimum at all times in combat. In these aircraft, when the pilot selects a certain force on his fly-by-wire control column, he will get the optimum turn rate and acceleration for the current circumstances of speed, altitude, angle of attack and fuel/weapon load, nothing more, nothing less. His manoeuvring will be all but perfect and all he will have to do is position his 'hot line gunsight' and the automatic SRAAM will release itself when it thinks the solution is within its grasp.

However, this is the next generation and I am not sure that I want anything to do with it. I am happy to live with my imperfections, to make the little errors that sometimes result in 'Fox 2' ringing in my ears as a kill is scored against me. Instead I can perpetually strive towards the total perfection that belongs to the machine while yet knowing I will never achieve it, for to err is human. I do not wish to exchange what I have, just as the combatants of the past air wars abhorred the coming of the retractable undercarriage, the jet engine, the guided missile, the onboard weapon-aiming computer and just as, I suppose, the children of today, fighter pilots of tomorrow will wish for nothing more nor less than the complete automation that is their lot, perhaps rightfully so. Nevertheless, the basic details will always remain the same, even though we have analysed the old lessons into mathematical precision – 'Height gives the advantage', 'use the sun', 'sneak up low in his six o'clock', 'look out for top cover', 'keep the speed up', 'never fly straight and level in combat for more than five seconds' – all true in 1917, all true today. The only difference is that today we couch these basics in the modern jargon peculiar to our trade. Thus I study and analyse, practise and practise yet again.

On Tuesday I am scheduled for 2 v 2 combat with some Lightnings from a base down the road. My Number 2 and I have already spent some time examining the graphs and we have drawn a few basic conclusions. Low down, the F4 will have the edge on acceleration and zoom capability, and our turn performance is marginally better. But the differences are so small that the deciding factor in determining success and victory must lie in the hands of the pilot. Here the fliers of the British-built machine will have a major advantage, for we all know just when and where the Lightning's smoother handling qualities as an aircraft will start to pay off, especially if the fight drags on up to the higher, stratospheric levels. My Phantom is an aerodynamic compromise, attempting to satisfy several requirements in the one framework, excelling at nuclear strike, ground attack, Fleet Air Defence, reconnaissance, close air support, all at the drop of a hat with no major equipment changes. So we decide our basic tactics will be to keep the fight low, where our machine is happiest. We tailor our formation around our superior weapon system. Thus we are prepared as we walk out to the jets and blast off to keep the rendezvous out over the sea.

GCI set us up on a 180-degree head-on split. We roll out and head towards each other, accelerating rapidly. I pick them up immediately on the radar and deal with priority number one – identify their formation. They are in five-mile trail (a tactic favoured by the Russians) and a quick lock-on confirms my suspicions. They are doing Mach 1.3. We are in wide battle, closing at a combined speed of twenty miles a minute. I report to my Number 2 – it is obvious they are getting set for a high energy zoom into the stratosphere, hoping to lure us after them. Sure enough I pick up the lead Lightning visually, glowing silver in the sunlight. He passes between us and lances upwards. I am not to be caught out so easily. I delay the break up after him. I am looking for his Number 2 and I suddenly see him, fast and 5,000 feet low, lurking, waiting for us to turn out tails towards him, at the mercy of his Red Top missiles. I call the run out on the radio as he flashes past us and starts to follow his leader up into the heavens. I know his leader should already have been pitching back down towards us both when he saw us failing to follow him and when his Number 2 reported that we were still coming on. Either way, as he pitched back he would be in a good position to slide into a commanding firing slot behind one of us. I am having none of that, which is why I call for our formation to 'extend'. I light the 'burners and unload the aircraft to 0 degrees AOA for maximum acceleration. We were at Mach .95 and instantly, it seems, we are doing Mach 1.2, and that is the last we see of the 'enemy'. When we have all regrouped on the master GCI frequency, we find the Lightnings are thirty miles away. They built up just a little too much steam and their Saturn Five-like zoom into the stratosphere had carried them clean out of the fight. First move – stalemate.

We set up the pieces again, revert to different frequencies and head back in for another attack. We decide to remain in wide battle again, with a height separation. My radar picks up the Lightnings at closer range this time. They are in very wide battle, high subsonic speed. I plug in minimum AB to clean up the smoke trails from our Speys while four pairs of eyes search trying to pick up the incredibly inconspicuous silver blobs. My Number 2 on the right spots the first one, coming down my right hand side. This means the other one is somewhere out on my left, dangerous. I call this warning, wait till he flashes past and above us and then call an upwards inwards turnabout. I crank hard right and upwards, my Number 2 does the same and we pass head on in climbing turns before he too races past and disappears behind me. I hope he manages to acquire the other Lightning who must surely have seen me turning away from him. But I cannot afford to dwell on this yet. My main interest is a quick kill on the lead Lightning who passed down my right side. He did not see my initial zoom, but I have gone high into contrails and now with reheats blazing he is turning hard upwards into me, his whole aircraft shimmering with the white mists of condensation Shockwaves. That man is pulling an awful lot of G, the thought drifts through my mind, abstract, as I pull up into an oblique loop. Simultaneously, I am asking my Number 2 of his whereabouts; he is engaged in a 1 v 1 with the other Lightning – invariably the way these multi-plane combats turn out, and not wholly desirable. As I top over the loop, I see the other combat progressing about one mile away, also in stalemate. I know we are not fighting our aircraft to maximum advantage. I remember my own briefing – stay flexible, provide mutual support and be prepared to take whatever shots turn up in any of the missile brackets. So far we have not achieved that aim and the fight has already lasted too long, over one minute.

Our two fights have drifted closer together and the opportunity to extend safely presents itself. I seize it. As I pass head-on with my target, I level my wings and unload (I have been in full afterburner since the fight started, but I know the Lightning will be much shorter on fuel than I, which could prove significant in the long run – sooner or later, he would have to try and disengage and run for home, a task fraught with danger!). I pass right through the middle of the other fight, where my Number 2 is engaged with the Number 2 Lightning. They also have just passed head-on to one another and the Lightning having just seen me go past decides it is safe to switch his attack and attempt a quick shot. My Number 2 meanwhile calls that he has engaged the Lead Lightning who is busy pitching back after me following my run out. The Number 2 Lightning has underestimated my run-out range, however, for as I reef back round to point head-on at him, he floats into my gunsight, my navigator gets an instant boresight lock. I count the necessary seconds needed for missile acquisition but they are rushed seconds as I squeeze the trigger, the range decreasing dramatically as we close fast with the target. 'Fox 1!' I call for GCI to record the time of kill, although on the radar film I will see subsequently that it is a marginal one, but right now I do not care. As he rushes past very close and vanishes, I switch my attention to the other pair just in time to see the other Lightning turning hard away from me, range one mile, with my Number 2 completing the other half of an oblique loop to drop down into his six o'clock. The Lightning is a perfect target for both of us as I select Sidewinder, lay the pipper on his jetpipe and squeeze the trigger. I call 'Fox 2' a second after my wingman who has also achieved a kill.

We all return to the master frequency and the Lightnings are already on their way home crying fuel shortage. We return at a more leisurely pace and stream in for a battle break and land. In the crewroom, hot and sweaty, sipping chilled Coke, we debrief and discuss tactics, film, manoeuvres, successes, mistakes – arms waving, multi-coloured diagrams on chalkboard, inheritors of the tradition writing our own small contribution for the rule books and tactics manuals. The name of the game is Air Combat.

9

···

Incident at Bitburg

There are times when I wish the earth would open wide and swallow me up. That time on the tanker before the combined audience of Chequers Black and Victor crew was one. Leafing lazily through my logbook, I recall another from early days on the squadron.

Bitburg Air Base, Germany, United States Air Forces Europe, and it is hot summertime on the German plains. 43 (Fighter) Squadron has arrived on one of its periodic NATO detachments. Our arrival itself created quite a stir. With OCA Flight leading, we steamed across the airfield in a battle four-ship and launched into the circuit for a thirty-second flurry of speedbrakes, G, swift deceleration, idle throttles, downwind checks, crank it tight round finals and onto the dirty grey undulating Bitburg runway perched on top of a hill, 'chutes streaming and 1,000 yards' spacing on the runway please, gentlemen. It is as well to point out that the usual standard American visual recovery to base is somewhat more conservative. Their strict love of adhering to laid-down instrument procedures in the airfield pattern was to prove my undoing the next day.

Following the time-honoured custom on detachments, that night is party night. Typical American hospitality reigns supreme and several bottles of cold Schlitz and Budweiser flow down my throat in the Officers' Club as we get to know our hosts, in this case the 525th (Bulldogs) Tactical Fighter Squadron flying F4Es. The midnight hour comes and goes and soon afterwards I wend my way back to my room. It comes as a shock to the system when the BOQ attendant enters my room at 06.30 and shakes me into consciousness. It takes a few minutes before my mind engages gear and starts to function as I recall that I am scheduled for the first sortie that morning (I drew the short straw), briefing at seven, take-off at eight. OCA is leading me on a 'sector recce' round the German country-side to have a look at the local area and a diversion or two we will be using during our stay.

The heat is already beginning to gather force for the noonday on-slaught, the air heavy and humid as I sit, flying suit sleeves rolled up in the briefing room (wherefore art thou, God of Air Condition-ing?) listening to erstwhile Flight Commander holding forth. OCA's brief is comprehensive and to the point, covering the strange SOPs, departure and recovery details pertinent to operating from a strange base for the first time. I will live to regret not having paid closer at-tention to this brief.

The plan is to take-off, carry out some general handling and then transit to Ramstein Air Base, our primary diversion, shoot a pairs GCA there and then return to Bitburg to practise various Tacan pen-etrations.

We gather helmets, harnesses and flight bags and jump (or should I say, step delicately) into the big Dodge station wagon allocated to us as squadron transport. Our aircraft are spotted around the air-field in the hardened, camouflaged shelters now common to NATO European bases. Each toughened revetment is a hangar settlement in itself, built to withstand a nuclear blast, seal itself off from the outside world and continue to give protection and support to both aircraft and men working within, and then to allow its beast to go forth and do battle. OCA's aircraft is in another shelter hidden away somewhere in the woods, for we cannot see it. However, American-style Houchin pumping international amps into electrical circuits allows me to switch the radio on and my leader and I are linked by UHF.

Engines start (deafening inside the shelter, despite helmets on and closed canopy. Head protests even more), checks complete and I gingerly taxi forward (wingtip-to-wall clearance is not generous) out into the now blazing sunlight. My navigator has a map of the airfield and we need it as we slowly thread our way round the maze of taxi-tracks-cum-roadways ('All vehicles will give way to moving aircraft'), the rabbit warren system that links the bundle of nests, till we arrive at a great steel-wire reinforced gate. I pause and fold my wingtips (the clearance on our FG 1 is too minimal for comfort, so we play it safe). OCA has already arrived ahead of me. A huge, black American sergeant pushes a button to send the gates sweeping open and flashes us a grin as we taxi past and turn left onto the main taxiway running parallel to the one and only east/west runway. We take the roller coaster route past the fenced-in technical site, the huge open transport and logistics delivery area, the multi-storey control tower (olive-green and almost 150 feet high) and finally to the 'quick check' area at the threshold where we pull up alongside a four-ship of F4Ds, all bombed up for a strike mission.

Another American foible, the quick check consists of a team of NCOs rushing around beneath the aircraft having a last look for hydraulic leaks, deflated tyres, pins still in place, panels loose or missing and any other potential hazards to the forthcoming mission. I sit patiently, hopefully, letting them do their thing until they reappear and give me the thumbs up. Ahead of us the four-ship blasts off while behind, another four F4Es are already rolling into the slots we have just vacated. This is a busy base.

OCA calls up Big Wham (USAF Bitburg equivalent of RAF Duty Pilot) for final clearance. Big Wham says go, so we go – to tower frequency, who also says go. No malfunctions with the aircraft, no problems with our flight plan clearance, we are committed to fly.

I line up echelon starboard. OCA glances across briefly and nods his head sharply, I release the brakes and proceed to carry out the best formation take-off I have ever done in my life. There are some days when the stage of life seems set in treacle, where events unfold in graceful slow motion and one has all the time in the world to react, but there is no need to react anyway because the treacle has created a static situation, the set piece has frozen in time while still drifting along the river of life. So it is with this take-off.

I select my reference points and hold them, and believe it or not, that trailing edge nav light does not waver more than an inch or two laterally or vertically from the starboard engine blow hole to which I have glued it. Fifty tons of combined machinery smoke down the runway as one, rotate as one, unstick into the shimmering heat haze as one, cancel afterburners and vortice trails draw as one, side by side, Siamese twins locked in an aerodynamic warp, so we coast upwards and outwards to the north-east. I have come close to such man-machine empathy in a pairs take-off since, but never quite matched it.

However, I do not want to dish out self praise at this exhibition of super coordination. We are now airborne, I can slide out into fighting wing, select 100 per cent oxygen and full cold on the cabin conditioning, engage autopilot and disengage brain, leaving all the work to OCA in the lead ship. Hope springs eternal in the breast, but I should have remembered Sod's Law which says that such a state of affairs remaining intact would have been too good to be true. Sure enough, ten minutes later, OCA calls up and explains that his Tacan equipment is unserviceable and that I must take over the lead. Inward groans and curses.

It is as well to explain that military navigation in Europe relies heavily on Tacan, adopted as the universal military system for getting around, and an excellent system it is too. It is because it is so excellent that the Americans (and so the rest of the Western world) have decided to shift the workload, the onus of responsibility for position keeping, right back from the ground into the cockpit. Hence in my cockpit, I carry the Tacan letdown procedures for every base in Europe, enabling me (if my equipment is operating correctly) to carry out a penetration and airfield approach without the benefit of radar vectoring, and without even talking to ground control if necessary. However, the process does involve a certain degree of average skill at instrument flying, and more important, a sharpness of mind to hit the various radials and gates at the right speed, right height and sometimes, at the right time. Mental and physical agility is the name of the game when homing in for a genuine Tacan dive, which is why the fighter pilot, when the weather gets rough or the going tough, invariably hands over the control of his recovery back to the guy on the ground who is paid to do just that anyway.

But, when the airspace gets congested, or weather clogs out his radar screen or he runs short of frequencies and control positions to work with or the going just becomes plain tough for him as well, then that guy on the ground is quite justified in insisting that everybody follows the published internal aids letdown procedures, which is why I have to be well versed in the same. Right now, I am digging out my TAPs for Ramstein, and after vainly trying to tune into several Tacan beacons and listening for mysterious ident codes, I decide to take the easy way out and call up Dusseldorf Clutch Radar for a vector to Ramstein and handover for GCA pickup. It is my day, I think as they come back loud and clear to inform me I am identified, steer 130 degrees, set QFE 29.33 inches and descend to 5,000 feet, calling Ramstein GCA on 381.4 megahertz. I sit back and sigh with relief as I call OCA into close formation and settle down for a routine GCA.

I should be able to hack this, I think. The GCA is routine alright and I make a nice high overshoot, looking down disinterestedly at the sprawling collection of green-grey buildings, metallic roadways and excavated gravel pits that go to make up Ramstein Air Base, Headquarters of USAFE and 4 ATAF.

100 per cent oxygen is beginning to have effect as we climb out and request a radar handover back to Bitburg, seventy miles away. Unfortunately that plan is stillborn, scotched by OCA on my wing who says 'negative, Chequers 01 and 02 request a Tacan to visual'. If looks could kill, his aircraft would have been a ball of smoke in the sky at that instant. I rack my brains trying to recall the briefing squadron IRE had given us all the previous day after arriving, and even OCA's briefing before take-off. Yesterday, we had been vectored straight onto the centreline by radar and I hadn't paid too much attention to events as I jockeyed to maintain position with the other three aircraft.

The normal visual approach involves going through various points which I shall call Points A, B and C. To the Bitburg veteran, Point Alpha is a roundabout on the autobahn, Point Bravo a large red house in a field and Point Charlie is probably a specially shaped bush. To me, Point Alpha is on a radial X and Y miles to the north of the airfield. From this point, steering a certain heading at a certain speed and height will eventually intersect me with another radial on which I should find Point Bravo, also a certain number of degrees and miles removed from the airfield. From Point Bravo I am supposed to hop to Point Charlie, following which a right turn should leave Bitburg Runway 24 dead in front of me by ten miles or so. A fairly simple process to the Bitburg man, even in poor weather. A little bit more difficult for RAF visitor until (as eventually happens) he gets used to it and learns the little short cuts and tricks of the trade hidden away in all such systems.

To me it is a question of sorting out the jumble of figures, bearings, ranges, speeds, heights, into some sort of recognisable sequence. Thank God for navigators. The secretary in the back isn't busy flying the aeroplane. He can use both hands to leaf through 'en route' documents. Between us, we work something out and gaily call Bitburg that we are commencing a Tacan dive to visual. A laconic 'Roger, sir, you're cleared right on in, we got one shootin' closed patterns and a two-ship comin' up for the pitch'.

I call OCA into close formation and we start the downward slice. The first thing I notice as we approach 3,000 feet is that the visibility, good on top, isn't so hot down here, like it's about one to two miles in haze. Again, no sweat to the local boys used to leapfrogging from one visual pinpoint to another. I am stuck strictly with heading, speed and time. Nevertheless, Point Alpha appears on time and we are cleared to Bravo two minutes' flying time away. It is getting hot and bumpy again, reviving that sweaty anxious feeling as my eyes strive to pierce the gloom, searching for something recognisable. OCA is still clinging on to my wing. Point Bravo arrives, no sweat, and I turn onto the next heading. Bitburg should be only three minutes flying time away, somewhere out to our right. I ease down to 1,500 feet. The navigator reminds me that Spangdahlen Airfield is out to our left, seven odd miles from Bitburg and displaced slightly to the left of the centreline, its runway on the same heading. This piece of information goes straight through one ear and out the other. I am busy trying to find my own airfield. We miss Point Charlie altogether, my headings and speeds have wandered. The Tacan needle starts to swing round inexorably, past the radial representing runway heading and further – we are through the centreline and its only three miles away!

I bank desperately to the right, eyes searching the drab green-brown countryside frantically. The Americans have done their job well, for this airfield blends effectively into the background of hills and valleys, woods and fields. Woe betide Ivan in his Flogger running in for a 'first pass' attack if his navigation is not up to scratch. Unfortunately for me, the high intensity strobe lighting common to American fields (and which will save me from further embarrassment later in the week) has not been switched on for this runway.

Nevertheless something catches my eye, and amazingly, like a jigsaw suddenly falling into place or like one of those trick reversed films when a broken object picks itself up from the floor and reassembles itself, so the whole airfield, runway, technical site, control tower, living quarters and surrounding dwellings instantly spring into crystal clear relief where they had been all the time if only eyes and brain had focused in the right spot. I reef my Phantom hard over to the right (spitting out OCA in the process) but it is way too late to make a proper arrival and break in the correct position over the runway. That is mistake number one. The laid down procedure after a missed visual approach is to climb out again and go through the whole business of finding Point Alpha and the rest, working round the pattern back onto the centreline. There is a very good reason for insisting on this, as I was about to find out. But right now I think – 'What, go through that rigmarole again? No way, not this boy', mistake number two. Instead I decide to carry out a left hand orbit and reposition on the centreline that way. Bitburg tower have been calling me now and again enquiring whether I have the field in sight. After a few curt 'negatives', I have decided to ignore the calls. Now as I start my left-hand turn, the whole world starts talking. OCA, who has been desperately hanging on, trying to follow me through my gyrations transmits something unintelligible; Bitburg Tower are demanding that I carry out missed approach procedures, sir!; navigator in the back is muttering something else and then a few moments later, RT wavelength erupts with strength five invective (OCA), admonishment (Bitburg Tower), desperate resignation (navigator).

A pair of USAF Phantoms in close formation flash past a few hundred feet away at a 90-degree angle, closely followed by another pair as we rock through their jetwash. Below me another huge runway complete with taxiways, control tower and base complex has suddenly appeared. With mounting horror, I realise I am flying right through the traffic pattern of Bitburg's sister base, Spangdahlen, just down the road. I imagine the nearest ground equivalent is waking up to find yourself driving up the motorway in the wrong lane against oncoming traffic. The air is full of aeroplanes as our two British Phantoms bounce into the circuit and just as quickly bounce out again, sending Americans scattering.

Right now I am resigned to my fate as Big Wham comes onto the air with a stream of advice that I find hard to decipher. Instead, I roll out on the centreline, pick up the runway (OCA is nowhere to be seen) and pitch in to break and land.

Back in the crewroom, the Boss chews me out about lack of professionalism, OCA (who has made his own way back) puts a further boot in over poor leadership, the telephone is hot as we apologise to Big Wham and Bitburg Local, persuade Spangdahlen not to file a violation report and generally try to appease all and sundry. Fellow crew members, British and American alike grin and guffaw as the tale is told. I grab a can of cold Coke, find a quiet corner and collapse into it, eyes closed. I am not scheduled to fly again that day.

That evening in the Officers' Club, the Budweisers flow again, it all seems like a bad dream and we all put it down to newcomer's luck. However, I secretly resolve never to go through such an experience again. I am green and new to the game, but even so, learning by one's mistakes can be a painful process to the tyro fighter pilot. Thus, to quote a favourite Air Force phrase, I sure learned about flying from that.

10

....

A Tale of Two Buccs

'90 Port ... Go!' We are three F4s, White formation, 500 feet over the dirty grey North Sea. I am leading. Numbers 2 and 3 are students. This is one of their last trips in the conversion phase. They are learning how to fly tactical formations at both high and low levels. For the past half hour I have led them a merry dance through the skies. Together we have wheeled and revolved our way through the neatly intricate manoeuvres employed in turning a large formation through the points of the compass while still maintaining some form of defensive cover amongst ourselves. 90s, 180s, turnabouts, inwards turnabouts, counters, hard turns, breaks, the two new guys are working hard maintaining their positions, keeping Lead in the right piece of sky, crisscrossing, sliding over and through, jockeying stick and throttle to hold the formation together in a neat and yet aggressively defensive package. When I am happy with them at medium level, I call 'line astern for tailchase, go' and give them a five-minute breather of 'follow my leader' through loops, and barrels, chandelles and reversals before reforming them into battle, setting QNH and Radar Altimeters on and heading for sea level.

We punch through a few thousand feet's worth of cloud before popping out at 2,000 feet still in immaculate formation. We start our turns at 1,000 feet and then gradually take it down lower. I have just completed a 90 turn to port when it happens. Out of the corner of my eye, I see two grey shapes curving up at us from sea level. A second of brain seizure, a moment of uncharacteristic indecision blended with shock before I shout 'White counter port, go!' but I know it is too late, way, way too late. We have been bounced, well and truly by two Buccaneers. I must explain that to be bounced by Buccaneers (the Banana Bomber) is to the fighter pilot a fate worse than death. The Buccs' normal habitat is very fast and very low in a straight line hell bent for the ships. Air combat does not figure in their defensive plans, unless of course they stray on a few sitting ducks (as we were), in which case it's fair game. We had been 'took'; took good too. Max mil power, 4G and pull, but as our formation hauls into them, they are already pulling up and away, laughing, their job done. Had they fired Sidewinders, two of us would be smoking heaps in the sea by now. As they fly through, smoking, I am close enough to see their upturned faces, pale, bonedome framed, staring back at us before they are gone in a flash of grey-white sea surface camouflage. We reverse and give ineffectual chase, all to no avail (they have a head of steam on). We have already been hacked and the point has been proven. I re-form the formation and deliver a salutary lesson on the responsibilities of lookout in the formation and for the next minutes, we manoeuvre in chastened silence before racing back to base, streaming onto the runway and retiring to the crewroom to choke on our crowfeathers. That night in the bar of RAF Honington, home of Buccs, I can well imagine the tales that will be bandied back and forth across the room coupled with shouts of derision. I gloomily hope no-one on 43 Squadron (Fighting Cocks) gets to hear of this …

The Buccaneer pilot in the low-level world of strike attack is a law unto himself. His primary role on the maritime squadrons is to attack shipping by day and night, and to do this he flies as low and as fast as possible. He does the job with a professional panache I have yet to see equalled. In my job as an Air Defence fighter pilot, I have clashed with Buccaneers many times on the numerous exercises that are our lot. Glancing through my logbook from 43 Squadron days, I see 'Exercise Quick Shave – Sept 18 – Phantom FG 1 XV 577 – 6.05 hrs – 1 × Buccaneer', therein lies a tale …

It is midnight. I have been airborne four hours in my usual position, capping over a task force steaming (very) slowly south-east. It is a clear and starry night, but below, patches of stratus serve to make the sea and lower levels very black. The fleet is expecting to be attacked by Orange (enemy) forces, which I happen to know will be Buccaneers operating out of Landivisiau in France. We are on CAP

100 miles off the coast of Cornwall in the Western Approaches. I am plugged into the tanker topping up my tanks when Anyface, the AEW Shackleton, pipes up 'Five-zero, we have a contact coming in from the east, range sixty miles, suspected low level. Request you investigate.'

'Rog,' unplug from the tanker, retract my probe, check the fuel is feeding and turn away towards the east, descending. In the back, Bill is already at work searching with the pulse doppler. There is something wrong with the set, he is not getting any contacts.

'He's forty miles from you heading 240 degrees, any joy?'

'Negative', I let down to 10,000 feet. Bill is cursing the set in the back. I am helpless. The pulses are refusing to travel. We must rely on the controller peering into his orange-tinted tube in his Shackleton orbiting at 2,000 feet.

'He bears 080 degrees, twenty-five miles, suspect there might be two ... come port heading 090 ... fifteen miles ... any luck yet?'

I am down at 5,000 feet flying half on instruments, half visually. Outside, beneath the five-eighths covering of cloud, the world is one huge bowl of blackness, sea merged with sky in black confusion. The occasional pinprick of light marks the presence of some innocent fishing vessel (or Russian trawler monitoring the aerial battle). The visual illusions are great, such that these lights appear to be above me, as if I were flying at five feet over the sea rather than 5,000, but my radio altimeter reassures me and I continue switching my gaze between the radar scope, the flight instruments and the outside world.

Bill has switched to pulse and is searching in that mode, the sea returns sweeping up and down the scope on the ten-mile range scale. I flick the filter down to diffuse the glow and transform green into red to blend with my cockpit lighting.

'Five-zero, he's ten miles, 35 degrees left, come port 360 and buster ...'

I bank obediently and ease the throttles forward to accelerate to 500 knots. If they are Buccs, I will need at least that to catch them ...

'Continue port onto 300 degrees, they bear 280 degrees, five miles, any contact? There should be two of them out there!'

I know the controller is wondering who are these two dummies in that aeroplane out there, unable to get such a simple pickup. Bill is searching frantically and I jig up and down in my seat with impatience. We are down at 2,000 feet. He picks up a contact, but the way it rushes down the tube shows that its a ship. He rejects it and searches on. If these contacts are low it will be difficult to spot them. A skill born only of experience is needed to recognise potential targets amidst the confusion of sea returns. Manipulating the radar controls is a delicate, finely tuned affair. Suddenly he sees something and pauses in his search; the contact, a tiny blip, holds its position, its range and bearing tie in with the information the Shackleton controller is passing us. Bill calls 'I have a contact bearing 270, four miles ...'

'That's them.'

'Roger, Judy!' and to me 'Tap the Heaters!'

With one sweep, I move the throttles through the gate, a slight pause followed by a punch in the back as the afterburners light up and we leap forward frantically. I am pressed back against the seat with the surging acceleration and the needle on the ASI scuds round to 600 knots, .95 Mach. I throttle back to min 'burner to hold that speed. I am having to concentrate fiercely on my instruments for I know the symptoms of disorientation under these circumstances well. The sudden acceleration has fooled the canals in my ears into thinking that we are in a steep climb. The natural tendency would be to push the stick forward and so fly straight into the sea. But the instruments tell me I am flying straight and level at 1,000 feet, and because I have practised this manoeuvre many times on instrument rating rides, I ignore the sensations and once my balance organs have readjusted themselves to the new velocity, it is safe to look outside once more. The blip on the screen is closing slowly but surely. However, we must be quick, the fleet is only thirty miles away, three minutes' flying at Bucc speeds.

'Switches!' the voice from the back calls. I hurriedly recheck the coolant, check Sidewinder is selected and indicated, ensure the Master Arm is 'On' and 'Ready', gunsight set at caged and glowing dimly in the combining glass ... 'Yeah, they're all set ...', we must film the kill for it to be confirmed. No Master Arm 'On' will show on the film and this means no kill – unprofessional.

Bill tries a lock, but we are still too far away, two miles and they are too low, and the radar doesn't want to know. The screen is covered by a mass of lines for a few sweeps, then the picture clears and luckily for Bill, he reacquires immediately. During those few seconds, the target could have evaded and disappeared forever. As it is, he must know that we are somewhere near behind him, but he is on his final run in to the target and so he must take the calculated risk of pressing on regardless and hope that he gets to the ships before we get to him.

However, fast though the Buccaneer is at low level, the Phantom is faster. I ease the throttles up to one half AB and the blip closes rapidly. One mile – Bill tries a lock again and this time is successful. I look out again and see a nav light flashing a few hundred feet below me. 'Visual', I call.

'Okay, you're in range, clear to fire.'

I ease forward on the stick and the nav light floats into the gunsight reticle, I hear the growl of the acquisition 'Winder in my headphones, I squeeze the trigger and there is sudden silence. 'Fox 2, splash; target destroyed,' I transmit this information to the controller as I recover from the slight dive. Back comes the reply from the Shackleton 'Okay, but there's another one in front of him!' I know this because I have studied the Buccaneer mind in our many clashes. I have built up my own mental dossier on his habits and modes of behaviour. Now I enjoy this game of trying to stay one step ahead, trying to guess his actions, anticipating his next move. Bill is searching again on the radar, but we are ten miles from the ships and too late now and I know what is going to happen next.

Sure enough, a few seconds later, night becomes day under the influence of a million watts equivalent candle power floating down on the end of a parachute. The Lead Buccaneer has pulled up and tossed his Lepus flares. Beneath us, the whole sea surface stands out in stark relief. The sea is calm and looking down, I can see five or six shapes comprising the destroyers and frigates of the task force with a few other escorts. One larger shape must be the Dutch cruiser, flag ship of the force and so probably the prime target of the attackers. The fleet is steaming peacefully, carving small furrows in the almost flat calm sea, casting dark shadows in sharply contrasting relief under the artificial sun. All looks quiet, but I know that in the bowels of those ships action stations hooters are blaring as crews man anti-aircraft guns and Seacat batteries, gunlaying radars sweeping out to find the range of the intruders. I know one of those blips on their screen will be me and they are not to know the difference between friend and foe in the MEZ. That is why I firewall the throttles and start hauling off in a steep climbing turn to port. That is the first reason I am getting out while the going is good.

The second reason is that I know the manoeuvres the Buccaneers will be carrying out next. The lead aircraft having tossed his flares will be rolling over and pulling back down and round to sea level and heading outbound to arm his weapons. In the next few seconds, he and his number 2 will perform a classic and confusing ballet as they run through the strike profiles peculiar to their trade. The action will be fast and furious, precise and co-ordinated, a symphony orchestrated at low level.

I do not figure in their tightly controlled plan of aircraft flashing about in close proximity in a small space of sky. That is why I mind my own business and return to CAP while Bill logs the time and position of our one kill.

11

En Route Episode

On idle days I leaf through my logbook, reliving bygone hours, and in doing so I find I cannot avoid the waves of nostalgia that sometimes attack me. Its not always the good things I reflect on either, because I have taken the rough with the smooth ...

Saturday morning and the Squadron detachment to Malta is drawing to an end. The farewell party of the previous night still lingers, an alcoholic haze nagging faintly in the subconscious. It is time to move 43 Squadron en masse back to the familiar environs of Leuchars fighter base, Scotland, UK. I am about to fit my little jigsaw piece into the whole giant planning machinery that is part and parcel of moving a squadron and its equipment a quarter of the way round the world.

We will depart in twos at hourly intervals, RV with our tankers off the coast of Italy and then simply let the tanker do the work of taking us across Europe, through the airways and TCAs that crisscross the European skies like some lace network. Our job is incredibly simple – to fly on the wing of the tanker for the whole three-hour jaunt. We will not even have to talk to any foreign controller on the ground. We shall simply sit back and enjoy the scenery. So I thought. I was not to know that the fates had other plans in store for me.

Phil is designated leader of our pair, making my task even more so one of 'airframe driver', period. I stuff some maps into my pocket just to show willing, but navigation does not figure in my plans for this trip. Mission brief, and this is the opportunity for all the squadron 'wheels' to stand up and put in their little bit of TCIC. We are briefed *ad infinitum* on route weather, available diversion fields, tanker RV points, emergency contingency plans, go/no-go criteria, all of it pours out and washes over me, but I am only a JP Number 2 and I will be following my leader who will be following a tanker and so half the pearls of wisdom filter straight through one ear and out the other. The brief ends with the traditional time hack and we all disperse.

I am allocated P-Papa for the trip, so I collect my duty-free bottles and cigarettes from the custom pound and make my way to the aircraft carrying a small holdall containing the immediate necessities of life for when I arrive back at base (Air Support Command will deliver my luggage four days later). My navigator and I spend fifteen minutes stowing equipment and bags in the many nooks and crannies that abound (amazingly) in a fighter cockpit. The ground-crew have opened Door 19 behind the navigator's cockpit and in here go shoes and other odd bits of junk to join the nitrogen cylinder nestling there. Thus all available crevices are filled with items which they were never designed to expect. We value our precious cargo and I make a mental note not to indulge in any form of aerobatics, however mild. To do so would result in several parcels of Maltese souvenirs and other mementoes shedding their contents into the bowels of the aircraft, never to be recovered again in any useful form.

Take-off time approaches and soon, for the last time, I am streaming down Luqa's great asphalt runway, thirty seconds behind my leader. Airborne call, after take-off checks, changeover to Malta approach and ahead of me Phil is already banking onto the first heading. I wheel after him. Below me, my shadow is sweeping across the brownish walls and fields surrounding the base, over the serried ranks of houses crowding Valetta, down Sliema waterfront and across Grand Harbour, the *Ark Royal* at anchor glinting in the weak sunlight, and as I roll out on heading we coast out over the deep blue of the Mediterranean. Climbing rapidly, the island dwindles to a green-brown jewel set in the surrounding blue before it disappears behind my port wing-tip.

I am flying fighting wing on my leader as Malta control hands us over to Rome control who will watch over us as we head north past Sicily before turning left just short of Elba to meet our tanker. The Victor has flown from the UK, having refuelled from his mate before continuing south to meet us. 43 is sending five pairs home so we are utilising ten tankers for the task.

We are flying in milky cirro-stratus which gradually gets thicker and thicker till I am forced to move into close formation. This is not nice at the best of times at the altitude we are flying (28,000 feet) but loaded as we are with three drop tanks and heavy with fuel, I need to concentrate to maintain what little performance margins I have left as I stay in close formation. Phil decides to ask Rome control for clearance to climb out of the cloud. We are cleared so up we go and finally, at 34,000 feet, we break out into hazy sunshine and I can afford to ease out into fighting wing again. Forewarning of possible trouble has been rearing its ugly head in the climb. The Static Corr caption has been flicking on and off, causing the instruments to give mad little jerks. I know there is a fault somwhere in the CADC. However, a failure in this component has been declared a 'Go' condition in the brief, so I inform my leader and we press on ahead. Nevertheless it sits at the back of my mind, niggling.

Our tanker is there waiting for us sure enough, and we pick him up on the radar at forty miles. He turns onto his course for the French coast and we close on him to join on his port side.

Below, there is nothing to be seen except the sea of milky stratus a few thousand feet lower. I hope it will have cleared by the time we cross France otherwise it will be a pretty boring old trip and my plans for photographing the Alps will have to go overboard. The Victor is talking to us on one frequency and to the ground agencies on another so we don't even have the light relief of trying to decipher Italo-French RT.

Our centreline tank is empty by now and Phil requests a top-up, as we are in the designated refuelling bracket. The tanker captain obliges by streaming the two wing hoses and we position astern each one. We are above our ideal tanking height and with the added handicap of three tanks, the task is made a little more difficult.

However, this is no cause for concern, as we are paid to do the job, not to worry about such details. Phil plugs in first time and I follow suit shortly after. In front of me the Victor's wing looms hugely, the green light on the refuelling pod winking to show that fuel is rushing into the depleted centreline tank. As we fill up, so the rate of transfer slows down, and as we become heavier, with the C of G moving further aft, so I need more and more power to stay plugged in and eventually I have to select one engine into min 'burner to prevent myself falling out. Under these circumstances we are using fuel as quickly as it is coming in, so after a minute, I call disengaging and drop back, the probe disconnecting and emerging from the basket in a cloud of fuel spray.

Probe retracted, all switches reset, centreline tank fuel selected and feeding and all is back to normal. With this method of airborne replenishment, I can fly nonstop from the UK to Singapore in fourteen hours. However, this particular journey is no such marathon, and with refuelling complete I can relax for a while. I reselect the autopilot in and decide to investigate the contents of the luncheon box that Luqa Mess provided for me. A short struggle rescues the cardboard container from its hiding place in the map container where I stowed it before take-off. Oxygen mask off, carton balanced on knee and lunch consisting of chicken, eggs and ham sandwiches washed down with orange juice. On my right side the Victor rides steadily, occasionally bobbing gently up and down. On his right is the other Phantom also rising and falling slowly in the rarefied air. All three of us are drawing long plumes of contrails from our jet exhausts, trails that stretch for miles behind us to linger before being finally carried away by the hidden currents of the air.

On the radar screen I can see Sardinia approaching and then disappearing below and to the left, unseen beneath the cloud. The navigator reselects another scale and starts searching for the French coast which should be coming up ahead at any moment. The sun is beating down strongly on the plexiglass canopy, producing a greenhouse effect which would have been unpleasant were it not for the cool blast of air issuing from the air-conditioning vents. As it is, the cockpit is pleasantly warm and homely with maps, charts, TAPs mixing on the coaming with empty orange squash containers and lunch boxes. On the telelight panel, the tank captions flash away periodically to show fuel is still feeding satisfactorily. Both engines are humming smoothly at 93 per cent, TGTs steady at 550 degrees C, fuel flow a constant 100 pounds a minutes. Leuchars is two hours away and I am already looking forward to checking out any changes in the downtown scene in the month we've been away.

I am busy staring drowsily out into space when the unexpected happens, that short period of terror that intersperses long periods of boredom. The Phantom gives an almighty lurch and rolls rapidly to the right and down. Maps, half-eaten sandwiches, food containers and sundry bits and pieces cascade everywhere. On the instrument panel, all the lights have gone out and I am confronted by a maze of red 'Off' flags, the radio and intercom are dead and I am in a silent world of my own, my ears are popping in protest at the rapid depressurisation of the cabin. The rapid pitch-up and roll has sent us heading rapidly down towards the sea of clouds, the whole event has lasted perhaps a second and a half, if that, but to me in my traumatic state it seems a lifetime.

Nevertheless, I have not spent many hours in the simulator training and practising emergency drills for nothing. The immediate actions are embedded deep within me. My reactions to the problem have been unhesitating and unthinking despite the apparent paralysis of the conscious mind. Born of instinct and long training, my hands have automatically hit the paddle switch to disconnect the autopilot and stab aug systems. At the same time, I am transferring my gaze to the standby ADI and rolling wings level and recovering from the dive in which we were established. Simultaneously my left hand has reached out to the port cockpit wall and pulled down a black and yellow striped lever to bring the emergency Ram Air Turbine popping out into the airstream on the left side of the fuselage. My mind has made an instant analysis – double generator failure. Definitely a no-go item. My actions have occupied fractions of a second, and mysteriously as the RAT starts generating, everything suddenly comes back to life with a clunk of resurrected gyros, flashing captions and confused chatter over the RT.

My navigator is shouting at me from the rear seat demanding to know what is going on. My own heart is in the process of slowing down from the mad race it had adopted when the emergency occurred. I look for and reacquire the other two aircraft visually some miles away from us. I take a few deep breaths before announcing on the RT that I have an electrical problem and would like to divert immediately. Lead agrees, so decision number one is made. Decision number two is not so easy. Where shall we divert to? We have several options open to us – return to Malta, head for Sigonella in Sicily, there is Decimomannu in Sardinia or we can keep going for

Nice or Istres. We decide to ask the Victor. It is his job after all to have the information readily at hand. Luqa is quickly ruled out. The weather has deteriorated and the last thing I want to do is make an approach on my leader's wing with the prospect of a visual-only capability should I lose him in the weather. Sigonella is scrapped, as is Istres, both too far to risk. The obvious choice is Decimomannu, a NATO base often visited by Phantoms. A quick weather check reveals that on the last hour the base was 'blue', no sweat. The decision is made. The Victor gives us a steer to Deci and we about-turn and bid him goodbye, leaving him to return to Marham, England on his own.

In my plane, the generators are still malfunctioning, the breakdown in electrical power causing the stab augs to cycle in and out resulting in the aircraft giving another of those sudden lurches that so frightened us minutes (or was it hours) before. I decide to select all three stab augs off, leaving me with a very sensitive aeroplane on my hands. The conflicts of demands for high performance in the corners of the envelope coupled with a need for reasonable low-speed handling characteristics called for a compromise in the Phantom. As with all swept wing, high wing-loaded fighters, the aircraft is not inherently stable, any excursions from balanced flight usually resulting in a rapid divergency. Flying the machine in this condition becomes rapidly tiring due to the need for constant small corrections to maintain equilibrium. Trimming becomes an impossible nightmare, each change of power or attitude demanding an instant correction on the stick. The engineers in their wisdom decided to remedy this unsatisfactory state of affairs by fitting a Stability Augmentation System consisting of a mass of sensing accelerometers, the system acting as a mini-autopilot to maintain the aircraft in whatever state or attitude selected on the control column. The stab augs operate on all three axes, but I can fly the aircraft quite happily with roll and yaw stab augs out. However, pitch stab aug is another matter and at high speeds with pitch aug out, life can become dangerous.

This is the first time I have experienced the problem in earnest and I tell my leader to keep his speed down as he forgets himself and pours on the coals in his haste to reach Deci. Nevertheless, I prefer to have a sensitive bird under complete control in my hands rather than one that is going to give me mild heart attacks every few minutes as the stab augs cycle involuntarily.

We are having trouble with the RT. I have declared PAN on 243 but this does not seem to arouse anyone's interest. Phil decides to go straight to Elmas approach, the controlling agency for Decimo-mannu. It is Saturday and probably a public holiday for we cannot get any sense out of ground control, we are unable to impress on them the state of emergency we have declared. We try to estab-lish whether the runway arrester gear is erected and whether the emergency crews are on alert. The answer in broken English is lost amidst the crackle of static, RT reception is poor. Neverthe-less we do manage to obtain a runway in use and so we decide to free call Deci tower. We eventually establish contact to find again the same lack of interest or urgency. I thank God for the refuelling we had carried out previously. Right now, fuel is not one of my problems. Suffering a total electrical failure and being unable to penetrate cloud to a landing is. Lead asks for a GCA into the field. Back comes the reply – GCA controller is off duty, no precision aids available. A conference takes place between our two aircraft and we eventually decide to attempt a Tacan letdown out to sea till we re-gain VMC and then turn back in to find the field. The 'Off' flags on my instruments are still flickering in and out of sight as I close up on my leader's wing and wedge my wing-tip solidly behind his and hang in.

We start the descent from 25,000 feet, thirty miles from Deci Tacan. Sardinia is an island with some big hills sitting on it. We have no QFE or QNH for that matter, so I will be watching the radio altimeter like a hawk. Almost immediately we sink into the stratus, still as milky white as ever, not very thick but all enveloping, no horizon, disorientating ... I edge in a little closer, too fast and the aircraft oscillates violently and I have to make a conscious effort to damp out the PIO and smooth down my formation. The altimeters unwind rapidly, Tacan needle swings round as we pass overhead the airfield and continue out to sea, but we see nothing, we are still solidly cloud-cloaked. We have heard nothing from the tower for quite a while. I don't care; I am only interested in that other aircraft twelve feet away from me. My faith is in the crew of that machine. He is the leader. It is up to him to get me down in one piece.

We begin to suspect that Victor's weather report when we finally break cloud at 1,200 feet over a murky grey sea, storm tossed and frothy, surrounded by ragged clouds and driving rain showers. The Tacan has broken lock (we are thirty miles out to sea), we have lost all contact with Deci tower, neither of us is familiar with the airfield local area, prospects look grim. I am not happy with the thought of trying to find a strange airfield set amidst a cloud-capped hill range. I say as much to lead and he agrees. He calls for a fuel check, and furious mental calculations follow before decision number three this morning is made. We will give Decimomannu up as a bad job and head for France instead. We inform Deci, but get no reply (I will not forget that place in a hurry); full power, tighten up into close formation again as we plunge back upwards into the murk we have just left. I am resigned now to whatever fate decrees. If I am to bale out into the Mediterranean sea miles from the nearest rescue services, then so be it.

However, our luck is already changing. As we climb, we suddenly burst out into a brilliant blueness, we are literally spewed out of the wall of clouds into a gin clear, typically Mediterranean day. Behind us, we can see the long line of clouds marking the edge of the front that has been affecting the southern Med and which is now gradually creeping northwards. In the clear air, our radios improve and as we level at 30,000 feet we immediately pick up France control. In a few short, well-chosen words, Phil explains our predicament (I am beginning to eye my fuel gauge anxiously) and requests diversion to Nice or Istres. A short wait and they come back with a clearance to divert to Istres. We are back in well controlled civilisation where the well oiled wheels of machinery run smoothly and efficiently.

The French coast appears out of the blue heat haze ahead and soon we are letting down to 2,500 feet, running down along the Riviera (the sands really are golden) and passing over the sunburnt scrubland of the inner coastal landscape. Istres takes control of us and I close up on Lead again as we position on the centreline for a pairs GCA. As a precaution I blow the gear down with the pneumatic air, just in case another generator failure results in the undercarriage folding up as we touch down. I decide against taking the 'wire'. Enough is enough, today. The giant runway appears ahead and at 100 feet Phil overshoots leaving me to land straight ahead. The wheels touch French soil (unscheduled) two hours after leaving Malta. Phil carries out a circuit and landing behind us. The tower directs us down a maze of taxiways till at last we are parked in a slot side by side somewhere on the sprawling base. It is with a sigh of relief that I select both throttles off through the gate and allow the two engines to grind down to a halt while I climb out to stretch stiffly in the hot sunlight, the sweat already cooling in the welcome whisper of a breeze that has sprung up, a forewarning of the front that is still advancing to meet us.

The front arrives that night, together with a Hercules load full of technicians who immediately get down to work in the pouring rain. It transpires that a faulty underspeed switch was the cause of our problems. Two days later, well sated with French cuisine, we blast off, follow a ruler-straight line across France to just north of Paris, turn left for the Clacton beacon and then race northwards up the east coast. One and a half hours after take-off, P-Papa is back on home territory to find an alert in progress. Its a case then of unloading aeroplane, booking back into the Mess (navigator drops his flagon of wine in the corridor) and so back on alert duty. We are already into the routine of squadron life. Memories are fading, like the coming of dawn after a dark and dirty night. The future beckons, and besides, looking back now, I see it was all in a day's work.

12

....

Posting

Variety, we are told, is the spice of life, and no-one upholds this philosophy better than our lords and masters in the Air Force. Hence, every two or three years I experience an upheaval in my life that involves a change of base, possibly a change of aircraft or role, perhaps a change of country (although this is less common these days with the dwindling Empire). Certainly a change in responsibility and outlook. It is all designed to keep me on my toes, mentally fresh and alert, ready to bring a new mind and new ideas to the problem-solving spheres of a new job. The arguments for and against this system are many. Certainly, change is good for the soul, for in the flying business I cannot afford to have the contempt bred by familiarity lurking in my subconscious. On the other hand, constant and regular uprooting does lead to problems in maintaining standards over a period of time. The danger of the Jack-of-all-Trades is an ever-present one when I look down the postings roster and see that we have received ten new technicians, all of whom have no previous experience (except from six weeks' introductory ground school) of Phantom systems, their previous backgrounds being VC10s, Hercules, Nimrods, Jaguars, Bulldogs.

They will spend two years learning the numerous foibles of the F4 Phantom only perhaps to be sent off yet again onto some other type. However, to be fair, this is becoming more a thing of the past. Today, we may shift bases, yes, but rarely do we change aeroplanes, or more important, roles. Eventually I suppose, we will end up like our Dutch and German colleagues, rooted to one base and its aeroplanes for year after year, exchanging variety for security. But who is going to have the courage to take it upon himself to sentence a man to ten years on some base out in the wilds? Who is going to be judge and advocate in the scramble for the choice postings? The efficiency of a fighting force depends on the well-being of its members. Trying to devise a system of long-term postings satisfactory to all is bound to raise discord and debate so perhaps the Air Force is right to shuttle us from place to place every three years or so. This adds an extra dimension of interest to everyday life, because as the 'Tourex' date approaches, so the crewroom chat turns to who is going where, when. At such times, even the favourite topics of pay, promotion, women and flying take a back seat while the question of postings is thrashed out.

Dwindled though the Empire may be, there are many exotic places the Air Force flier may find himself. Every year on my confidential reports, I can bid for one of these postings and compete with my fellow officers. Depending on what takes my fancy, I can opt to go and fly F5s with the Norwegian Air Force at Rygge, near Oslo. I can apply for a slot with the German Luftwaffe flying reconnaissance Phantoms out of Leek airbase in northern Germany, or I could volunteer to join the famous Richthofen wing at Wittmundhaven flying slatted F4Es. If I am partial to skiing and the Bavarian Alps I can apply to go to Bremgarten in southern Germany on another reconnaissance squadron. There is a slot available piloting F104s at Grazzanise in Italy. My wife is partial to French food, so I can apply to go to the French Test Pilot School at Istres in the South of France.

The States is a New World, in more ways than one for the Royal Air Force man. I can exchange into the United States Navy flying to the carriers from Oceana Naval Air Station. The US Marines have an exchange vacancy on F4s at Cherry Point. I can swop Coningsby Phantom OCU for the giant USAF training base at Davis-Monthan in the Nevada desert, where 100 Phantoms on the flight line every morning is nothing to marvel at, and Las Vegas just down the road. On the other hand, I could become a Squadron Joe, operating out of George Air Force base in the deep south and there is even an F4 posting in Alaska – the Frozen North. With my American squadron I can deploy to Honolulu, Hawaii, Turkey and Japan. In my two-year tour with them I can go on a junket around the world, all at Air Force expense. I don't even have to fly F4s. There are exchange jobs on F106 Delta Darts, defending the US borders. I can apply to fly F105 Thunderchiefs tackling the Aggressors on Red Flag war exercises. I can convert to A7 Corsairs flying low-level strike missions. If I were a transport man, there is a job for me on C-141 Starlifters.

But wait; suppose I am tired of flying for the moment and am interested in furthering my career, which means chalking up a few good marks on the Staff side. Why, then I can apply for defence attaché jobs in Stockholm, Brussels, the Solomon Islands, Hong Kong, Peking even. The world is my oyster, as far as such exchange postings are concerned.

However, there are many thousands of us chasing after these (relatively) few plums. What else is there for the average run-of-the-mill aviator, either down on luck, otherwise inclined or possessing no special talents either on the aviation or the blue-eyed-promotion-prospect side to warrant his being sent abroad on an ambassadorial post (which is really what an exchange tour is all about)? Well, the RAF still has a base in Hong Kong, it still maintains a presence in Cyprus. I could apply for these if I happened to fly helicopters, or Nimrod maritime patrol machines. But for the F4 driver, choice of posting is limited to few bases, three in the UK and one in the Federal Republic of Germany. If I wished, I could widen my choice of bases slightly by applying for training on the Jaguar, Harrier or Buccaneer, but my affair with the Phantom is one I am not prepared to end, so I juggle with the four optional postings available. But really, there is no question which I will choose, because even if I forget that I have already spent five years at Leuchars and Coningsby and do not really wish to visit Wattisham, Suffolk, for any length of time, even if I forget all these facts, the lure of the European continent and Royal Air Force Germany in particular is much too strong to ignore. When all the favourite exchange postings have been filled up, then the RAF in Germany is the next logical choice.

Let me forget for a while the material aspects of this choice. Let me forget a wide and varied continent waiting to be explored, strange and different people to be met, resorts and tourist centres that up to now have been merely names in colour brochures. Let me ignore the duty-free goods and the 'local overseas allowance' that enables the serviceman to exist in the affluent European environment. Let me cast these aside and concentrate instead on the tension, the tautness, the exhilaration of being at the centre of a complex vortex of power structures, of experiencing at first hand the manifestation of that state – cold war – that overshadows the workings of man in every corner of the world.

It is true that sitting on this 'Nook Shotten Isle of Albion', even today and despite the magnetic attempts of the Common Market to draw us closer into the European fold, we in Britain still retain that insular outlook. In my job of Air Defence of the UK airspace, I am seldom given any impression that there really is any threat of war. The only exception, possibly, is when I meet the occasional Bear on patrol up in the Iceland/Faeroes gap, but apart from that, the buffer of water conveys a nice sense of security and well-being. The annual exercises give us a taste of what we might expect with mass low-level raids, but these do take on the air of war games and picking off F104s and dicing with Mirages is great sport, chaps, but afterwards, I return to my rural non-hardened airfield, park my aeroplane in the open and stroll down to the nearby mess for tea. Germany, that battleground of two world wars, is to be a different kettle of fish.

So it is that one sunny July afternoon, the Wing Commander calls me in to his office to inform me that I have been posted to RAF Wildenrath, Germany, as Deputy QWI to 92 (East India) Squadron – the Cobras – which up till now has been flying Lightnings out of Gutersloh and are about to reform at Wildenrath with the F4 Phantom. Variety is about to commence.

13

....

RAFG

I am sitting here staring at a poster on the wall of my room in the Mess. It is a colour photo portrait – wide-angle lens – of a great, round shadowed globe hanging miraculously unsupported in a ghostly blackness. It is the earth, our planet, suspended in space and photographed from a distance of half a million miles by one of the Apollo moon projects. A thought drifts up to the surface of my mind – if I were a creature from another world looking on, if I were a Venus probe, a Voyager orbiting Mars, an Explorer looping past Jupiter, why, I would report back to Command HQ – 'This planet shows no sign of being inhabited by intelligent life. From this range the surface appears barren.' Such is the air of innocence the globe projects to the casual onlooker with its soft blues, greens and greys.

It so happens that this particular shot of the earth shows the European continent (half covered with perennial cloud) and my thumb and forefinger can encompass London to Moscow in one spread. I can make out the boundaries of the German mainland and I know where the border dividing East and West, Communist and Capitalist should lie on my poster-map. I know where that great curtain of Iron stretches, from the Baltic to the Black Seas. I know where they should be, but are they to be seen? Well, let me come closer, let me approach this glowing jewel travelling silently through the infinity … the spaceship Earth.

Eight miles high on border patrol off a Battle Flight scramble, I sit in my jet and because border patrols are routine, boring and inactive I have plenty of time to look down from this dizzy height and take in what the eye sees. My report back to the Command Module still in orbit high above (were there such a vessel) would still be – 'No sign of life.'

Jet flight has often been called 'remote' and on occasions like this, I realise once again why that should be so. The deep, deep blue of the sky above contrasts sharply with the patchwork quilt of mountains, valleys, plains below. That aspect is familiar enough. What interests me more today is the complete sense of loneliness, the 'cut-off' sensation about which the Aviation Medicine specialists love to postulate. If I stare really hard, I can make out the beetle cars crawling along little ribbon-strip highways. If I gaze for a long time I can detect the metallic centipedes of trains creeping slowly along silver-latticed tracks. As for signs of human life as such, I could be in the year one million BC with mechanical prehistoric beasts crawling on the surface beneath me. So I am alone in the sky apart from the occasional fellow pterodactyl drawing streaky white cons in the air. However, such euphoria is seldom long lived. Professional military aviators do not indulge in prolonged daydreaming and these feelings last a few seconds at the most. The imperious voice of ground control invariably sees to that. Nevertheless, I still continue to gaze at the ground, as I patrol the border, and I look for this Iron Curtain that I have heard so much about. I see nothing. Although my instruments tell me that I am flying a few miles on 'our' side of the border, the visual picture tells a different story. Surely 'our' side should be bright, cheerful, enlightened and airy, while 'they' should be dark, dank, grey, gloomy and under a perpetual cloud. Isn't that what the propaganda machine has told me? That 'they' live in a continual slough of despond? My eyes receive a different story. The fact is, the grass is just as green on their side, the same sun beats down on their soil, we seem to share a common breeze. Why, from up here, this road, that railway displays no favouritism, they run a constant course across the whole landscape. The river cares not about nationality as it flows on. Thus my eight-mile-high vigil tempts me to believe that there is no such thing as division, because from my perch there is no such thing as discord, there are no such things as boundaries, the world is at one, peaceful and in united harmony. Is the physical evidence not there right before my eyes? The aviator, residing temporarily in his element is indeed divorced from reality as soon as his wheels tuck into the wells in the fuselage. He translates into another dimension for the short while and he is able to look on with new perspectives … or so he thinks.

Flying can be a dangerous drug, setting traps for the unwary. Medusa is ever present and temptation, the forbidden fruit, lurks in the most innocent of situations. Then if I were a romantic fool, I would be in trouble. Instead, I am a hard-headed fighter pilot, a veteran of several thousand military flying hours. My senses are in full control and self-discipline overrules all. While I may look at the ground with a faintly pastoral interest, I know that if I altered heading by two degrees and held it for five minutes I would very soon have to start dodging volleys of Sam 3 or 4 missiles launched from the ground, 23-millimetre bullets fired from MiG 21 interceptors, air-to-air missiles launched by MiG 23 Floggers and for good measure, a hail of radar-guided lead thrown up by ZSU 23–4 track-mounted anti-aircraft guns.

All these nasties exist on the other side of that thick blue zig-zag line painted on my map and marking the boundary between 'them' and 'us', and that line (though invisible) is well represented on the ground, as I would see if I, like the outer space visitor, chose to come nearer. I would see the barbed wire fences, the minefields, the border patrolled by armed guards, the dogs running free, vicious and hungry, the tanks, artillery, planes, soldiers, all physical manifestations of that blue line, very real and very solid, should I dare to touch them.

So, although I may sit remote, up there in my cockpit looking down at the friendly earth, apparently still and barren, I know that it is not friendly at all, I know that there is a great deal of evil festering down there like a subcutaneous sore waiting to burst open and because I know surface beauty can be deceptive, I approach with care, for the Iron Curtain is there, and respective ideologies have decreed that these barriers shall continue to exist. So the reality of life goes on.

The Boeing 737 punches through the few remaining octas of cloud on its final approach and the first I see of RAF Germany is a large autobahn and the cars driving on the wrong side of the road. The next sight I catch, as the wings dismantle themselves with high lift devices, is a battery complex of drab olive-green Bloodhound missiles – sixteen of them – and all facing eastwards. A few seconds later, the Boeing touches down, rather hard, and very quickly slows to a walking pace under the influence of reverse thrust.

'Welcome to Royal Air Force Wildenrath' the big notice board says at the air terminal – drab olive-green – as we dismount from the trooper. I step down onto German soil – my home-to-be for the next three years – and I am confronted by a Martian creature brandishing a sub-machine gun. At least he looks like a Martian to many of my fellow passengers; wives, friends, relations of people based here in Germany. Some small children start to cry, and I don't blame them. In fact, I recognise the standard NATO issue gas mask and a query to the Duty Air Movements Officer reveals that the base is under (simulated) gas attack. An alert is in progress.

A bus deposits me at the Officers' Mess where I check into my bachelor accommodation. Over the next week I settle down to explore and get used to this strange new habitat. I say strange only in the sense that there is a semblance of permanency to my stay this time. I have been to Germany many times before on Phantom 'leaps', the nickname given to those weekend forays from the UK to sample Löwenbräu, Mosel wine, King Edward cigars at £2 for 50, and to stock up on Chanel No 5, Worth and Fidji for wives and girlfriends. On other occasions I have made sorties across to attack NATO airfields, flight refuelling over the Channel, striking their bases at first light and then returning to my distant base on the Island. On more friendly visits I have detached to American and French fields where we have wined and dined by night and flown in friendly rivalry by day, learning a little more of the ways of operation of our allies. No, none of it is new to me. But on those brief visits, I have always been the outsider, the visitor, experiencing for a short while but never being quite sure what the total picture consisted of. On those occasions I have returned to the UK base, baffled and puzzled by the rules and regulations I have encountered, confused by the terrain over which I have flown – littered with tanks, guns, missile batteries – amazed by the procedures I have been forced to adopt. Now I can get down to sorting out some order from this great jungle of tangled information stretching before me.

To start with there is no walking anywhere on this base. That is, if I wish to arrive at any destination on time. From my room in the Mess to the barbed wire gate leading into Squadron Operations is two miles as the bus drives. Should I wish to visit our sister squadron I am faced with a further two-mile journey along the twisting perimeter road. Continuing along the same road for a further three miles would bring me right back to my squadron, having travelled full circle, literally, around the base area. It is big.

So the first thing I do is acquire a bicycle and kill two birds with one stone – achieve a certain degree of mobility and promote physical fitness. My body seems to have quietly forgotten the latter aim over the past few years. A squadron crew bus is provided, but I will try to avoid using it. The next feature that strikes the casual observer about this base, and indeed about most NATO bases, is the colour, the same colour that struck me as the 737 swept low over the approach lights. The whole world is green. Everything is painted green. The mess buildings, the hangars, the squadron accommodation, the network of aircraft shelters, the refuelling bowsers, the executive mini-cars, the firetrucks, our flying suits, harnesses and helmets, the Phantom aircraft, the Bloodhound missiles, the ambulances, they are all painted *green*. Mind you, the shades of green do vary, from deep jungle green through an emerald tinge to a muddy ochre type of green. All designed, naturally enough, to blend in with the surrounding countryside. Anything that isn't obviously green must expect green jungle netting to be draped over it. Confusing to the enemy it may be but invariably this 'tone down' can also prove baffling to friend as well. This airfield is very difficult to find from the air if you do not happen to know it is there. I fly many sorties out of here every day and yet still find it difficult, almost impossible sometimes in the frequently gloomy German weather, still tricky when the air is clear and I am boring in at 500 feet on a low-level recovery. It is a fine task of navigation for me, and I know it is there. How will my fellow fliers from across the border feel as they penetrate, harassed all the way by fighters and missiles? So, needless to say, we feel confidently secure on our base, hidden away amongst the tall green trees that seem to proliferate everywhere, apart from on the German plains to the north of us. Camouflage has always been a number one weapon of defence and here it has been developed to a fine art.

Some people (some!) think that flying a supersonic jet fighter is something difficult; that handling twenty-five tons of raw energy requires some exceptional, super-human qualities of alertness and instant reaction. Far from it. The fact is, I could teach my grandmother with a wooden leg to fly a Phantom with ease and confidence. My ten-year-old nephew, with a little practice and instruction, could climb into the beast, start up, take off, carry out a circuit and land it back onto the ground. My wife, with a detailed briefing, could fly down to Nordhorn range and deliver a simulated nuclear weapon within the broad limits necessary to obliterate a city. All it takes is a little practice, some know-how and an appreciation of the tricks of the trade. A lorry driver could do my job, so could a surgeon, or a lawyer, or the local accountant. It's just like riding a bicycle ...

These thoughts came to me after I broke into the circuit just now from a medium level Air Combat sortie. I landed, taxied, in, shut down and strolled back into the squadron crew room. Now, I and my fellow pilots and navigators sit (or rather sprawl) at comfortable ease in the stuffed red leather crewroom chairs, legs propped up on tables, wreaths of vapour from steaming mugs of coffee mingling with the less pleasant streamers from burning cigarette ends. Thus we adopt the relaxed pose beloved of military aircrew the world over.

As I sit, vaguely listening to the desultory chatter floating about me, I think about the circuit I have just flown and what could have caused me to contemplate the ease of it all. I must analyse it, because there is a faint danger that familiarity might be breeding contempt here and I must nip it in the bud before disaster looms. So I ask myself – is it really as easy as I think? Well, let me re-fly that circuit ...

It starts with a close formation penetration through the cloud. It is dusk, with the onset of twilight. A misty drizzle cloaks the world, the cloudbase ragged at 1,200 feet. However, visibility is reasonable which is why Dave is electing to carry out a visual approach. I have been sitting tucked in close on his starboard side for the cloud penetration, and because I feel comfortable and in the groove, I decide to remain in close formation for the break. The Wegberg ring road slides past beneath us, the signal for Dave to tilt his aircraft in a smooth starboard turn to line up with Wildenrath Runway 27 as yet unseen somewhere out in the mist. I am concentrating, but it is a relaxed concentration as we forge along together at 350 knots. My movements are sub-conscious as the runway lights loom up in the gathering dusk and Dave pitches into the visual circuit pattern.

'Two second pause … wham … stick to the left, throttle back, speedbrakes out, pull G … grey world revolves onto it's side … pull G … 2 … 3, climbing from 800 feet break height up to 1,000 circuit height, a 180-degree turn onto the downwind leg … put Dave's aircraft on the horizon … what horizon? He is barely visible in the mist ahead … oh, well I'll fly at 1,000 feet on the altimeter, stuff what Dave's doing, nobody can see us from the ground anyway … runway's just visible out to the left side … smoothly roll out on heading 090 degrees downwind … thumb hits RT button – "75 downwind roll, climbout for ILS" … "Roger, you're cleared to continue, one ahead" the man in the control tower says … right, how are we doing … time for checks … engines are still whispering at 60 per cent idle RPM, speed is decaying … 250 knots … speedbrakes IN; undercarriage down … rumble, thud, clunk … three wheels indicating … speed decays even faster … leave the throttle back at idle, we're catching Dave up, bunching, we'll be in his slipstream in a second, move it out to the right a bit … 210 kts … reach for the flaps and notch them down … indicating down okay … 180 knots … 90 per cent power to hold it … do the rest of the checks … fuel – 4,000 pounds … On-Speed – 148 knots … hook – checked up … harness – tight and locked … taxi-light – ON … antiskid – ON … hydraulics and pneumatics all indicating 3,000 psi … Dave is turning finals … wait till he's passing my beam on his way round to runway heading then … "75, finals gear down, Roll" … "Clear to continue, one ahead", the man says … hands on stick and throttle, feet on rudders rearrange the dynamics and here we are in the finals turn, no trouble at all … there goes the scrapyard below us … there's a queue of cars waiting impatiently at the traffic lights for us to complete our approach … what kind of bomber circuit is this that we're flying anyhow? … the airfield's almost disappeared, all I've got are the runway lights, this is going to take forever, no hurry … oh, yes, I need to get the ILS warmed up, I forgot … change hands, left mitt on the control column, head in and right hand groping at the rear of the starboard console ... find the switch ... switch it ON ... ear shattering beeps ... the volume control is too high ... turn it down ... swop hands back to normal order ... look up ... we have not fallen out of the sky ... throttles are still where I left them ... speed is decaying through 160 knots on its way to a target 158 kts ... nail it there with 92 per cent RPM a side ... what next ... the ILS indicator lights are too bright in the increasing darkness ... we're trimmed out aren't we? Right ... hands off the stick and turn it down ... the jet flies itself, hands off ... we do not fall out of the sky ... approaching runway centreline and Dave's still airborne a quarter-mile ahead of me, I've caught him up ... shit, I'm going to hit slipstream on this roller ... I think I'll hold on-speed plus ten knots all the way down to the runway ... not much crosswind ... so roll out on centreline ... runway disappears under the nose as the Phantom adopts its normal praying mantis approach attitude, so ... swop hands again ... reach down to a switch on the right hand side of the ejection seat ... buzzing sound quite audible above the muf- fled whine of engine compressors and the seat raises itself by six or seven inches ... now the runway and Dave (still airborne) reap- pear ... useful gadget this seat-raising, Concorde has to drop the whole nose section ... threshold is creeping towards me, excruci- atingly slowly ... subconsciously blip trim button, adjust throttles, counter drift with rudder, I don't even think about it, I've got all day to do it ... trooper flight's arrived, there's Britannia's 737 sitting outside the Air Terminal ... red-white on the VASIs, everything's looking good, smooth air today ... I wonder what Brian's doing in the tower in this sort of weather, better get up there quick to relieve him ... beep, beep, beep ... inner marker of the ILS sounding in my headset ... we must be at 300 feet or so ... look in at altime- ter ... sure enough ... look out again ... Ah, at last, Dave's touched down ... "Tower, am I cleared to roll?" ... "Affirmative" he says, "and after roll, climb straight ahead to 1,500 feet, turn left heading 120 degrees and call stud 12 for your ILS. Three others in the radar pattern." I acknowledge "Roger, that" ... runway's wet, but there's no rain so ... juggling act with hands and controls again ... reach down to rain-removal switch ... turn it OFF ... right hand back on stick ... navigator makes some observation about his radar and we discuss it a while ... all the time descending down the funnel that terminates at the piano keys on runway threshold ... Dave's climbing out ahead ... 100 feet ... 50 feet ... a slight tension now ... the necessity to fine down the movements, hold it steady in the groove ... the earth flattens and expands, but life is still graceful, relaxed as my eyes tell my brain to tell my hands (don't ask me how) that the time is right to make a little backwards movement to check our rate of descent slightly (the purist never crashes the Phantom onto the ground as the QFIs taught us to do at OCU Conversion) and at the *moment critique,* draw back the throttles and settle the main wheels ... feather soft and belying our 170 mph onwards race ... onto the damp runway ... easy. How do I do it? How do I make this beast dance to my will, respond to my every whim and fancy? It is truly amazing, the capabilities of man. Oh well – "75 rolled. Going to stud 12 for ILS!"'

But the fact is – from breaking into the circuit to wheels touching occupied forty-six seconds of real time. I climb out – perform a routine ILS approach, land back on and taxi into dispersal where the aircraft is pushed back into the HAS and the sortie ends. That is when the thought strikes me ... it's money for old rope.

But when the heady euphoria of flying has died down, as I trudge through the cold drizzle back to my car, I realise yet again what I have known all the time and what I will always know. It is not really easy at all, it is not a 'piece of cake', it is not a sinecure. The reason my grandmother is not a Phantom jet pilot is because she does not have the speed of reaction or the physical stamina to manoeuvre at 500 mph and 6 G. She does not have the alertness of mind to withstand these stresses and yet make instant decisions in Air Combat. She does not have the mental agility to solve intercept problems at twice the speed of sound. She does not have the self-discipline to withstand rigorous hours of training, training and yet more training. I am fooling myself by trying to pretend that it is not damn hard work. I am forgetting that the apparent ease with which I perform my tasks is born of many thousands of sometimes desperate hours in classrooms and cockpits, on the ground and in the air, in simulator and in aeroplane. In fact, I have practised and practised so much that I have forgotten just how difficult it all is. Thus does familiarity breed contempt, and as I drive back to the Mess through the now pouring rain in the solid darkness I resolve to be on my guard.

I have before me a little sticker, a phrase coined by some wag and intended as a gentle needle to our earthbound fellow Air Force friends, the non fliers. It says

'The business of the Air Force is flying and fighting.
The business of those who don't is to support those who do.'

It may hurt, but it's true. The whole purpose in life of the clerks in Administration wing, the fitters in Engineering wing, the controllers in Air Traffic, the telephonist in Operations Headquarters, the cooks in Catering section – their whole aim in life is to ensure the continued well-being of that pinnacle, the 'sharp end', the flying squadrons with their aircraft and aircrew. They are the be-all and end-all of the base's existence. Needless to say, not everybody sees it this way, and sometimes it is a struggle to convince some of the support staff that there are any aeroplanes on the base at all. But happily, being in the 'front line', this is less often the case out here.

The base is a slave to its aircraft, a mother to the little beasts that carry their deadly stings every time they venture from the nest. The base feeds, nourishes and replenishes its hosts. It provides the roosts to which the war machines return after combat for rearming and re-fuelling. The base is a King Bee, not a Queen, because it looks after its workers and in return the workers provide it with protection so that their own well-being may continue.

The priorities are laid down and everybody takes his allotted place, his allotted task. The hierarchy is very definite, the responsibilities clear cut. It has to be so, because when dealing with precision material there can be no room for error and this applies at all levels, whether to the aircraft fitter servicing a hydraulic union on the port aileron of an F4, or to the C-in-C RAF, Germany weighing up the pros and cons of putting his forces on alert following a border violation and so creating an international incident. The margin between success and disaster is very small.

Thus the base is geared to ensure the continued efficiency of the two resident squadrons – 19 (Dolphins) and 92 (East India Cobras) who have now taken over the Air Defence mantle from the Lightnings, scourge of Germany strike squadrons ('Okay boys, standard transit speed through their CAP – Warp Factor Ten!'). We live on the other side of the airfield, isolated in a nest, secluded from the remainder of the station. Hopefully, when the bombs start falling they will be directed at us and not at the families living on the married patch.

The Operations complex of the base is in five main sections, all surrounding the main east-west runway (8,300 feet of grey asphalt). On the one corner, just off Runway 27 threshold lives the Bloodhound squadron, owners of those missiles that I saw as we came in to land. In the other half, also a few hundred metres back from the runway, is a huge air-conditioned building called the COC – Combat Operations Centre. I shall return to this building later. On the opposite side is Delta dispersal (92 Squadron). In the middle lies Charlie dispersal (reserved for visiting squadrons) and at the extreme end, opposite 25 Squadron, is Bravo dispersal, the hideout for the Dolphins (19 Squadron). The whole base area is surrounded by tall barbed wire and at night the police patrol with dogs, big, mean looking animals.

Perhaps the only suitable word for describing this whole complex is – hard. A few years ago, the word went out from the NATO bosses to the various member governments; get your aircraft under shelter. The damage wreaked by the Israelis on the Egyptian Air Force in the Six Day War might have had something to do with it. Or perhaps it was just a question of relearning old, old lessons. But, nevertheless, a widespread and extensive building programme started to put NATO combat forces under some sort of hardened accommodation. As usual, the Americans have been way ahead of the rest of us. They have been living in hardened shelters for years, the Germans not so long behind them. We in the RAF have taken a little longer to convince the government that today's nuclear fighters need a little more than the blast revetments that have been our lot over the years.

The result is a futuristic network of hardened aircraft shelters (abbreviated to HAS by the aircrew) and protected briefing facilities (PBF). The whole issue is an architect's exercise in reinforced concrete, and to be fair, money has been no object in creating these great eggs within which the aeroplanes hide. Each squadron dispersal possesses ten of these grey-green shelters scattered around the woods in a haphazardly crescent shape. A network of taxiways links each HAS and then in turn radiates in towards the off-centre hub, the PBF, where the aircrew and engineers normally live. The HAS itself is a massive, angular structure, almost semi-circular. Two giant wedge-shaped steel doors seal off the entrance. These doors open outwards in a clamshell fashion. The edges are stuffed with asbestos seals denying entry to napalm, gas, or other NBC-type clouds. A form of air-conditioning within also helps in the fight to keep the air clear. At the back of the shelter is another pair of steel doors running vertically on roller bearings, left and right respectively. These also open, to allow jet exhaust at 600 degrees C to escape harmlessly into the countryside, via two ducted channels.

All doors are painted – jungle green. The concrete of the HAS itself is impregnated with a chemical substance that tones down the original whiteness into a form of pale lime green. The HASs are built onto the necks of what were the old revetments and these already have banks of weed and grass-encrusted earth built up all around from over the years; hence the whole nest blends with the trees amongst which the whole complex lies, hidden from prying Soviet eyes on the roads running outside the base.

The HAS is big. The Jaguar squadrons keep two of their breed in each HAS. We can only manage one Phantom in each, but there is plenty of room. There has to be, because come war or peace, we (aircrew and groundcrew alike) live our lives in this HAS. During peace-time operations, routine servicing and minor repairs take place inside. During a practice alert, I go into the HAS at the start of the day, fly my missions and return to the shelter, fly again and return, take my meals, perhaps sleep, fly again, and return once again to the shelter. I do not leave until I am relieved or the war is over. We remain there in our own little world, linked only by telephones, tannoys or land lines to the outside world from which we receive our instructions and orders. It is a self-contained world. There is even a winch at the back of the hangar to haul the aircraft back into safety at the end of a mission, although the normal peace-time practice is to use a tractor and tow arm to push the aircraft back in. Inside the HAS we have our own generator for electrical supplies, our own communications switchboard, our own minor repair facilities. The only thing that would ruin our happiness would be a direct hit from a 1,000-pound HE bomb. Near misses we can live with.

The PBF is a similar, even more sophisticated set-up. In the Squadron Operations Room, we can seal ourselves off from the outside world and live in an air-filtered environment, pressurised and air-conditioned to keep out the nasty bugs the enemy might throw at us. The walls of the briefing room are covered with photographs and dimensions of silvery machines with red stars on their bodies. In war-time the crews on stand-down would live in here, sleeping and eating in the crewroom while the squadron executives run the war from the squadron operations centre. Through a bewildering set-up of communication options, information about the state of the war, number of aircraft and crews available, weapons readiness, intelligence and the thousand and one other details arising in any battle, all flow backwards and forwards up and down the chain of command. Thus, sitting in my HAS waiting to scramble, I might not know exactly what the big picture is, but I have a pretty good idea.

So, as I launch off out into the hostile open with my war load to do battle, I know where the front line of troops is, I know the position of the enemy fighter squadron and which types of aeroplanes I can expect to meet. I know the movements of the Warsaw Pact regiments in our sector and I know what ground fire to expect. I know the routes our friendly fighters will be using to and from the battle area and I know the heights and speeds at which they should be flying. I know what IFF modes they should be squawking at each regular interval and I know the codes of the day. All designed to promote the efficiency of war. But one thing is very clear, the principles have not changed one iota from those employed in the Second or even the First World War. The requirements and solutions, the tactics even are still basically similar. It is just that, today, electronic wizardry has put a finer edge on the whole campaign. It has streamlined the business of killing.

Bravo and Charlie dispersals are laid out similar to our own. The Bloodhound operations centre is buried under mounds of earth. The missiles themselves, however, stand, starkly naked out in the open, blatantly facing eastwards, a dire warning to any intruder seeking to penetrate this sector.

Dotted around the airfield are little camouflaged nests (that is exactly what they look like) and during every alert, these nests fill up with Rapier low-level point defence missiles, handled by the RAF Regiment. These Rapiers take a heavy toll of attacking fighters both in fair weather and foul. In fact these boys are so nasty and trigger happy that I take great pains when recovering back to the airfield to ensure that I am right in the middle of the designated safe lane, squawking the correct IFF, at the correct height and speed and following the prescribed landing procedures. Doing anything else is to invite disaster – a (simulated) Rapier up your jetpipe (and a Station Commander's interview for persistent offenders). They tend to be a highly suspicious group of individuals, quite rightly so when the price of hesitation or doubt could be a neutron bomb raining down on your head from a MiG 23 Flogger that you thought was a Phantom.

To get into the Combat Operations Centre needs a special pass and a convincing story to persuade the suspicion-filled corporal at the gate to allow you through the treble system of interlocking gates, doors and airlocks into the main building itself. The COC is the brains of the base. From here, the base commander runs his war: everything in sight, from files and books to newspapers (it seems!) is stamped 'secret' in big red letters. The Operations staff regard everyone else with suspicion, or so it appears, although it is probably my imagination. But it is hard to blame them when you appreciate the information that lives in this building.

Wars run on intelligence and so this building (hardened, air-conditioned, filtered, green) runs on intelligence, both our own and from fellow NATO (or any other) sources. With current information at his fingertips, the Commander can keep a ready eye on the ebb and flow of his particular battle. Updated on a daily basis, this information forms the background for squadron planning of where to route CAPs, when to redeploy and where to reinforce. I am a fascinated observer when I look on this map, because it drives home once again the purpose of our being here and it is because of this ever-present threat of a surprise attack that we maintain a proportion of the force on constant alert; a state we call Battle Flight.

At Wildenrath, there are two special HASs; with doors that open automatically as soon as a button is pushed by the sector controller to sound the scramble hooter. Inside these HASs live two fully armed F4s, just like in the UK. However, the alert posture we hold here seems rather more strained. I must be able to get airborne and be heading for the border within five minutes of the hooter button being pressed, even if I am in a deep sleep. This state is held for twenty-four hours every day, every month, year in, year out and in whatever weather. So I sleep, fully clothed and sometimes wearing my harness, ready for instant reaction. And I scramble. Most times it is to intercept a light aircraft straying off course across the border and without a flight plan. Most times it is for a border patrol. Sometimes it is in retaliation for the 'other' side in East Germany scrambling their MiG alert aircraft and making a dash towards the border, a feint, before returning home again. One time it is to patrol in readiness awaiting a skyjacked Lufthansa Boeing with the threat of a suicide destruction of Bonn. The skyjacker instead goes off to Mogadishu ... One time it is to intercept a MiG 21 that has gone astray on a training flight from East Germany and wanders around in our sector of the ADIZ for a few minutes, lost. By the time we get there, he has gone. We learn later that a fellow MiG 21 scrambled to lead him home also gets lost, strays into Czech airspace and also has four MiGs scrambled against him. Confusion.

Yes, Battle Flight out here certainly has its moments, but it is a tense, nervy, keyed-up existence. There is none of the relaxed nonchalance of a UK IAF. There is none of the friendly camaraderie of a Bear intercept up in the Iceland/Faeroes gap. No, here on the NATO borders everyone is on their toes. Down the road at our fellow RAF bases at Bruggen and Laarbruch, Buccaneers and Jaguars also sit on alert, but they never fly practice flights because they are waiting for the Big One.

Thus we all wait in NATO, in our alert hangars up and down the borders in the various countries. Across on the other side, our opposite numbers do the same. They too sit in hardened shelters, they too study war routes and targets. They too sit and wait expectantly. Sometimes, it all seems like a game, but it is a deadly serious one.

14

··

Runways, People and Things

When I've got nothing better to do on my Battle Flight stand-down days, I like to go out onto the airfield to watch Phantoms landing. I park my car off the ring road and walk across the grass to a position just off the threshold, by the last line of runway approach lead-in lights. There I sit down and watch. I make sure that I am in line with the traffic lights on the ring road, so that I am not an object of attention for some curious patrolman passing by. From this vantage point I can observe these birds in flight.

The curious thing is that, as I lie there and look up at the black birds wheeling across the sky, I forget that I am also a pilot. It seems to me then as if I know nothing whatsoever about flying Phantoms. I am ignorant of the goings-on inside the cockpit. I am a stranger to the sky and all that takes place up there. Instead, I am a casual, ignorant observer, an outsider watching these birds at play. As they whistle remotely overhead, I feel that I have nothing in common with them, that they are not actually my brother aviators. Strangely, I enter a world of the dispassionate observer. The result is that I look on even simple things with a detached and critical eye. Perfectly ordinary and everyday manoeuvres and events become new sources of excitement and wonder. So it is that an apparently routine event such as an F4 making its landing approach becomes, for me, watching from the outside, an event worthy of great attention.

A four-ship comes smoking over my limited horizon. They are at 800 feet, in a tight starboard echelon. A strong wind is blowing down the runway, so their sound does not reach me, not until they are going past overhead, still tucked in tight together, a good, neat, package. They look mean, birds of prey indeed, with their black snouts and their wings and tails up and down at all sorts of angles. They are coming home to roost, after the hunt.

The leader breaks, a sharp sudden motion and one by one the others follow at a two-second interval till they are spaced out evenly along the horizon line. The lead machine has fitted itself into a groove in the sky and the others follow along similar tramlines, four carbon-copy images stamped against the blue. All is silent again, the initial thunder of their arrival gone. I watch and wait.

They move quite slowly now as their legs lower into a waiting position in the wind. I concentrate on the leader, as he has already tilted his wing in a smooth, steady, curve to line up with the landing ground.

As he comes around, head on to me and rolls out level again, images flash through my mind. The world is still silent as he homes in on a steadily descending path and as he slows even further, so his nose rises higher and higher until I see, not a Phantom, but a praying mantis with its exaggerated nose-up stance. The image instantly changes as I take in the gaping black intakes either side of the main body and now I see a king cobra, hood erect, swaying slowly and poised ready to strike, its beady eyes staring steadily and unblinking.

A blink of my eye and the image disappears, but another one remains. The cobra balanced on its long, thin body. This creature is balanced on a hazy, shimmering plume of jet thrust. The jet is angled downwards, resisting gravity and keeping the machine poised, cobra-like in the air. It too sways gently left and right as it corrects for the wind, back onto the centre-line of the strip. The poise is delicate, the balance precarious. Even I, watching from the ground can see that. Flap devices hang down from the front and rear of the wings to accentuate their shape and produce more lift as it slows yet again. The stabilator angles down to counteract the forces on the front part of the aircraft and so maintain balance. The rudder and the stabilator are working to maintain balance in the fore and aft axis. The ailerons and spoilers move spasmodically, subconsciously, to maintain balance in the lateral axis. The drag from the wheels, the flaps, the body of the aeroplane itself and the unseen, aerodynamic drag are balanced by those mighty plumes streaming rearward, and this plume is working the hardest. I can see that, because the plume says – Energy. It is heavy and turbulent and every now and again its texture changes. At one moment, when the balance is perfect, it is quite smooth, and clear and I can see the world (albeit blurred) through it on the other side. But as something acts to disturb the balance, as the bird sinks into some hidden wind shear, the jet wake becomes dark and smoky, thicker, as it restores the equilibrium, and if the correction has been too much, the plume disappears altogether as the engines slow their pace and allow the machine to settle back into the invisible groove. Down it comes, towards me, the oleos dangling down at their full extension, the rubber tyres waiting anxiously for their burning, 170-mph contact with hard concrete.

The other three Phantoms have lined up behind their leader and they too are setting up in the landing attitude as they float in towards the threshold that marks the start of the resting ground. They too are in various states of equilibrium, their balance changing minutely as they weave around each other's jet-wake and drop silently down, wings outspread.

Suddently, there is a howl of compressors as the first Phantom goes past. I turn to follow him, as, with nose still cocked up to the sky, it feels for the earth! However, this feeling has no finesse because the wheels meet the ground with a great jar, the oleos compress viciously in protest before expanding again, and great blue puffs of smoke shoot up from the tyres as they are galvanised from zero to maximum effort in an instant. There is a dull rumble of sound from the turbines, borne on the wind, followed by a hot blast of air from the engines, their job finished and sulking back into idleness, the vapours dissipating into the airstream but still strong enough to rock me on my feet. A parachute pops out and quivers rapidly in the slipstream as the machine slows down.

Thirty seconds later there is another thump as the second Phantom arrives, followed by the third and the fourth, till they are all proceeding down the runway in a great gaggle, their chutes wagging like tails behind them. At the end, they all turn and hustle off towards the woods, into which they disappear. All that remains in the air then is the acrid, pungent smell of fumes, Avtur, jet aviation fuel. I go back to my car and drive off towards the Mess.

A sailor recalls ports when he thinks back on his career. A judge remembers cases and a doctor recalls his favourite operations. I remember runways.

To me, a runway is not just a strip of concrete or tarmacadam. It is not simply an expensive piece of ground for getting aeroplanes airborne. It is a lot more than that. A runway is a springboard. It is a point from which I can jump off into a whole new way of life. It is a magic carpet on which I can step, and a few minutes, or hours, later find myself in a totally new environment, be it Hong Kong, Malta, Akrotiri, Decimomannu or even Bruggen just down the road. Runways may look alike, but in fact each one has a different character of its own because as soon as my wheels touch, I am filled with new expectations, new anticipations about the base at which I have arrived. This feeling persists even if I have been there before. The runway is the feature that links all these places. Because every runway forms an association in my mind with the type of approach to it, and this leads on to the terrain surrounding it which in turn is followed by the base area to which the runway belongs. This results in memories of the people on the base and the associations I formed with them, followed by the character of the local town and the people there, which in turn is followed by experiences of the country itself. This is why I am filled with expectancy every time I line up on the threshold markings at the start of every 'landaway', whether it's a one-day mission to Hahn and back, or a weekend tanker-refuelled jaunt to Akrotiri, Cyprus, or a one-week detachment to Leuchars for a TAC Fighter Meet, or a four-week expedition to Decimomannu for Armament Practice Camp.

Thoughts of a springboard are quite strong in my mind as I race down the runway, gathering speed, the nose-wheel thumping on the runway centre-markings, the main undercarriage oleos flexing as I pass over slight bumps and irregularities. The barrier at runway's end rushes inexorably towards me, as I sit patiently waiting for the laws of aerodynamics to manifest themselves and transfer my weight from the wheels to the wings. At night, the wait seems even longer as I rush onwards into the blackness with the runway lights blurring past me. But aerodynamics never fail on take-off, only the engines, and so it is that we unstick and punch up into the clouds. Ahead of us is a half-hour hop, or a fourteen-hour flight-refuelled leap, depending on whether the destination is Jever,

North Germany or Singapore in the Far East. In between are short conversations with faceless bodies in ground control centres, numerous radio frequencies and IFF squawks, multitudes of heading changes and miles that simply fly by underneath before a letdown commences and another runway finally appears at journey's end. Sometimes I will take-off and go straight into the cloud at 300 feet, fly several hours without seeing the ground, let down through cloud again and at 300 feet look up into the gloomy rain to see a wet runway looking exactly like the one I left hours ago, but I know it's different as I jump back onto the board and go to the end to get off.

Different it may be, but unfamiliar? Never. As fellow fliers in the 2nd and 4th Tactical Air Forces of NATO, we aim to maintain a closely linked net and the net covers every aspect of operations, both on the ground and in the air. This has to be so, because come the war, I am likely to go into combat not with a fellow RAF flier, but with a German in his F4, a Belgian in his F16, a Dane in his Draaken, a Dutchman in his F5, a Canadian in his F 104 or an American in his F15. We are all part of the team on this side of the border and so at every opportunity the links are forged and strengthened. Therefore I go on landaways at the bases of fellow NATO nations. There the ground crew will familiarise themselves with refuelling and re-arming my aeroplane ready to go back to war. I practise joint airborne missions, affiliation training as it is euphemistically known, when we attempt to perfect mutual tactics. Thus we rendezvous with F104s from the Belgian base at Beauvechain and proceed to the Ardennes low-flying area to carry out 'Manoeuvres', perfecting low-level interception techniques using our superior pulse-doppler radar and the 104's superior acceleration performance. We join up with F15s from the American base at Bitburg and set up coordinated CAP patterns to attack low-level raiders. We intercept German F4s from Bremgarten, carrying out formal attacks to exercise their lookout and RWR evasion tactics. We escort six F104s from Norvenich, the German base to the south, on a one-hour simulated strike mission into Holland and North Germany. These are all official, planned commitments. But Germany is one big battleground and our 'affiliation' training unofficially runs into everday operations. Thus a visual sighting en route is the signal for wings to bank, 'burners to light and G to come on as combat is joined for a few hectic minutes before fuel or the prime needs of the sorties dictate that both forces disengage and smoke out in opposite directions, high speed and low level.

I am amused when I look through Standing Orders and see the official limits for these affiliation engagements. AS1 A10 says, 'Once an aircraft is recognised as belonging to a non-RAF body, the intercept is to be terminated. Engagements with RAF aircraft are to be limited to a maximum of two 360-degree turns only.' However, the fighter pilot's interpretation of these rules tends to be somewhat liberal. Nevertheless, the trade of Fighter Pilot requires degrees of unwavering self-confidence, whatever the situation. Therefore the squadron work-up training programme has to build up the pieces slowly, taking the new pilot through the stages, from high level combat gradually lower till he is ready to mix it with the 'enemy' on low level affiliation exercises, safely and (hopefully) successfully. Now and again the Commanders fly on these missions, but the sight of multi-plane air battles running over the plains is enough to send them back to their desks with a silent prayer and fingers crossed. Indeed, now and again someone plunges into the ground, but no-one denies the training value of these engagements to all concerned so we seize every opportunity to develop the skills until they become second nature. We all know now that when (if!) the war comes, we will all be well versed in that specialised art – low-level air combat. As for the strike crews, our opposition on these engagements, they have steeled themselves to the problems of fighting through to the target while maintaining accurate navigation and weapon delivery. In such fashion does the NATO war machine attempt to mould itself into a credible, unified fighting force. Politicians may fight and squabble over defence budgets, newspapers may mock and deride the ratios vis-à-vis the Warsaw Pact. The machinery of bureaucracy and decision-making may grind along with interminable slowness as the nations strive to standardize on procedures, bomb carriers, refuelling couplings and other basic equipment, but these are all mere details. My main interest is to get to know the man in that aircraft on my wing. I wish to know his quirks and foibles, his likes and dislikes, just as he wishes to know mine. We wish to discover each other's limits because the heat of combat is no time to start having doubts. We must build up mutual trust and understanding and this is

151

why we train and practise together.

Fortunately, the leaders at the top recognise this need for mutual training which is why, in addition to localised cross-training with neighbouring bases, they organise the giant NATO exercises that attempt to exercise the whole chain. I have already come across these in the UK; Germany is no different except that we have more of them. Cloudy Chorus, Cold Fire, Active Edge, Black Label – the names are meaningless, but the exercises spell days of patrols, strikes and 'official' combat. In these exercises I really get to know my fellow fliers. The strike aircraft are all routed through our Air Defence CAPs. Our interceptions and kills are logged and tabulated. In addition, the Rapiers, Hawks and Nike-Hercules SAM sites put in their claims. The strike elements also submit their reports on who 'tapped' them along their route. The whole mess is handed over to computers to sort out and eventually a report emerges, stating the effectiveness of the respective forces, strike and Air Defence. Weak spots in defensive areas and strategy emerge and the commanders sit down and scratch their heads as they seek remedial action.

However, that is their problem – understanding the big picture. At a local, squadron level I am more interested in devising my own tactics to deal with the 'opposition' and so I get to learn what to expect each time we meet. Thus I learn that I can very rarely 'bounce' a formation of Harriers without being seen, such is the high standard of their lookout. I try sneaking up on them, hiding low in the trees in their 'deep six'; I try running in on the beam, at high speed; I try dropping down on them from on high, but invariably I am spotted and a fight ensues, the Harrier using its moveable nozzles to prevent me bringing my missiles to bear.

Several 2 v 2 engagements with German 'Ginos' – Fiat G91s – have convinced me what an aggressive team they are, although we point out to them that the 'stick, search and report' tactics of their wingmen (a hangover from World War II and Korean days) might need modifying. Similarly 'punchy' are the Dutch in their F5s and the Belgians in their Mirage 5s. The Americans, on the other hand, are ultra-conservative in their approach to operations and this is evident in the flying of the American-trained German F4 force. However, I often meet exceptions to the general rule and this helps to convince me that they are operating under peace-time constraints, perhaps with a healthier respect for the rules, and that come the war, they too will adopt the aggressive approach necessary for success in the fighter combat world.

I also learn about my fellow squadron pilots. I know who I can rely on to fly the correct combat formations and make the right tactical decisions, and I know the ones who need to have every move spelled out for them on the radio. I know the ones who I can trust to lay on a 6-G break at 200 feet above the trees and I know the ones who will take an age to pitch back into the fight to take the heat off me. There is no ill feeling or bitterness involved, no recriminations are passed. Its just a question of knowing what to expect from any given situation. War and peace ride side by side, because the fact is that peace-time it may be, but we are still training for war. These sentiments are printed in bold black letters just inside the main gate at Bruggen, our sister base down the road, for all to see. At Wildenrath we respect the same rules even though for us they are unwritten.

Part and parcel of getting to know an ally in the air is getting to know him on the ground, and we all make a big effort to socialise. This can happen in various ways. Landaways, either for the day or the weekend are fairly common. The aim is to provide foreign groundcrew with experience in servicing my Phantom. More popular are the detachments. Europe is not new to me. My days with 43 Squadron have ensured that. But with 92 Squadron we explore new ground. Thus we are the first unit to take Air Defence Phantoms back into the Italian base at Decimomannu for Armament Practice Camp. Memories are hazy, because, looking back, life consisted of long hot days with the sun beating down on Sardinian scrubland. Fuel shortage was rife and so flying proceeded in fits and starts from the great multi-national air base. When we did fly, it was a case of getting airborne, rushing off to the range over the sea, spending twenty minutes hammering away at the banner in an effort to gain an ace qualifying score and then smoking back to base to turn round for the next slot. Short, busy, clean-wing sorties.

The nights were spent in traditional fashion – long drinking sessions with the aircrew of the other nations. Thus the evening started at the Royal Air Force Mess, gravitated round to the Italian Mess for flaming sambucas, and finally down to the German Mess for good, old fashioned German 'frosties'. The German Mess was particularly popular because they, in their typical thoroughness, had managed to install a big-busted serving wench behind their bar and this was easy on the eye in what was to all intents and purposes a monastic and celibate atmosphere on the base area.

Weekends saw mass moves to downtown Cagliari, where if you tried really hard, you could force yourself to enjoy Sardinian 'Sea Food Salad' – whole baby octopus and sliced squid garnished with blue ink and all looking very fresh indeed. We ate, because after all, experimentation was the order of the day.

Dijon is a different proposition. Here we exchange with the 3/2 Alsace Squadron of the French Air Force, flying Mirage III interceptors. With typical hospitality, the French bend over backwards to make our visit memorable. The days are spent flying high-level combat missions – 3 v 3. This supersonic combat does not often figure in our training schedules and the Mirage is a slippery eel at 40,000 feet, so a rapid re-think of tactics is required.

The nights are spent visiting vineyards, wine cellars and local restaurants, they even lay on a visit to Paris for the weekend. I learn to eat snails and frogs legs. I fly the Mirage.

The Squadron deploys to Cyprus for another APC. We do not have tankers for this particular trip, so the long haul out to Akrotiri is via an overnight stage through Bremgarten, then on to Brindisi and the final hop across into the land of olives, kokinelli and kebabs. Now we fly early in the morning and in the afternoon rush down to the beach at the bottom of the airfield to soak up the blistering heat, sailing, water-skiing and scuba-diving. Yet again I marvel at the benevolence of the government in granting me this paid holiday. Even as I sweat it out at 6,000 feet trying to track the banner behind the Canberra with my pipper and trying to ensure that as great a number as possible of my 20-millimetre bullets pass through that piece of airborne hessian, why even then I still refuse to believe that this is *work* that I am doing. No, I am being paid to indulge in my favourite hobby.

In the evenings, Hero Square in Limassol is still a source of amusement even though life has quietened down since the ravages of the Turkish–Cypriot war. On these squadron detachments, we are all as one, together in the same boat. It is now that we really manage to knit together as a squadron. At the end of the day, there is no rushing off to wives and families somewhere off base. Instead, we work, eat and play together, from the Wing Commander down to the lowliest SAC. We get to know each other.

Over the years, these visits and detachments have crowded in my mind, until only fragmentary memories are left. The sun still shining brightly at midnight (Oerland RNAF, Norway) ... the heady taste of grappa (Grazzanise, Italy) ... Budweiser and Schlitz beer in the BOQs (USAFE, Hahn) ... Smorgasbord and topless bathing beaches (Aalborg, Northern Denmark) and many more to which the Squadron goes but I remain back at home base for some reason or other. It is one giant exercise in diplomacy from the Air Force Board's point of view, but for me it is a chance to meet different people, see different places, do different things all of which I would probably never have remotely considered. Instead, the Air Force provides me with a twin-engined fighting machine, fills it with limitless supplies of fuel, provides me with diplomatic clearance, hands over sheafs of foreign currency notes as pocket money and says 'Go forth and experience' ...

Wildenrath, being a major air base in the NATO chain, plays a major part in the socialising area. Various Tactical Air Meets are held every year at differing NATO bases and Wildenrath has to do its bit. Thus at midsummer, dozens of aeroplanes descend on the base from all points of the compass. For the next three weeks competitions run to see which crew amongst the nations can fly the most accurate navigation routes, perform the most accurate reconnaissance sweeps, drop the most accurate bombs, achieve the best strafing scores, and so on. In short, everyone gets down to what fighter pilots love doing best – competing against each other. In the fighter world, egotism runs just as high, if not higher, than in any other walk of life. Hence it is the natural ambition of every pilot to be the best in his particular field, whether air combat, bombing, navigation or troop dropping. It is a natural, healthy outlook.

Sometimes it is the Americans who put everybody to shame when they fly across from the States, flight refuelling across the Atlantic in their A7D Corsair fighter-bombers. Then, in spite of unfamiliar weather and terrain, they manage to out-bomb and out-strafe everybody else. Nevertheless, the margin between best and worst is small indeed and we raise our hats to their professionalism, although everyone knows that questions will be asked ...

The Squadron is invited to a party at 349 Squadron, Belgian Air Force, at Beauvechain. They are celebrating the thirty-fifth anniversary of the foundation of their squadron. The party lasts long into the night ...

Wildenrath decides it is time for a NATO Beer Call. The fact is, apart from the Tac Air Meets, which are of necessity formal, long-drawn-out affairs, we rarely get the opportunity to gather together all the different nations in one place, exchanging ideas over a few beers. At least that is the aim of the planners – a quiet drinking session with some 'jawing' thrown in. However, the 'Boys' have different ideas.

A giant hangar in a remote corner of the airfield is set aside for the purpose. (Some naive admin officer had suggested 'Why don't we have it in the Mess?' We look at him pityingly.) Various derelict cars and vans are somehow acquired and left lying strategically in front of the hangar. Many barrels of beer (good, strong, German) are connected up to the cooler outlets. Several trestle tables are loaded with mugs and steins. Steaming hotlocks of bratwurst and rolls sit in the corner of the hangar. We wait ...

The invitations have been sent out weeks before. At midday they start arriving in dribs and drabs, generally in pairs, like animals coming aboard the Ark. Two F15s from Bitburg. A Mirage and a Mystère from Dijon. Four Dutch F104s from Leeuwarden, a USAF F4 from Soesterburg, Holland. Three F5s from Gilze Rijen (Holland again), two German RF4s from Bremgarten, another couple of German F4Es from Wittmundhaven. A Fiat G91 from Ahlhorn, three Belgian F104s from Beauvechain, a couple of British Phantoms from a UK base, an Italian Starfighter from somewhere in Italy. A transport lands and disgorges ten German fighter-controllers from a radar unit somewhere up to the north. A few RAF 'wheels' – Deputy C-in-C, RAF Germany and his side-kicks also sweep in in their limousines, all curious to see what the evening holds. On 92 Squadron we have tried to upstage our fellow fliers on 19 by inviting some World War II heroes – Stanford Tuck, a former member of 92 and the German General Adolf Galland, his foe at one time, but friend now. Both of them have already attended our sixtieth anniversary celebrations. Several other local dignitaries arrive, bent on finding out what the fuss is all about.

The evening turns out to be a memorable one. A Scottish pipe band and several litres of Dortmunder serve to set the ball rolling. One very brave WRAF officer has turned up as the sole representative of womanhood, but she wisely decides to beat a hasty retreat half an hour later when the extent of the wantonness becomes clear.

The Dutch fliers are particularly 'evil', with a limitless capability for destruction and the hangar takes on the appearance of a major disaster area. The derelict cars are soon burning fiercely, having been manhandled around the apron in front of the hangar and then smashed and battered with sledgehammers. Several spectators are lucky to escape severe burns as dull 'whoomphs' signal a petrol tank going up in flames. When all five cars and vans are burning fiercely, attention turns to a giant rubbish tip lying innocently nearby. Half a dozen bodies in flying suits (for that is the rig of the day) descend on the wooden structure and haul it into the centre of the arena. The sledgehammers set to work and very soon there is a blazing pyre that overshadows that of the cars, now fully burnt out and simmering gently. A smoke pall climbs thickly into the gathering dusk as the station fire brigade arrives to deal with this unscheduled fire. They are liberal with their hoses and the main culprits are soon drenched to the skin as the burning tip relapses into a steaming, charcoal mess.

The firemen, now in the mood also, turn their hoses on the other wrecks and pretty soon all the fires are out. They stand around their fire vehicles, waiting expectantly, defying us to start more fires. They are somewhat disappointed when we don't. The effect of their water hoses and the gathering evening chill has served to drive us back into the relative warmth of the hangar where the beer pumps are still working overtime. We leave the firemen still waiting outside, the whole apron area awash with water.

Inside, the hangar is packed full and the lights are glaring down from the roof high above. I notice that the 'wheels' have long since left. The Deputy C-in-C has decided that discretion is the better part of valour and has departed with his entourage, leaving the Station

Commander to 'keep an eye on things and make sure it doesn't get out of hand, old chap'. He is now making a brave effort to persuade the mad Dutch not to tear down the lockers and other fittings lining the walls of the hangar. The netting and decorative bunting, hung up as a welcome, have long since disappeared into the various fires.

However, the night is yet young and we still have plenty of steam left to get rid of. The pipe band makes a nervous entry again, but their presence is short-lived as a new game starts. A 'bombing area' of beer bottles is lined up and 'bombs' are lobbed in an attempt to demolish the target. Unfortunately the bombs are beer glasses and once again the Station Commander has to make a timely entrance to prevent all his stocks of glassware disappearing at one stroke.

It does not take long for the ingenious mind of aircrew officer temporarily-turned-animal to dream up new forms of diversion and so thunderflashes start sailing from one side of the hangar to the other. The explosions in the confined hangar space are deafening. All of a sudden, I acquire a great deal of alertness, despite the pints of alcohol washing around in my veins, and while I stand trying to hold a conversation with an F15 pilot above the hubbub, my eyes are constantly scanning the skies for inbound fizzling projectiles. My new-found American friend and I cover each other's six o'clock, guarding against the joker who sidles up and drops a smouldering banger at our heels and then departs quietly smirking to himself. Every now and again, there is a mad flurry as bodies scatter away from a thunderflash that has landed amidst some group.

A 'bomb' lands in the middle of a circle of admin officers, but they have not developed that necessary early-warning sense of self-preservation. They continue chatting, while we wait expectantly, perversely refusing to warn them. The explosion, when it comes, is shattering. The circle splits outwards and beer from mugs fly outwards, drenching bystanders. One or two of them are bowled over by the shock, while the others stagger out of the smoke haze, coughing and spluttering, their ears ringing. One of them has his spectacles dangling from one ear. Yet another has had his beautiful No 1 uniform drenched with his neighbour's Dortmunder. I feel sorry for him, but he should have known better. The rest of us, knowing these occasions well, are dressed in tatty old 'drinking' flying suits. Mine is already soaked through.

The Station Commander sets off on a witch hunt, trying to discover who is launching these missiles, but his task is fruitless, because while he is in one corner, there is an explosion in another. Some of our Belgian and German friends have also brought their own stockpiles. The bangs only cease when the supplies run out and that is late in the evening. By then, the admin officers have long since made an exit, muttering curses at the 'stupid, irresponsible aircrew', and they are probably quite right. They will reckon the damage with us in the days to come, but right now blood lust is in the air and it's a brave man who confronts the aircrew in that state.

The floor of the hangar is littered with broken glass and literally awash with beer. We now indulge in swopping flying suits and uniforms. I exchange mine with a German officer of similar build, his bright dayglo-orange suit a stark contrast to my drab olive-green one. Danish blue is exchanged with Dutch grey, French green with Italian brown. My fellow British pilots are recognised by face only. On their bodies are bewildering arrays of uniforms, rank braids, name tags and flight suits. In the days to come we will lovingly attach our own rank braids and name tags to these souvenirs and hang them up in our lockers next door to similar trophies of previous occasions; a hobby indeed, like any other.

The ritual complete, several bodies melt into the darkness en route to hotels or Mess bedrooms. It is now well into the early hours of the morning and only the diehards are left.

Somebody with a great deal of bravado climbs a rope ladder up to the moveable gantry running along the roof and used to transport heavy jet engines from one end of the hangar to the other. He is joined by several other similarly hardy comrades. They converse in whispers high above our heads for ten minutes before the whole hangar shakes and rumbles as they somehow manage to get the electric motors going and zoom backwards and forwards, balancing precariously on the framework of the gantry, in serious danger of plummeting to the hard concrete floor at any moment. An engineering officer is hopping up and down with rage and demanding that they descend and cease forthwith. They ignore him, either that or fail to hear him above the racket. The unfortunate officer (the hangar is probably on his inventory, which is why he's still hanging around) rushes around looking for the Station Commander, but he has long since given up and gone home. Finally, 'Black Fergie', our Squadron boss, decides enough is enough and climbs halfway up the rope ladder with the rest of his 'boys' cheering him on and persuades the recalcitrants to come back to earth.

The engineering officer stands glowering in the corner, nursing a pint of beer, but he is soon given something to do when the rowdy element gets to work again, dismantling the trestle tables and setting fire to them in the middle of the hangar. He makes a quick phone call and the fire brigade zooms into the hangar in a flash and once again turns the hoses on the fire and all nearby.

It is now 04.00 and we are freezing to death, so a mutual halt to proceedings is called. I walk back to my room in the Mess, a 300-yard trek through the bushes. En route I stumble across several bodies that have chosen the most comfortable and convenient place to pass the night, on what is a warm, early midsummer's morning. I wake them and together we meander back to the Mess where they collapse into spare beds and I strip off my soaking 'new' flying suit and drop rapidly into a deep slumber.

The following morning comes the reckoning. The two flying squadrons on the wing, 19 and 92, are up early and into the hangar where we make some attempt to sweep up the mess and generally tidy up. We work in silence, for our heads are splitting with hangovers, the legacy of German beer. In the days to come, our two squadrons will be presented with a giant bill for broken tables, damaged crockery and shattered glasses. We will have to pay for repairs to the gantry and we will have to pay for the construction of a new tip.

We pay gladly. The night's events have had a cathartic effect on many people. Whatever tension or bad feeling or frustrations associated with our task and role that had been built up over the past months have now been eased. I have been an observer, rather than a major participant, but I have had a small insight into the nature of the wild parties beloved by our forerunners in the Battle of Britain, Korea or South-East Asia. Admittedly our own stresses and strains are very small compared to theirs, but, nevertheless, they are there.

Our NATO guests surface around lunch-time and they all depart quietly throughout the afternoon. They will not be charged for anything. These events occur in strict rotation and next year it will be the turn of the Americans or the French or the Dutch to host the NATO Beer Call. Meanwhile, we all agree that it has been a great evening and we'll meet again next year. New friendships have been forged and relations amongst us have been strengthened. Now when I land away at some base, I often meet some flier and I will say 'Weren't you at the NATO Beer Call?' and we will stop to reminisce on the crazy things we got up to. Then perhaps we will take-off together to go and exercise and as we run together in formation, at 500 knots and 200 feet, we will not be strangers.

15

....

Living on the Limits

This evening, I went down to the base cinema with my navigator, Brian, to while away the time gazing at the big screen. A short documentary entitled *The Display* preceded the main feature. This documentary opened with a short epitaph dedicating the film to its main 'starring' character, an internationally famous light aircraft aerobatic pilot who unfortunately was killed in a flying accident shortly after the film was completed. I settled back to watch ...

The film opens with shots of this pilot climbing into his Pitts Special biplane, starting up the engine and taxiing to the threshold of the main runway. As he starts his take-off to commence his display, the scene shifts to the view seen from a camera mounted on the top plane of the aircraft and facing aft, looking past the pilot in his cockpit to the tailplane and the world receding beyond. The photography is splendidly panoramic, in full graphic colour accompanied by an appropriately classical music score, a Viennese waltz, as the aeroplane rockets down the runway, lifts off and at ten or so feet (as the background commentary assures us) goes into its first manoeuvre.

The whole world revolves slowly and very smoothly through 360 degrees as the pilot carries out a slow roll at what seems to me a suicidal height. He then flattens out and holds the Pitts very low, indeed at ground level, as is confirmed by the wide expanse of runway and blurred green verges streaming backwards into the distance before he decides the speed is sufficient for a quick tug rearwards on the pole that sends the little aircraft shooting upwards in a vertical climb, leaving the world receding rapidly. It is a view much beloved by NASA photographers who mount their cameras facing downwards at the base of Saturn 5 boosters as they launch off the pad. At one moment the world is flat, wide, expansive and dynamic, full of infinite varieties of detail, the next it shrinks and dwindles rapidly into a nothingness of curved horizons. In the Pitts, the effect is accentuated by the use of a fish-eye lens.

The pilot then gets stuck into his sequence of manoeuvres and the Pitts tumbles through the sky, seemingly oblivious to gravity. It is a poetic and lyrical affair, but all too short-lived as the film comes to an end with the pilot in his aircraft paying aerobatic homage to a great orange ball – the setting sun.

However, my mind keeps returning to that initial sequence, that ultra-low slow roll, with the wing-tips only feet from the hard ground. Now, there is no way I could try such a manoeuvre in my heavy Phantom. The laws of dynamics forbid it. But in a Pitts Special, in the hands of a fully trained, skilful and accomplished aerobatics pilot, it is a perfectly safe manoeuvre ... or is it?

I now sit here, debating the question as the clock ticks towards midnight. One thing is perfectly clear to me – that man was living on the limits. Yet he had infinite confidence in his own ability and skill to fly such a manoeuvre to perfection and nothing else but per-fection because, being right on the limits, there was absolutely no margin for error. As I have already observed the dividing line be-tween success and disaster can be very thin indeed, especially when luck is balanced against professional training. And yet, time and time again as I progress through my flying life, the thought con-fronts me – we are all living on the limits at some time or other, and often at those times, we live on by the grace of God. Let me give one or two examples ...

I am Duty Pilot in the control tower. The weather is clear, visibility good although the Met Man is forecasting snow showers. Looking behind me to the north-west, I can see one approaching, for the sky is a gloomy grey over there, contrasting with the sunshine and blue sky to the south of the field. The local controller is a new boy being supervised by one of the older hands who sits beside me on a raised platform at the rear of the visual control room, that expanse of tinted glass that sits at the top of every control tower. The air waves are quiet at the moment because nobody is in the visual circuit, but we are expecting four aircraft to recover shortly. This new controller is just about to get a painful lesson in how quickly ordered tranquillity can turn into sheer chaos and helpless panic, how normal routine can rapidly escalate into Emergency – 'Red One'!

I flick a switch on the console before me so that I can listen to the radar controllers talking in their dark room two floors below me. The first aircraft, an F4 from 92 Squadron, is already on final radar approach, slotting in for a GCA talkdown. A second F4 is still with Clutch radar, being given radar vectors through the various Air Traffic 'gates'. The two other aircraft, Belgian F104s, are still with Lippe, the high-level German radar control agency for this area. They are due to land here for a debrief with our two squadrons over some affiliation training we have been doing over the past week. They are from a sister Air Defence base, Beauvechain in the Belgian Ardennes. They will be spending the night at Wildenrath.

A few flurries of snow have started to drift down. We are flying State Bravo which means aircraft are quite entitled to make a visual approach to the airfield without the assistance of ground radar. I decide to consult the Met Man – he tells me that Bruggen, six miles up the road to the north, is reporting heavy snow with visibility down to 2,000 metres. A glance behind me confirms that the weather is indeed worsening, although the visibility to the south is still several kilometers.

'You'd better get them down quick' I call to the controller 'or we'll have some diversions on our hands.' He replies that the two Wildenrath F4s are on radar finals and the 104s are in the process of being handed over to Clutch radar who will position them for the base radar heads to pick up. The question is, will they get in before the weather clamps? A faint air of tension has crept into the room.

I see the first F4's landing lights at three miles and he touches down safely. The second F4, two minutes behind him, reports snow on final approach with the main cloudbase at 600 feet and visibility four kilometres. He too touches down, streams his 'chute and disappears through the woods into Delta dispersal, the home of 92 Squadron.

The snow is falling heavily now, great thick clusters, flakes bigger than I've seen for a long time. All around me, various visual pinpoints – the church steeple at Erkelenz, the chimneys at Wassenberg, the cooling tower at Kipshoven – all are disappearing one by one, fading into the gathering murk and telling me better than any Met Man that the visibility is falling rapidly from four kilometres down to 3,500 ... 2,800 ... 2,300 ... 2,000 metres. Our normal rockbottom limit for take-offs and landings hovers around the 1,000-metre mark, although Battle Flight will launch for an operational scramble even in thick fog if the pilot can see two runway lights for take-off.

When the first 104 touches down, the visibility is down to 1,500 metres and I do not even see him cross the runway threshold. The world has turned into a solid sheet of snow, swirling across the airfield in spasmodic drifts.

Downstairs the boss of Air Traffic Control has taken over the GCA talkdown chair. He is the best. He knows it and nobody argues with him. The F104 pilot will be on the limits all the way. He knows that, when he fails to see the runway lights or the runway at his break-off height of 240 feet. All we hear in the tower is the characteristic howling of his J79 as he rams the throttle forward to carry out an overshoot. We do not even see him go past as he climbs back up through the murk.

'Okay, we'll have to divert him. Get me Bruggen's weather' I call to the local controller. But the lines to Bruggen are engaged and precious seconds are wasted while he tries to get through. He finally makes it, listens for a second and then turns to me – 'Bruggen's out. They're Red in snow like us, visibility 500 metres.'

Shit – 'Try Norvenich!' and I speak into my headset to the Controller below – 'Look, we're Red out here, tell him he's got to divert, we're trying for Norvenich.' The reply comes back rapidly, 'It's no good, he's turned downwind for a "quickie" GCA. He's only got 600 lbs of gas left. He's got to get in this time!' It's as well to mention that the normal safe minimums for the 104 approximate to 1,500 lbs of usable fuel. I look outside again. I can barely make out the runway 400 metres away, so thick is the snow. I think to myself – if this man gets in here today, it will be only by the grace of God. A glance to the north confirms that there is no chance of the snow shower dissipating within the next five minutes. The 104 is already turning onto a short GCA finals at four nautical miles.

The Supervisor has ousted the trainee from the local controller's position on the console below me and he has alerted the crash crews who are already climbing into their great, green fire-wagons. Theirs is, of necessity, a normally boring existence. Occasions like this make it all seem worthwhile. The Rolls-Royce engines throb into life and the convoy – Crash 1, 2 and 3 – advances onto the taxiway that is already wet with snow. The Controller turns all airfield lighting up to maximum brilliance.

Events have developed so fast that I have had no time to inform the Base Commander or OC Ops Wing or indeed anybody else in the chain of command. Normally these gentlemen would come running up to the control tower in the time honoured fashion to take command in any emergency and offer advice that was mainly superfluous or obvious to the trained crew in the aircraft above. Today, mercifully, we are spared.

The GCA talkdown controller's voice comes out on the loudspeaker, clear and confident, deliberately low key and calm – the 104 pilot must already be at a high arousal state, for a missed approach this time would mean climbing out and finding a safe ejection area. The pattern is set for disaster. Visions of Boards of Enquiry loom before my eyes ... 'Why did you permit the aircraft to commence its initial approach with a storm already in the vicinity? ... why did you not pass diversion airfield information sooner? ... why? ... why? ... why? ...' A gloomy chill grips my spine.

'Begin your descent now for a 2½-degree glide path ... right 263 degrees to maintain centreline ... rate of descent is good, you're on the glidepath ... looking very good for your landing, final check of gear and flaps to land, acknowledge ...' A strangled acknowledgement comes over the radio. The 'quickie' GCA involves a shortened pattern and the final approach leg is barely three to four miles in length, so it's all over very quickly. 'Approaching your decision height and starting to go above the glidepath ... above the glidepath now, increase your rate of descent, increase your rate of descent, advisory information only will now follow!' I feel for him. It happens to everybody. Looking up from the instruments at decision height and searching for runway lights, the natural tendency is to tweak back on the stick, to slow that inexorable rush towards the hard, invisible ground and so to go high on the glidepath, which is the last thing you want to do in a poor visibility landing.

He is past decision height now and there is nothing anybody on the ground can do. We all wait in a long agonised silence. There is no sound of engines, so he hasn't overshot yet. (I learn later from John, who was sitting in the Battle Flight HAS at runway's end and watching, that the 104 crossed the runway threshold at 150 feet instead of the normal 10 feet.)

'There he is!' someone shouts as a glowing landing lamp highlighting a shadowy needle-shaped form appears out of the snowy mist.

'Jesus, he's still airborne!' this from me as I see him hurtle past the 5,000-feet-to-go marker, 'there's no way he's going to stop. Get the barrier up!'

The Controller jerks himself forward as if in a dream and stabs the button that sends the huge net affair called the Jet-barrier springing into the upright position ready to catch runaway aeroplanes. The Belgian 104 has no hook to seize the over-run hookwire lying in wait 1,000 feet before the Jet-barrier. In the Phantom, it is infinitely preferable to take the wire rather than go into the barrier which is why many pilots prefer to land with the barrier down. I personally have my doubts as to whether the Jet-barrier will be able to dissipate the kinetic energy tied up in 25 tons of Phantom moving at 100 knots plus, despite what the designers say.

These thoughts flash through my mind in an instant as the 104 finally touches down with 3,000 feet of useable concrete left on the 8,000-foot runway. In a Phantom, this is a guaranteed wire or barrier engagement situation and I see no reason why this should be any different in a 104 making its final approach a good twenty to thirty knots faster than the F4's 150 knots. I subconsciously notice the crash wagons roaring off down the taxiway in anticipation.

To stream the landing 'chute too early in the F104 is inviting it to get ripped off in the slipstream, which is why there is a slight pause before we see the 'chute pop and flutter as the little fighter rockets past the 2,000-feet-to-go marker. The pilot has been very wise and very cool in sticking to standard procedure rather than making a panic-stricken grab at the 'chute handle as soon as the wheels touched. Now we all sit back and wait for the inevitable. But we have all forgotten one thing – the fact that Kelly Johnson and his Lockheed team designed some very good brakes into their lightweight fighter. The 104 disappears into the snow shower once more, its nose dipping heavily under obviously savage braking, the grey 'chute oscillating madly in sympathy as it too carries out its part in the retardation process.

So it is that the next call from the 104 pilot is not one of engaging the barrier but rather one requesting taxiing instructions as, much to the amazement of those assembled in the tower, he reappears in the murk, taxiing very fast to cool down his smoking brakes, with the convoy of crash vehicles hurrying along disappointedly in his wake.

I give him a wave as he races past the tower on the taxiway and disappears once again into the snow (which is already easing up its spiteful fury) in the direction of Visiting Aircraft Flight. I scratch my head and sigh – that man has been living on the limits.

It's amazing, what you can see when you sit minding your own business and watching. In my room at Coningsby looking out of the window, I see a 41 Squadron Phantom start its take-off run, accelerate to 'burner light-up and then suddenly abort the run, disappear from sight, hook down but no tail 'chute, straight into the RHAG wire with smoking brakes … RAF Valley, Advanced Flying Training on Gnats, standing in the coffee bar with fellow students, first week of ground school, watching the little red and white machines going round and round those invisible grooves in the sky called circuits; one makes a roller landing, lifts and climbs away. Suddenly, at 700 feet, it noses down, ever steeper, and plunges into a farmyard three miles off the end of the runway, ugly red ball of flame, there are no 'chutes. Death … Taxiing out for take-off at RAF Coningsby, a Phantom overshoots. Suddenly on the radio – 'Mayday, engine failure!'

Another voice cries 'You're on fire, eject, eject!' I look back over my shoulder to see the aircraft falling, inevitably, disappearing behind the trees, that same ugly short-lived gout of flame to be replaced by thick oily smoke. I see two multi-coloured 'chutes floating serenely down … A fellow squadron pilot on patrol in the Eifel Mountains, at low level just north of Buchel Air Base. He spies two American F4s at just about the same time that they spy him. An engagement takes place, short sharp combat, mutual training, friendly hassling that suddenly turns deadly. One of the American F4s decides to disengage and reposition. He 'unloads' and runs, with full afterburners, descending ... straight into a hill. Silent explosion ... Friends, acquaintances, fellow fliers, here today and gone tomorrow.

Such is the innocently deadly nature of this airborne sport of ours. The Air Force community, that of the fighter world especially, is such a close-knit one that just about everybody knows or has heard of everybody else. So every disaster is a personal tragedy in one way or other, and this is peace-time. God help our generation if the war comes.

So it is that before every flight, I often wonder – will this be the flight upon which disaster falls? Will this be the mission from which I will not return? It's not that I seriously think such will be the case. I dare not think seriously. But fear (subdued) is a passenger on every flight, and human nature being what it is, I must appease Hubris, the God of Fate. I must not tempt him and therefore I acknowledge his presence, while at the same time loading those odds in my favour. After all, my survival problem is a very easy one. I simply have to obey the rules and stay inside some very safe limits. Life would be vastly more complicated were I an Israeli Mirage pilot strapping into my cramped cockpit for a sortie over the Golan heights, or a Thunderchief driver penetrating Thud Ridge north of Hanoi at 600 knots chased by MiGs. My problems and fears pale into insignificance compared to theirs. But then perhaps it is this very fact of having little to worry about that sometimes makes me think about what little problems I have. There are no big problems to overshadow the little ones and because life isn't life without something to puzzle over, so therefore the minor problems grow out of all proportion to their significance. Yet, in this flying game, these little problems can be just as deadly as the big ones. Playing on the limits, it can sometimes be very easy to lose.

I have lived on the limits many times, and brushes with fate have left me a frightened and wiser man.

One morning I oversleep, awake with a throbbing head and a dull ache behind my eyes, and am late for briefing. I should have swallowed my pride and remained on the ground. Instead (like thousands before me) I elect to fly and proceed north up to CAP 1 on the North German Plain. The sunny day is one mass of bright lights

169

penetrating my darkened visor. The cockpit noises hammer at my eardrums.

Flying past the Dummer See, just to the north of the Osnabruck ridge, I am 'bounced' by a clean-wing German F4F. Headache or not, I am not about to take my punishment lying down, so I engage the afterburners, lay on 5G and break into him. We 'wheel and deal' for a few seconds and it is as I attempt to disengage (he is making grounds on me) that I come closer to disaster.

The 'fight' has been at low level, see-sawing between a start at 1,000 feet and a peak at around 5,000 feet. It is at the top of one of these peaks that I roll inverted and attempt to disengage. However, I am looking back over my shoulder at the opposition and not at the ground ahead as I counter roll and push downwards, seeking to gain the energy that I need to smoke away into the distance down in the 'weeds' at zero feet or thereabouts, where his pulse radar will be unable to pick me up.

The speed is low. I can tell from the feel of the aircraft around me even without looking at the ASI. It feels mushy, so I automatically plug in the 'burners again, still looking back at the 'enemy'. This morning it seems that the decisions come slowly. So it is that I do not realise that the nose is burying itself quite steeply. Only the sixth sense makes me look forward just in time to see the ploughed fields rushing towards me, the world accelerating and expanding with an insidious finality. The navigator is shouting 'pull out!'

Time stands still. I snatch back on the stick, but not so hard that the Phantom enters a super-stall from which there will be no re-covery at this height. The G meter registers 6 as the aircraft buffets madly and rotates about its lateral axis, sinking all the while. I wait and pray.

We do not have time to consider ejecting before we flatten out at a few hundred feet and race away into the distance, no doubt leaving our German foe shaking his head in amazement. Luck was with me. The crisis was past almost as soon as it arrived. But I recall the incident with the American in the Eifel a few weeks previously and I break out in a cold sweat.

Many such incidents follow every flier through his career. An unfortunate few do not live to learn from the experience. They become statistics in Flight Safety reviews, leaving the rest of us publicly wondering why a Jaguar should fly into the ground on a perfectly clear day; why a Buccaneer should fly into the sea during a formation turn; why a Lightning should disappear at night on a vis-ident approach to a low-level target; why two Harriers, in perfect visibility, should collide and lock in a deadly embrace, fluttering to the ground in a flaming mass of showering wreckage. The Boards of Enquiry publish their results, which invariably have to be conjecture. Meanwhile the rest of us secretly cross ourselves, recall hidden skeletons and never-to-be-forgotten experiences, and pray – 'There but for the Grace ...' It's all part of going too near to the borderlines.

I am reminded of a hairy fly-past that we did at Gutersloh. Every pilot has his favourite fly-past story because every pilot, at one time or another, is involved in some fly-past. Everybody loves a fly-past – great masses of aeroplanes in formation thundering overhead as the band plays a stirring march and the parade comes to attention. Pilots love them because it is a chance to show off their steely steeds to some admiring public gathering, so fly-pasts are generated at the slightest drop of a hat.

The size of the formation depends on the relative importance of the gathering. Hence the Queen's Jubilee involves months of planning and just about every aircraft type in the Air Force. On a slightly smaller scale, but still involving max effort from masses of aeroplanes, is the Queen's Birthday. Visiting generals or Cs-in-C warrant a turnout by most of the aircraft on the station being visited. Lesser occasions have to make do with a lowly four-ship from the station. The transfer of the squadron standard from 92 Lightning Squadron to 92 Phantom Squadron is just such an event. The plan is for four Phantoms to rendezvous with five Lightnings, join up in formation and carry out a fly-past at Gutersloh (home of the Lightnings) where the handover parade is taking place.

At first sight a ridiculously simple task. Unfortunately, the Gods often take a hand in these events in the form of inclement weather. The result, invariably, is a shambles and an experience best termed by the aviator as 'hairy'. This sort of fly-past is the aircrew's favourite because it provides a source of conversation for ever after when such topics come up – 'Were you on that fly-past at RAF So and So back in nineteen something or other? You remember when we were still in cloud in a diamond nine at 300 feet with thirty seconds to go to the overhead? The Boss had to call for a check-in at the end of it to make sure he hadn't lost anyone in the trees.' It is amazing how many such tales there are, all recounted with an air of glee of one who has suffered some expiatory process and come through unscathed.

Cobra formation briefs at Wildenrath. The Leader, Ali, gets on to the hotline to Gutersloh. The weather isn't so hot. In fact, it's pouring with rain, the cloud base is at 800 feet and the parade will be held indoors in a hangar. The question is – will the fly-past take place or not? We sit around waiting for some 'wheel' to make a decision.

Twenty minutes before the deadline for take-off, a 'Go' decision is received and this triggers a mad scramble for the door as we gather harnesses and helmets and run for our respective HASs. Apparently somebody has decided that the noise of nine aeroplanes going overhead at the General Salute will be better than nothing at all.

We crank up the turbines and, right on time, stream off into the damp air. I am Number 4 in this formation which means that I bring up the rear end. Chris and Hylton are Cobras 2 and 3, the wing men.

Gutersloh is a good ninety miles away, but we have elected to transit out at low level. This is fine, until we cross the Rhine in low arrow formation and start heading eastwards towards the front lying stationary in the Gutersloh area. The cloudbase gradually lowers and the visibility slowly drops until the four of us are forging along almost in close formation, driving through the mist, still in visual contact with the trees, bushes and autobahns flashing below, but not much else.

We know the route well. The terrain is flat, there are no high masts, which is why we are happy to bore along at 300 feet with visibility in the vertical plane only. The air is moist and the three aircraft ahead of me leave long, curling vortices trailing ribbon-like back from their wing-tips, so it is easy for me to position my Phantom in air that is clear of jetwash turbulence. I do not look in at the instruments, but rather keep my eyes glued on those three aircraft

172

ahead. They are my horizon, my altimeter, my airspeed indicator. Trust in the Lead is implicit. At this moment, if for some reason he flies into the ground, the rest of us will make holes in perfect formation beside him.

However, the survival instinct is strong and this state of affairs cannot continue for much longer. But the decision to pull up is tempered with the knowledge that immediately above us is a network of teeming airways leading into the civil airport complexes at Dusseldorf and Köln-Bonn. So we press on.

Soon enough, the inevitable happens and we fly into a thick bank of low stratus and the whole world turns dark grey. The decision is made for us. 'Pulling up!' the Leader calls. As for the rest of us, it's a matter of every man for himself. I have been on the right-hand side of the wedge, so I immediately bank to the right and select 30 degrees of nose-up pitch on the ADI, at the same time pushing the throttles forward to the max military power position. I maintain my divergent heading for twenty seconds before turning back onto the original track.

Cobra Lead calls the formation across to Clutch radar who, fortunately for us, are on the ball as usual. The Clutch controller stacks each of us at differing heights and informs us that we are all split up by five miles or so. The survival instinct of gaining separation has been very effective. The only problem now is how to get us back together again as a formation in order to get down for the fly-past. We are still in the cloud but my air-air Tacan is locked on to the Leader and showing I am four miles from him, but whether I am ahead or behind, to the left or the right, I do not know.

Clutch radar sets to work disentangling the mess. He identifies each of us by calling us on the radio, having us squawk an IFF code and then relating each squawk to the blip on his radar tube. Then by a series of turns he manages to get each member of the formation in a position to pick up another Phantom on radar. Five minutes later we are all strung out in one nautical mile trail behind the Leader and even in the correct formation sequence of numbers. We feel confident again.

A further five minutes and we are orbiting in Gutersloh's overhead, still at 5,000 feet and still in cloud. Clutch gives us up as a bad job and hands us over to Gutersloh Zone control who will be responsible for getting us down VMC below. The check-in on Gutersloh's frequency is smart and crisp. Ali calls up – 'What's the weather like down there?' 1,000 feet overcast in drizzle, four Ks vis is the answer. Not good, but then not bad. 'What are the Lightnings doing?' Just getting airborne. Well that settles it. The gauntlet is down. 'Can you get us down below this stuff?' Affirmative. The controller gives us the regional QNH and asks us to turn onto a southerly heading, away from the great Osnabruck ridge that runs east–west like a rigid finger a few miles to the north of Gutersloh airfield.

We set off down the hill, still in radar trail. I am passing 2,000 feet, the last man in the line, when the Leader calls that he is VMC below at 900 feet and that he is turning back north for the holding point just south of the ridge and to the north-east of the field. This galvanises me into action as I retract the speedbrakes and push the throttles forward to close up on the guy ahead of me. The radar lock is already getting 'noisy' as the set fills up with ground returns, and I am afraid it will not hold for much longer at these low levels now that I am stretching in range. If I lose the formation now, I may as well go home because I'll never find them again in time at low level in this weather.

I break out of the cloud at 1,000 feet doing 450 knots just in time to see the first two aircraft go past heading north, with Cobra 3 in a hard left turn after them. I almost grey out as I reef the aircraft around to follow them, clouds of misty condensation surrounding the wings and canopy as I pull G. I roll out heading north and pick up the other three aircraft smoking along in the gloom below the nebulous grey of the cloudbase. Drops of rain are splashing against the front windscreen as I fly through intermittent squalls but despite the rain removal being switched on, the windscreen remains blurred, making it harder to see the others.

I am in such a hurry to catch up that I underestimate my overtake and I am pushing 500 knots as I come up to the rest of the formation. Despite idle/idle and full speedbrakes, I go sailing past on the port side and have to dumbbell viciously left and right to kill my speed before repositioning in low arrow once again. I am sweating in spite of the cold air gushing from the air-conditioning louvres.

The Lightning formation checks in on frequency with the Approach Controller, who will be responsible for controlling us in the holding pattern and then giving us the countdown for the start of the run-in. The aim is to fly-past as a section of five Lightnings in a close arrow formation followed by the Phantoms in box four. The timing calls for us to blast over the hangar at the instant the Air Marshal raises his hand to take the General Salute. A stooge on the ground with a walkie-talkie will relay the progress of events on the parade to the control tower, who will in turn give us the state of play so that we can adjust our timing.

At the moment, however, our main aim is to get joined up with the Lightnings so that we can establish our orbiting holding pattern. Ali has been busy chatting to the leader of the Lightning formation and both have agreed to rendezvous overhead the holding point, a small village strategically picked to lie at the start of the straight two-minute line for the run-in and fly-past, heading from north to south.

Well picked for timing the run-in it may have been, but as a holding pattern for nine aeroplanes in poor visibility it definitely is not. Five miles to the north lies the ridge of Osnabruck, festooned with masts and power cables, the tops of which are poking into a cloud-base fluctuating between 700 and 1,100 feet above the low ground, but considerably lower over the ridge itself. The visibility is indeed around the four kilometre mark in drizzle which means the join-up is going to be interesting. And so it turns out to be.

The Lightnings have already reached the RV point, running along the ridge line on an easterly heading before making an easy, 90-degree starboard turn onto south for the holding point. We are still racing up north from the position where we broke cloud some miles to the south of Gutersloh. Zone control has been giving us bearings to the other formation, but nevertheless the first we see of them is when they loom up out of the mist on an opposite heading, all five of them in tight formation, trailing a black wall of smoke from their Avons.

Everyone shouts over the radio at the same time but it is too late and the Gutersloh controller suffers a mild seizure as the two blobs on the scope merge, coalesce and then split again. In the air, we have no time to act as we slice past each other, one formation rocking in the other's turbulence as we head off in opposite directions, fading away into the mist like ghost ships. Well, they do say that a miss is as good as a mile.

There is a slight shocked pause, a tense and expectant freezing of the controls at the moment of passing, a microscopic hiccough in the passage of time before the action resumes. The moment has passed instantly, the memory already fragmentary and disjointed as new priorities crowd in, clamouring for attention. We have arrived too close to the ridge to turn safely inside it to follow the Lightnings. We are closing at 400 knots and there is no way to go (if we are to stay visual with the ground) but over the ridge into the valley on the other side. Before us is the classic pillar box effect, with the cloud fifty or so feet above the ground on the top of the ridge.

Once again it's every man for himself. We all pick our line and dive through. One by one the F4s ahead of me squeeze through and disappear down over the other side. It is all over in a few seconds. I grit my teeth and push the stick forward (I must stay visual with the ground at all costs) and my only recollection is of tree trunks and branches heavy with rain streaming in crystal clear detail below my belly, a pylon off my left wing-tip with its cables invisible and a red latticed TV mast flashing past my right wing-tip, then I am through and into the next valley which seems cosmic in its relative clearness. Why, the cloudbase here is all of 1,000 feet.

I have no time to dwell on this luxury because we have to get back on the other side of the ridge, pronto, to join up with the Lightnings for the fly-past which is only three minutes away. To my starboard I see three steaming balls of condensation in 500 yard trail on each other with sheets of flame jetting from the rear end of each ball. The flame is crimson, a peculiar colour against the contrasting background grey, a surrealistic canvas that would be dear to the heart of any avant-garde artist. But it is another part of my consciousness that takes note of such inconsequential detail. My main attention is focused on the very existence of that flame, the need for it. A good idea, I think, as I also select the throttles through the gate and command the afterburners to peg my speed as I buffet round behind them in a 5-G starboard turn, 700 yards behind.

The Leader, Ali, has spotted a slightly larger gap to the east of the one we have just punched through. There is a slight dip here in the ridge line, giving a gap of about 150 feet for us to penetrate – miles.

He straightens, cancels his 'burners and makes a beeline for it. The rest of us follow suit and set off hard on his heels. Not a word has passed between us so far. There is nothing to be said. This is just a question of survival.

So we all dive once more back across the ridge, slow down to 350 knots and get vectored onto the Lightnings who pass a mile in front of us in a left-hand orbit, still in a tight serene formation. All we have to do is jink slightly to tack onto the back and close up from the 'loose shambles' formation we have been maintaining so far into a tight, professional-looking box. We even have time to waltz around the holding pattern twice before the time comes for the actual fly-past. The preceding five minutes have been nothing but a bad dream.

We roar across right on the second to ecstatic exclamations of congratulation from Air Traffic. We then circle around back to the holding point which the Lightning formation leader has mysteriously (and wisely) moved four miles further away from the ridge. The Lightnings break off and perform a fly-past for the benefit of their wives and families. We follow two minutes later, just to demonstrate that we can fly a tighter, smoother formation than they. The (high level) recovery to Wildenrath is uneventful. There we wheel around the circuit, still in box four, showing off for five minutes before fuel gauges shout 'Land!'

I suppose that, discretion being the better part of valour, there were times when we should have called a halt and cancelled the whole show, but the thought never entered our minds. After all, there is a code.

I have learnt a great deal about flying from incidents such as that one and I have tucked them away in the back of my mind for future reference. Some of these incidents have aroused excitement, others fear, still others shame. One or two have simply caused an excessive expenditure of adrenalin and aroused nothing more than amused amazement. Amused, that is, when I look back on it, but certainly not funny at that time. But the common denominator is the experience I have gained, and with this experience, I can explore the boundaries of my limitations in greater safety.

16

The Simulator

Some of my fellow fliers hate the simulator. Not me. I love it. Some of the Squadron pilots will try all sorts of tricks to avoid making that journey down to 'The Box'. Not me. I leap at every chance. You see, to me the simulator is one big game. It is a game played between my navigator and I and the simulator crew on the console in the next room. It is a battle of wits, 'Mastermind', chess and blackjack all rolled into one, with a touch of 'University Challenge' thrown in as well. But the good thing about this game is that I know all the answers already. I have met all the problems before in similar games. The tasks are not new to me, the gambits are well worn. The solutions are familiar, the problem-solving mechanics are all well tried. A predictable and boring game, therefore ...? There lies the rub.

The Phantom simulator lives at RAF Bruggen twelve road miles away. Bruggen is home to the Jaguar Strike Squadrons. Their simulator, for some reason best known to Ministry of Defence planners, lives at Wildenrath. So every day we cross in our squadron buses, both sets of crews en route to each other's base. The Harrier simulator also lives at Wildenrath so we cross with them as well, as they drive down from RAF Gutersloh. It is all a strange exercise in logistics and mobility.

The requirement is for every Phantom crew to carry out at least one simulator session a month, preferably two. Each session consists of two sim rides lasting about an hour and a half each. The whole affair takes up half the day. The simulator crews are invariably ex-Phantom operators serving the usual ground tour. I know most of them – Arthur, Tony, Jim – from Coningsby days. 'Jace' is ex Phantom reconnaissance (2 Squadron, Laarbruch), Clive I remember from 43 Squadron at Leuchars. They are our friendly opponents in the games that we play with the Phantom simulator.

Bruggen (unlike Coningsby) has one Phantom simulator, living (like Coningsby) in a giant corrugated steel building. The Coningsby sim building was painted white. This building is painted – inevitably – green. The simulator itself is a strangely amazing contraption. A Phantom cockpit sits on a giant platform held fifteen feet off the floor by a complex system of hydraulic stilts. These stilts cause the platform to sway, tilt, rise, pitch, rock and roll in a fashion designed to convince the pilot operating the controls in the cockpit that he really is airborne at 30,000 feet or whatever, and not rooted solidly to the ground. The interior of the building, as well as the simulator itself, is painted matt black, but in front of the cockpit is what appears to be a large, white cinema screen. On to this screen is projected a technicolour visual picture from three projectors mounted in parallel at the rear of the platform above the navigator's cockpit. The cockpit canopies themselves are painted an opaque white. Only the pilot's front windscreen is left clear and through this he can see only the visual picture projected on to the screen ahead. This picture can be of a runway or airfield complex or it can be of an airborne target, or it can be a ground complex of bridges and railways or it can be of an academic weapons' range. In fact, the picture can be of anything the training machine wishes. Thus the crew can take-off, fly a low-level navigation route to a target, perform several attack profiles and return to base for a GCA to land, all on the visual picture. If they so wish.

The computer is Lord and Master of this simulator Empire. It is the computer that senses the million and one inputs and triggers the million and one commands to actuate the hydraulics and the electrics to ensure that the whole machine responds just like the real thing, that the instruments all rotate and revolve in sympathy with what the pilot is doing at the controls. It is the computer that controls the giant three-dimensional model of the terrain that lives in a separate twenty foot high room all by itself, lit by brilliant white spot lights. The computer commands the television camera to trundle along a gantry – fore and aft, up and down – to scan the simulated terrain over which the Phantom is flying and then to project it onto the screen in the other room as a three-dimensional, real-time view of the world.

So yet again, as I go away and stare at the banks of chattering computer tapes, glowing lights and clicking relays in the air-conditioned room that the device lives in, I am forced to acknowledge that the computer is King. The science fiction writers are not joking when they predict that one day computers will rule the world. Here, in this Phantom simulator that Redifon have created, I see a hybrid forerunner, the fusion of Man–Machine.

However, right now the computer is Man's tool, a slave to his intentions and as I climb the long ladder up to the platform and into the cockpit, I think it is all perfectly natural and proper that the simulator should respond perfectly. In fact, I get upset and complain if it does not. I take it for granted that it will.

So, having laid out the pieces on the table, the game begins. The first move is mine as I carry out normal engine starts and functional checks of the instruments and controls. It is now that the subtlety of the game emerges. The simulator crew sit next door in a clinically white room that always reminds me of an operating theatre. They sit before a large console that surrounds them in a semi-circular curve. Every instrument in the cockpit of the aeroplane next door is represented on the console so they can see instantly just what I am looking at on the gauges. In addition, every time I move a switch or minor control, a warning light comes up on their console, so that they can also tell what modes I am in and whether I am carrying out the correct checks and drills. That console is Big Brother personified. To the left of the pilot's position on the console is a large bank of press studs each of which lights up when it is pressed. A random look at a few labels under one or two reveals – 'LH Eng Fire'; 'PC 1 Failure'; 'Double Generator Failure'; 'Turbine Overspeed'. There are about 100 more of these studs, any of which can be pressed simultaneously in any combination. The aim is to make my adrenalin flow. The purpose is to bring pressure to bear on me until I reach the limits. When I reach these limits, the aim then is to push the boundaries of those limits further away.

When I first started flying the Phantom, my limits were very narrow. An engine failure coupled with a hydraulics failure and one or two other distractions was enough to blow the fuses in my head and send me crashing into the ground out of control. Now, with 1,400 hours sitting in the cockpit of the Phantom in the air, I have got to know a few things about this aeroplane, which is why I now enjoy having the pressure heaped on me, fielding the 'curve balls' and generally seeing just what new limits I can explore. Yes, I know the answers already, but the questions come from different angles and at different times. I have to recognise the question and produce a solution before it bites me. The Phantom is a very forgiving aeroplane, but like any mistress, it will not tolerate inattention. I must remain in control at all times. The simulator teaches me to stay alert and so stay alive. It is a training machine and in it I can make mistakes and still live to discuss it. That is why I like playing the games.

As soon as the engines are started, the moves come thick and fast. I am ready for the old favourites – 'TGT Overheat' comes up, and I immediately shut down the engine. 'Check Hyd' caption fails to extinguish after starting the right engine; Starboard Utility failure. Abort the mission. As soon as I spot the fault and act on it, the mentors on the console remove the problem and we proceed anew. I taxi and line up for take-off. Check the circuit breakers. Another favourite console goody is to pop the flap or undercarriage circuit breaker as you are distracted by radio calls. Then you wonder why they don't work after take-off. Sure enough, the flap breaker is out. I push it back in. Ready for take-off, and I know what to expect here. As I accelerate through 150 knots, a 'FIRE' caption comes on. Drill – don't do anything. Continue the take-off, get airborne and away from the ground, have a good look at things and then sort it out. I always remember a Phantom accident where the pilot shut down the wrong engine after take-off due to an over-hasty diagnosis of which engine had failed. The result was a Martin-Baker parachute let-down for both himself and the navigator. So I take my time and identify which engine is actually on fire before coming out of afterburner and carrying out the appropriate drills.

The sense of realism is complete as I fly around the pattern on what seems like a dark and dirty night, with the cockpit lighting turned fully up. As I fly the heavyweight single-engine GCA pattern, I anticipate the next move and to be sure, it comes. The generator on the good engine fails, leaving me in effect with a double generator failure. I have to revert to RAT power. No sweat. My navigator reads out the drills and confirms I have blown down the gear and flaps with pneumatic air and that I have lowered the hook for an arrested landing. He reads out a numerous list of important services (nosewheel steering, navigation aids, stability augmentation, radar) that I have lost. RAT power is a get-you-home facility only. So round we go and land back on.

Clear the problems and line up for take-off again. No engine problems this time but I am expecting something else. As I bank onto the climbout heading the ADI does not move, it is frozen. 'ADI failure' I call out to the nav as I transfer immediately to the BAI (Back-up Altitude Indicator). I have been caught out before by insidious ADI failure with no 'OFF' flag warnings and I have lost control and had to eject from the simulator. Those were in the old days. I am not to be caught out so easily now, which is why I watch it like a hawk, always cross-referring.

I cancel the 'burners after take-off and watch the nozzles as I do so. One nozzle refuses to close. That means I have lost about 60 percent of my power on that engine. Go through the drills … satisfactory, okay, fault cleared. We go off to practise some intercepts and it is here that I have to be most wary in this game, for it is when I am deeply engrossed in an attack that a fault will be fed in which I will not then notice for several minutes. So my eyes never stop roaming. I know such faults are rare in the actual aeroplane, but in the simulator they are dead certainties. The fuel gauge fails. The AOA 'OFF' flag sneaks into sight. The ASI freezes. The oxygen runs down to zero. Cabin pressure fails. The altimeter sticks. I pick all these up quickly because I expect them to occur on a simulator ride. The only question is when.

Some of the malfunctions require some thought and analysis. 'Check Hyd' caption comes on. All the gauges show everything at 3,000 psi, so what's wrong? I know my systems, therefore I know that the left hand utility pump has failed, because this pump runs at 2,750 psi and the gauge continues to register the higher pressure of the starboard pump, so I carry out my drills, confident in my knowledge.

The sim instructor sets us up on a supersonic intercept. Warning bells ring in my brain. As we accelerate through Mach 1.3, I wait. There we go – double engine flame out. A ramp malfunction. More important, however, is the fact that I must remember the RAT limiting speed – Mach 1.1. If I put it out at 1.3, I will tear the thing off. So I must steel myself to wait till the speed has bled off, and in that time I sit in a black silence, save for the eerie glow of the red utility wander lamp operating off the battery. Below 1.1, I can put out that RAT and restore some electrical power to the aeroplane and get on with relighting the engines.

Returning to base, the radio fails. No-one will talk to us. Immediately, out comes the emergency Tacan letdown plate and we carry out a Tacan penetration without Air Traffic Control. On final approach, I wait expectantly and sure enough, an engine seizes. Into 'burner, select half flap, increase 'On speed' by 10 knots, carry on with the landing. On touchdown, the brakes fail. Lower the hook, check 'chute streamed, engage the hookwire. As we come to a halt, the good engine catches fire. Emergency shutdown, rapid egress drill.

Back in the simulator crewroom, the sweat cools rapidly on my face, although my flying suit is still damp and sticky. We debrief our performance. A good average session is just about all he can say. Average performance means that I noticed all the failures and reacted promptly and appropriately with no major slip-ups. He has a few small criticisms about the order in which we carried out the drills or some of the decisions we took, but the criticisms are minor. However, this trip was quite straightforward. The game was a familiar one and the moves were relatively uncomplicated. It was a warm-up.

The next sortie has me searching the depths of experience and knowledge for solutions. The game is fast and vicious. The faults, still basically familiar, come in a bewildering order of combinations, with the complications of drills for one emergency having repercussions on another failure occurring at the same time. As I carry out each drill, I am left wondering about what point of significance has escaped me regarding this system or the other. The cockpit switches and levers rearrange into a series of positions never normally seen as I battle to keep airborne what has turned out to be a wreck. Sometimes on these occasions, the simulator guys win the game and I know that today I have reached a new limit, as I resort to the ejection seat handle.

There is a great danger that a simulator instructor will get 'button-happy' when things are going too well for the crew in the cockpit, and start pushing in every fault in sight. Some crews have experienced this and this has led to their aversion to the simulator. I am fortunate. We have some intelligent people on our simulator, and all the faults, in whatever combination, are plausible, and the aim is to make the crew think about the problem. The odds on such multiple faults occurring for real in the air are remote, and even the little individual faults like ADI failure, engine failure or trim runaway are rare. However, while that one chance remains, I will be trained to prepare for it. The name of the simulator game is – Building Up Experience.

17

....

Air Wars

Germany is a battleground. It always has been and it always will be. Every time I get airborne I am convinced of this. Every time the wheels slot into the wells and I set course across the Rhine, I am confronted with past, present and future manifestations of conflict. Why is it, I wonder as I fly along en route for my CAP, that this part of the world has been the focus of world attention for the past couple of generations? Why has this whole planet come to blows with itself on account of machinations in one relatively small nation? Why is it that today, two great armies stand and glare at one another across a barbed wire fence? Why must it be that the whole future of mankind could quite well swing in the balance depending on the moves that take place on the soil of this divided nation?

Well, the questions come thick and fast to me, but it is not for me to indulge in such philosophy, the dichotomy is not mine to solve. My only concern is that my missiles and bombs arrive at the appointed place at the appointed time. Let the historians puzzle over such quandaries. Let the politicians continue their attempts to shape the future. My immediate interests lie with 'real time', what is happening now.

But even so, as I fly, I cannot help wondering, because even though I race over Nike-Hercules and Hawk SAM sites, littering the countryside by the dozen, even though I fly over innumerable barracks with hundreds of Chieftain and Leopard tanks on display, even though I flash across many training grounds where troops and armoured personnel carriers manoeuvre in the mud, despite all these manifestations of the present, I am still surrounded by ghosts from the past.

Germany is one great low-flying area. This means that, within reason, I can fly anywhere over the whole of Germany at 500 feet. It is a good idea because it spreads the low-flying noise load over a wide area, rather than concentrating it in the narrow link route corridors, as in the UK. However, we still have several low-flying areas set aside within which we may descend to 250 feet. Thus in one flight, I can view at close proximity the flatness of the North German plains, the smoky haze of the Ruhr industrial complex, the rolling beauty of the Eifel Mountains and the majestic grandeur of Bavaria and the Austrian Alps to the south. It makes for an interesting and varied flying life. The only problem is the density of the airborne forms of life. Our particular bugbear is the glider. Apparently there are more gliders in Germany than in the rest of the world put together. On some hot summer days I can well believe it, as our formations surge through masses of them spiralling up their thermal corridors.

Light aircraft also abound, so much so that we have been instructed to avoid the layers between 1,500 and 5,000 feet which is light aircraft territory. Now hang gliders, dropping from the high ridges, have decided to join in the party, so the skies of Europe are crowded indeed. Frequent air misses are the order of the day.

I fly down to the Nurburgring, fourteen-odd miles of track that swoops and dips round the Eifel Mountains. Floating overhead, I watch the Porsche Turbos winding round the tortuous course. To them, on the ground, 140 mph is a headlong and frantic race. Yet to me, 500 feet above and drifting through at twice that pace, life is leisurely. When I tire of their sport, I raise my flaps to accelerate down the home straight, sweeping past with disdain, 300 ... 400 knots towards the grandstand, over and away, mocking them with my three-dimensional freedom. My course takes me onwards to the Mohne Dam. It is one of our standard CAP datums. The dam itself is a giant structured affair holding back the great wall of water that forms the Mohne See. The ghosts of 617 Squadron Lancasters live around this lake and as I thunder across the dull grey waters at 400 knots, I marvel at those men of a bygone age. The dam, with its lake, sits surrounded by peaks and ridges. An attacking approach to the dam involves steep turns round the ridges and valleys and a leap over a wooded island jutting out into the lake, before settling down for a suicidally short run up to the dam itself. I try it.

In my Phantom, travelling at 400 knots and with a huge radius of turn, it proves an impossible mission. The Lancaster, at half my speed, should have had an easier task. But I make my attempt in broad daylight and fair weather, and I am very familiar with the geography. Guy Gibson and his men have to fly across war-torn Europe, low-level at night. They do not have radio altimeters, inertial navigation systems and mapping radar to pave the way. Then, having arrived in the area, in massed formation, they have to find their way round the peaks in the darkness, jump the ridges and projections before flattening out at sixty feet over the black water for the short run; nerves must be steady, heads cool and hands firm on the controls to meet the critical parameters for the successful release of the bouncing bomb, and afterwards the heavy, slow, awkward bomber must be manoeuvred out of the confined spaces to escape the deadly guns on the dam and the even deadlier trees on the hills. Then comes the long haul back to England.

As I circle overhead, the scene is calm and peaceful, but I am sober because the ghosts are with me and I have nothing but profound respect and admiration for those men who went into battle with such huge handicaps. Certainly, wars are still the same, but truly the quality has changed.

I fly at night over Germany and I learn the meaning of a Bomber's Moon. Our high-level patrols take me over the same territory visited by the Lancasters, Halifaxes and Stirlings thirty-five years ago. It is a fascinating sight. Whereas I have been used to the empty, gloomy blackness of the North Sea on my night flights from the UK, with only the lights of fishing fleets and oil rigs punctuating the blackness, here on the Continent the lights of the cities almost make night into day. Certainly, as I practise my night close formation manoeuvres, the other aircraft is lit up by the electric glow from below, so much so that I can read the lettering on his fuselage.

Below me stretches the Ruhr – target for tonight. Duisburg, Cologne, Essen, the marshalling yards at Hamm, Koblenz, Aachen and in the distance to the north, if I am high enough, the glow of Hamburg. It is one great illuminated daisy chain, each ocean of light being linked by the thin pencil glows of the autobahns. Today, the complex shouts 'industry', just as it did thirty-five years ago and here again, at 20,000 feet, the sky is filled with the ghost-riders of thousand-bomber raids. I see Me 110 fighters hanging like vampire bats against the yellow moon. I see waving searchlights and I see the dull red glow of heavy anti-aircraft fire. I see the blazing infernos of fire storms in the hearts of the cities below. I see bombers falling, trailing great long banners of flame, victims of the night-fighting marauders, Ju 88s, or even simply of a mid-air collision as hundreds of the machines converge haphazardly on the same spot, the same target marked by the Pathfinders, I see ...

I shake my head and tear myself back to the present from the night-dreams. The air is peaceful. The ghosts have fled. The stars above mingle with the lights below and I fly carefully on the instruments because disorientation comes very easily over here in such conditions – clear but with hazy stratus at all levels. The moon is full, but benevolent, its ridges and mountains shadowing the surface quite clearly, a yellow ball close enough to touch.

I redirect my gaze to the ground and puzzle for a minute over an inch-long object that is crawling across the black ground. It is a collection of very small lights, beads strung together. I realise that it is a train. Now and again the lights fade completely, only to reappear again and it takes me a second or two to deduce that it must have run through a tunnel. My memory is triggered along yet another track and I remember this hairy old pilot who visited the Squadron a few months back. He used to fly Mosquitos on night-intruder missions over Germany during the second half of the last war. His favourite sport, so he informed us, was train busting.

He would fly along some known railway line at low level and look out for the tell-tale glow as the boilers were stoked on a train otherwise blacked out for night travel. His target identified, he would then stalk the train, weaving and circling behind it at a slow speed until the train disappeared into a tunnel. His navigator having assured him that the tunnel was of sufficient length, he would then clean up his aircraft, accelerate round a turn and attack the tunnel entrance with his multiple cannon. The usual effect of such an onslaught of bullets was to cause the tunnel mouth to cave in. He would then rush at full speed up to the other end of the tunnel and carry out a similar attack, sealing off that end also and so (if all timings worked perfectly – which he admitted was rare) leaving the train buried beneath the mountain.

Now, as I look down at the express making its way cross country, I think – there's no way I could carry out such an attack in my Phantom. There's no way I could fly down a street and a lob a bomb through the windows of a particular building as the Mosquitos did. Yet again, I feel very humble sitting in the cockpit of my multi-million pound jet fighter.

As I fly my lonely Tacan route, high above the surface, I can forgive myself for indulging in idle fantasy because the environment over Europe at night is conducive to just that. I fly in my Phantom, a fantasy itself to me as I cruise along in the night sky, a faint distant thunder to everyone but myself and my navigator sitting silently behind, the two of us suspended in space, held up by invisible forces. To be sure, the fantasies run riot at times like this and then I feel I will soon wake up from this dream and find myself in another world.

Dave and I are selected to represent RAF Germany (Phantoms) at the Strike Command Tactical Fighter Meet up at Leuchars, Scotland. Dave, like myself, is no stranger to Leuchars. A Scotsman himself, he used to fly Lightnings out of Leuchars before transferring to Phantoms and an exchange posting with the Royal Navy on *Ark Royal*. He has a never-ending fund of hairy stories to relate concerning the trials and tribulations of operating off the pitching deck of a carrier out in the middle of the ocean, far from land.

Chris, his fellow 'crab' on board the *Ark* also has his supply of tales of night deck landings, or rather night deck 'bolters' that result in minimum fuel diversions to strange runways at Gibraltar or Rio de Janeiro. They love to recall cruises to Barbados, Miami Beach and 'Cecile Field, Florida'. Well, this is usually the excuse for John to start telling us about his Hunter days, 'wadi-bashing' out in the Oman desert, or for Dinger to reminisce on his days flying Javelins from Singapore and Hong Kong. The stories are all invariably amusing and entertaining and the thought occurs to me that one day I shall sit down and put their little anecdotes on paper, because some of these people, both young and old, have really lived life to the full.

We fly up to Scotland on a Thursday evening. Leuchars has to be my favourite base in the UK and I never stop going back at every opportunity. Perhaps it's something to do with the clear, fresh High-land air and the limitless visibility that prevails 95 per cent of the time. Perhaps it is the fact that I can get airborne, and, ten miles off the coast, go straight into the first combat split. Perhaps it is the fact that I can go straight from tower frequency direct to my operating frequency without the palaver of routeing through Clutch radar and Lippe radar and innumerable IFF squawk changes that is our lot in Germany. Maybe it is the fact that over the sea I can operate with freedom from 200 feet up to the 60,000-foot ceiling of my aeroplane without bouncing into an airliner on an airway. Over the land I do have to watch out for airways, but up in the hills, I can fly for half an hour and not see another solitary aeroplane. It is indeed free air-space which is naturally why they choose to hold the bi-annual Tac Fighter meet up here.

While I was at Leuchars in 1971 and ever since Phantoms had arrived there three years previously in 1968, not one aircraft had been lost from that base. But after I left, the airfield itself suffered a number of knocks at the hands of fate. A Navy Phantom pitches into the circuit to land, the pilot draws both throttles back to idle, but inadvertently goes through the shut-off detents and suffers dou-ble engine failure, both pilot and navigator eject and the Phantom plunges into the woods next to the northern taxiway … 43 Squadron practising for a four-ship Battle of Britain display; they go into a 'Canadian Break' manoeuvre; one pilot flicks and loses control and both of them are forced to eject; the Phantom crashes into a field near Arbroath to the north of the field … A Navy Phantom suffers a utility failure and comes into land, its hook dangling; it touches down, but somehow the hook bounces over the RHAG wire and it careers on down the runway, with no brakes, heading straight for a line of parked Victor tankers; the navigator decides he has had enough of this and pulls the ejection seat handle and departs the aircraft with a bang; the pilot stays with the aeroplane, nar-rowly misses the Victors and comes to a shuddering halt while his navigator floats down to the ground nearby … A Navy Phantom en-gages afterburners at the start of the take-off roll. There is a muffled thump from the engines, quite different from those of the 'burners lighting up; great sheets of flame cascade from the exhausts and blowholes; there has been a catastrophic failure of both engines; somebody coming in to land behind him sees all this and advises him to eject; he and his navigator do so forthwith, leaving the flaming wreck to trundle off the edge of the runway ... It is midwinter and a JP on 43 is carrying out a take-off; as he accelerates away, something malfunctions in the nosewheel steering mechanism and the Phantom lurches viciously and swings off the runway onto the hard, snow-packed ground, carving furrowed grooves and flinging mud everywhere. The navigator decides he doesn't like the look of this and ejects; the pilot hears the bang and decides maybe the nav knows something that he doesn't, and also decides to carry out a Martin-Baker departure; the two of them float down safely under their 'chutes.

All of these events occur within a few years of each other. The Tac Fighter Meet has an inauspicious start when this record is continued. A Naval officer gets airborne in his Phantom to practise a low-level aerobatics display. All is going well until he completes a derry turn and drops his wheels and flaps in preparation for making a low pass down the runway. Something goes horribly wrong. The aircraft starts sinking towards the threshold, but the power does not come on to arrest the sink. A crash is inevitable. It just misses the QRA sheds before crumpling into the ground and dissolving into a great ball of rolling flame, sickening to watch. Dave is standing watching. The navigator is his friend from *Ark Royal* days; we were talking to him in the bar the previous night. The navigator dies instantly in the inferno. By some miracle, the pilot is ejected and his seat bounces along the grass, shaving his legs to the bone as he decelerates. The 'chute does not deploy, but he is saved from death as the seat rotates and passes through a wall bottom first and comes to a halt on the other side. He survives, but we hear that he is paralysed and his memory is apparently gone.

Wreckage is strewn along the runway threshold and many of the aircraft arriving for the Meet are diverted and the airfield is closed for several hours. The wreckage and the ugly gouge in the earth will remain there for several days while the Board of Enquiry deliberates and it is there as a sobering reminder when we return from our missions to land, a morbid object of curiosity that drags our eyes away from the landing strip as we make our approaches. Even when the wreckage is finally cleared away into the hangar, a grim blackened scar remains (despite the efforts of the groundsmen) to remind us that this game we play can have tragic and sudden consequences.

However, nobody dwells on the event. Most of us have seen similar events before or experienced the loss of a good friend in a flying accident. So call it callousness or what you like, we retire to the bar and drink to the dead while laughing and joking. Life is too short to waste time in sorrowful regret. Life must go on, until it too comes to an end for each one of us. So, I fly CAP the next day and we bounce two Harriers up in the hills, Dave and I, and we engage in five minutes of thrilling combat, ducking and weaving round the cloud-topped hills, racing down one steep-sided valley in hot pursuit and pulling back savagely on the stick to cream up the slope on the other side as the Harriers wriggle to escape, bending low down against the rocky outcrop. At the back of my mind lurks the thought – one little mistake here and you're into the ground, but I persist until the navigator has managed to get a lock on the radar to confirm my missile launch.

Our main task (the RAFG Phantom element, that is) on this Meet is to develop Escort tactics for the Jaguars who are unfortunate enough not to carry any self-defence weaponry. So it is that we fly round the route with them to defend them against attacking fighers. The aim is that the escorts take the heat off the bombers by engaging the CAP fighters, thereby allowing the Jaguars to sneak off unnoticed.

The Operations men plan a mass raid on a simulated target in the north of England that houses different SAM installations. Six Jaguars of 14 Squadron, RAF Bruggen, are detailed for the strike. Four escorts are allocated to them. Dave and I will be fighter escorts. Two F4D 'Wild Weasels' will act as SAM Suppression, flying one minute ahead of the main formation.

The route meanders up through the Scottish Highlands to the west coast by Oban and Loch Ness, before running down past the Isle of Arran to re-enter the mainland north of Dumfries and Carlisle, then to attack the target, finally recovering to Leuchars via

St Abbs head. Anywhere along this route, we will be liable to get 'tapped' by defending fighters.

Well, Dave and I know the CAP positions because we were flying Air Defence missions only yesterday and we have the Air Defence CAP plan. So we know that four Phantoms of 43 Squadron will be CA Ping near Dumfries and four Lightnings of 5 Squadron, Binbrook will be lurking beneath their tanker overhead St Abbs head, ready to plunge downwards at the expected time of arrival of the strike force.

The aim is to get some 'interaction' as the planners euphemistically put it. To the rest of us, it seems like good ingredients for a movie entitled *Air Wars.*

Our ten aircraft head off in a great, wide-spread gaggle, the 'Wild Weasels' out ahead scanning for ground radars to attack with their Shrike missiles. Ten miles behind, I am sitting with the leading pair of Jaguars. In trail five miles behind is the second pair of Jaguars. These four are all carrying four 1,000-pound bombs, a weighty load that inevitably has to cut down manoeuvring performance. To this end, they fly at 480 knots, to maintain the margins. A further four miles behind are the last two Jaguars with Dave riding shotgun between them. I, in the vanguard, am supposed to use my pulse doppler radar for early warning of attacking fighters, but this is easier said than done, at low level in the Scottish hills.

As we enter the hills, to the west of Perth, the formation splits up and disappears, every man taking his own route down different valleys and ravines. This is the new style of tactical flying – the result of technical innovation. It is a far cry from the 'stick-search-and-report' tight, low arrow formations of Chivenor days years ago. Then, the wingmen had to rely on their leader for navigation, so wherever he went, they went.

Today it is different. The Jaguar has a sophisticated inertial navigator with moving map display. The pilot can see instantly where he is on the map and so he can devote much more time to looking out and getting down to some really low-level contour-flying. This, coupled with their relatively small size makes them very difficult to see. The end result is the opening of a whole new world of tactical freedom for the Jaguar pilot. Constraints on formation positions disappear and his operational outlook takes on a flexible air. But there are variations on the theme, and the UK Jaguar boys from Coltishall tend to fly a tighter formation at this Meet, more reminiscent of Chivenor days. The fact that one of their leaders, Cyd, is an instructor of mine from Chivenor days might have something to do with it.

But as far as escorting goes, this present formation is giving me a headache. At any one time, as we bend down great valleys or race across giant lochs (keeping to the edges), I have only one Jaguar in sight and it is a full time job keeping him visual as he merges into the background vegetation, vanishes, only to reappear again. Every now and again, there is a confluence of valleys and gorges, and the sky is suddenly full of aeroplanes as Jaguars criss-cross, weaving past each other, only to disappear again at different angles down other valleys. Then I have to latch onto the nearest Jaguar, whoever he may be and set off behind him once again. I started off flying formation on Black Lead. Only God knows who I am with now, but he is carrying bombs, so it must be one of the lead four. I have no idea where Dave is. We are supposed to keep track of each other with Air–Air Tacan, fine in flat terrain but impossible up here in the hills. However, we are all heading in the same general direction, so I hang on to the Jaguar ahead who is now flying extremely low, jinking and banking all the while, hugging the edges of the valleys, rolling over and pulling down past the ridges to reduce his skyline time to a minimum. Everyone knows we are approaching the first danger zone, in the relatively flat expanses surrounding the Blackwater Reservoir. We would love to detour round it, but the rules say that we must stay within ten miles of the nominated track so that 'interaction' might take place.

The Jaguars are hoping that by being so widely spread, the odds are that only one or two of them will be engaged. Today they have not reckoned with Steve, nicknamed 'AWACS'. Steve is the leader of the 29 Squadron Air Defence formation. He has been christened AWACS (after Boeing's Airborne Warning and Control System) because of his tactic of sitting over Loch Ness, picking up incoming raids on his radar and then directing his fellow Phantoms and the Lightnings on visual CAP far below in to the attack. From the heights, he shuttles his forces backwards and forwards as he detects the 'enemy' invasion on radar to cover the valley outlets until visual contact is made and combat joined. We learn from the subsequent debrief that he spots us coming in on the radar at some great range. The weather is on his side today, crystal clear with unlimited visibility. I do not wonder that the Air Force Selection Board places great store on visual acuity. The ability to spot small objects at extreme ranges is the fighter pilot's greatest gift. Good eyesight is a natural prerequisite but thereafter, with training and practice, it can be developed even further, because without 'eagle eyes' the would-be fighter pilot is wasting his time. What he doesn't see he can't shoot at.

Steve looks down from 10,000 feet and spies a solitary Jaguar sneaking unprotected round a hill. He plummets down like an avenging angel from 10,000 to 200 feet in seconds. He closes. Today has been declared guns' kill day. All the Phantoms have been fitted with gunsight recording cameras. We must close to inside 500 yards and deliver a one-second burst of cannon fire on the 'enemy's' fuselage, all on film, before a kill will be validated. Steve closes very rapidly and fires. The Jaguar doesn't even see him. Only on the debrief will he discover that he had been 'smoked'. As for the rest of us, we know nothing, until Dave shouts from the back – 'Cobra Lead to 2, there's a Phantom dropping in, in your area.'

It is Steve's lucky day; he barrel rolls off his target and hops into the next valley. He sees a shadow, tracks it for a moment and then picks up the owner of that shadow, another Jaguar, going hell for leather. It so happens that this is the Jaguar that I am escorting at the moment. We are running along the south of Blackwater Reservoir, in a steep-sided valley, the walls towering way above us. I am about a mile directly behind the Jaguar, Black 2 it turns out. On the other side of the valley is Black Lead.

As Steve crests over the ridge and drops into our valley, that is when Dave gives his warning cry. My navigator and I, we start checking six and sure enough, I see a Phantom coming over the top of me travelling very fast. I do not know it, but it is the AWACS man himself. He has called in reinforcements and they pitch in. They are all behind us, but as Mike, one of the Jaguar pilots flying in formation describes it – 'Suddenly everywhere Phantoms came tumbling down from the cliffs.' It now has to be every man for himself as Dave dives into the midst of the attackers to draw their attention. Their combat moves rapidly skywards, up to 20,000 feet.

But all this is happening way behind me. I call 'Black Lead, Buster', the signal for them to run out. In fact, Black Lead has already disappeared, diving down a convenient ravine that appeared on the right. Black 2 has no such escape route, he must continue to the end of the valley before dropping down and turning left into another loch-filled valley running at right angles to our present one. With his bomb load, he cannot hope to barrel upwards out of the valley and into the next before being overhauled. He must hug the valley floor and hope the attacker loses sight of him. I watch the attacker. He is pushing 600 knots as he closes, but I am not sure whether he has seen me. I am hoping that he will fly past me and present his tail pipes to my guns. In fact, I am dreaming because he has seen me all right. But his prime aim is to get to the bombers. These principles have been the same throughout the ages. So he makes a feint towards me, forcing me to go into a 5-G energy-dissipating break upwards. I reverse just in time to see him go blazing past, his afterburners as white as the sun above. I set off in hot pursuit but I am too late. The Jaguar ducks down into the next valley, the Phantom does the same and they both disappear, a shimmering haze marking their vanishing point. Ten seconds later I reach the same point, roll over and pull down into the valley below, the mossy rock-face and waterfall of the higher valley streaming past my canopy as I fall down to the loch, flatten out and rush forwards, but it is all over. The killing ground. Death has struck. Steve's machine suddenly arcs skywards, its task done, vortices streaming from the tips. He knows I am behind him. I follow him half-heartedly, zooming up to 7,000 feet. He is beginning to manoeuvre towards me. I remember the brief – stay with the Jaguars at all costs, avoid prolonged combat. I decide to disengage. To the north, high above us, I see dots diving and climbing – Dave, still hard at it. I imagine Steve will go across to help his comrades out, in which case Dave will have to look after himself and get out of it as best as he can – that's what we decided in the brief. So I have no qualms as I roll on my back and plummet down towards the earth.

I learn later that I made an error not harassing Steve there, for he struck lucky a third time and spotted Mike in his Jaguar trying to sneak round the battle without being seen. Mike's Jaguar carries no bombs, so he leads Steve a hectic dance across the lochs and trees and down the ravines, but once a Phantom is locked into your rear quarter, it's only a matter of time (if the pilot has any fighter spirit in him at all) before he closes 'In-Range' to deliver the killing burst, and so it was with Mike.

In the meantime, I look down, and just as Steve had done earlier, I spot a Jaguar hurtling across a brown rocky outcrop. I drop in behind him. He immediately lights his 'burners and starts jinking madly. He obviously thinks I am the devil returned to finish his business. I transmit – 'Jaguar with 'burners in, it's Cobra 2 behind you!'

His reheats immediately cut out and his course straightens. A laconic and sheepish 'Roger!' comes over the radio.

The big problem now is to regroup the formation and get the strike force together. The 'Wild Weasels' have been having an easy time of it, sailing peacefully ahead. They are now about five minutes in front of us. The hitherto silent radio erupts into cross-chat as we try to identify which aeroplane is flying alongside whom and by a succession of check-ins and wing waggling we manage to sort ourselves out into the correct order, although I am now mysteriously flying with the rear pair and Dave, his combat successfully terminated, has somehow managed to link up with Black 1 and 2 in the lead. However, infinite flexibility is the name of the game as we cruise down the relatively peaceful sea leg, running south down the west coast, past Oban, Arran and the Mull of Kintyre, scenic grandeur that I never cease to marvel at, no matter how many times I fly down there.

It is hot and sweaty in the cockpit. The air-conditioning is doing its usual poor job at low level of maintaining cooling air. We coast in and run towards Dumfries. The visibility is not so good in this part of the world. It is hazy and there are patches of thick cloud. I can imagine the 'mud movers' brightening up. This is their sort of weather.

The 'Wild Weasels' run smack into the next CAP. Everybody else alters course and leaves them to it, sneaking past in the murk. The Jaguars are rapidly approaching the IP for their run-in to the target. The plan is that the Phantom escort leaves them at this point and runs ahead sweeping down the route, three minutes ahead by the time the Jaguars have completed their attacks. We will then tie up the Lightnings while the Jags run for home.

Dave has already set off on his sweep, twenty miles ahead of us, although God knows what he's using for fuel. The first pairs of Jaguars are already running in to the target and I hear their short sharp transmissions as they check in, 'Over the IP' ... 'Thirty seconds' ... 'Splash! Out!' as the target is hit.

My two Jaguars, Black 5 and 6, reach the IP and turn starboard while I continue ahead on a north-easterly track. I have been craning my head looking for any other fighters around, but see nothing. I turn back and watch the Jaguars disappearing into the mist, just in time to see a Phantom crest a ridge and turn starboard in behind them.

'Black 5, Buster out; there's a bogey in your six o'clock, one mile!' The call is automatic as I haul back towards him. With 'burners lit and at light fuel weight we close fast on the other Phantom who is getting set to open fire on the Jaguar, although he is still out of range at about 700 yards. But there is a sixth sense inbred in fighter aircrew that sounds warning signals when all is not well. Talking to Mike in the bar that evening he discusses his encounter with Steve earlier, up in the hills. He says – 'Well, I was flying along quietly, by myself, when all of a sudden I got that funny prickly feeling – you know how it is – that tells you a mate is not alone in the skies. I knew there was somebody else around.' So he drops the wings, kicks the rudders and sees the ugly snout of a Phantom, airborne 'Jaws', sneaking up on him for a surprise kill.

Well, so it must be with this one and I have to congratulate him, because all of a sudden he lays on 5Gs and hauls off the Jaguar, ruining his own attack but also ruining mine. He and his nav, they have seen me and now they are bent on survival. Their break has destroyed my tracking solution and the gunsight throws its hands up in despair and drops to the bottom of the sighting glass as I follow them round the break.

I have to balloon slightly and yo-yo upwards, but even so, I slip to the outside of my opponent's turn and lose ground as he straightens, unloads his aircraft and smokes off to the north-west. I do not know it now, but his plan is to lure me towards the general area where his Number 2 should be so that the two of them can set upon me. Unfortunately, his Number 2 is not where he thought he was and never manages to reach the fight, so it will be a 1 v 1, me versus him, just the way I like it.

I check my fuel and decide I have three minutes in which to get a kill, so I set off after him. Now, at low level, Phantom versus Phantom, the two aircraft are pretty evenly matched as far as our performance is concerned. I have the slight edge because I am lighter on fuel, but even so, as we both race away at 300-odd feet … Something has to give, and on this occasion, it is the sound barrier. Even with tanks on, the Phantoms will exceed Mach 1 quite easily at low level such is the excess of thrust available, especially when light on fuel. In fact, chasing Buccaneers over populated land, I have to make a physical effort to check the onward rush of the beast. But here, in the remote Highlands, caution is thrown to the winds of combat as I push the throttles into the far left corner.

He too has engaged his afterburners and he stretches to 1,500 yards on me, three-quarters of a mile, much too far for a guns shot, but ideal for a Sidewinder missile shot, especially with that beautiful belching exhaust for the heat-seeking missile to home on to. I curse the exercise constraints that require me to close to 500 yards for a cannon shot, but if that's what they want …

The pressure instruments all flicker and revolve violently as we go supersonic. The aircraft is buffeting, but even at 300 feet it is still quite steady. I have no misgivings. Haven't the Americans flown it at 800 knots plus, below 100 feet during world record testing days? I'm only doing 670 knots, even if that does equate to Mach 1.05 today. The only thing that would upset my day right now would be a generator problem leading to a Stab Aug transient. (That happened to Dave, chasing Jaguars at 600 knots and 500 feet two days previously. It made his eyes water.) But I am not concerned with Ifs and Buts only with results, so I press on regardless. Our supersonic chase lasts thirty seconds, by which time I have closed to 1,000 yards, still too far. My opponent has been busy chatting to his Number 2 (it turns out) and has decided it is futile to rely on the cavalry coming to his rescue. In fact we have been flying away from his Number 2, not towards him. We are up in the barren hills to the north-west of Moffat. He has the opportunity to try and disengage up into the clouds or to try and lose me by flying down the valleys. The problem with going up into the clouds is trying to get back down below again when surrounded by big, hard hills. Besides, his pride dictates that he tries to shake me off his tail and forces me out ahead so that he can get a shot at me. He must try and reverse positions. Time is on his side because he has more fuel than I. However, having been trounced by 'AWACS' and his men I have no intention of going home just yet without a 'kill'. I am only going to take the easy way out and plunge up into the clouds if I think I am about to lose, and that thought does not enter my head.

He cuts his 'burners, flicks out the speedbrakes and breaks hard to starboard. I close rapidly, all right. Too rapidly. I stand no chance of getting my gunsight to bear, let alone tracking for one second, before I am inside 200 yards. I have also come back to idle-idle on the throttles with the speedbrakes clutching at the airstream in a vain effort to stop my closure. I fly through and immediately balloon upwards, the standard fighter tactic to counter an overshoot situation. I have been caught out by his attempt to reverse positions, a crude and basic manoeuvre. I pop into cloud, shove the stick forward and pop out again in time to see him reversing on my beam. His nose is coming on to me, his aircraft framed by the canvas backdrop of dirty green woods and dry brown scrubland, the river beds long exhausted. My mind races on to what my next move must be. My subconscious does the work, a computer scanning a memory bank of tapes (label – Air Combat Tricks) choosing and rejecting solutions. The debate is instant, the decision immediate as my muscles react on the controls. I must gamble as ever to outscissor him, so we shudder across each other's paths, 1,000 yards apart at the extremities, only feet at the closest point as we criss-cross, both engines at full power now as I slip down the back side of the drag curve. Because of the cloud above and the ground below, it is a flat, horizontal scissors and success will come from flying a perfectly timed reversal and taking the aeroplane down to the minimum controllable airspeed. As my speed falls I dump half-flap, and at the same time engage full AB. The Phantom hangs in the sky, balancing on jet thrust, as my opponent gradually slides in front of me, 100 yards, 200 ... I start my reversals a little earlier each time till I am in phase with him, turning at the same moment that he does, kicking the rudder to reverse the instant he does, forcing him ever further ahead.

It requires a great deal of confidence to operate the aircraft in these regimes, but I am happy because I have years of jet combat experience behind me. My time in Germany has given me months of daily combat practice in close proximity to the ground, and I know that there is no way that he, based in the UK, can have the same confidence. So I sit and wait for him to break out of the see-saw, to leap from the swing and run. Although he is now in front of me, the crossing rates are too great for me to bring the sight to bear. But if he stays in the scissors much longer, I will be able to track him through each reversal and then his days will be numbered. He is no beginner to this fighter game (he has many hours on Light-nings) and he realises he is losing this particular move so he picks the time to disengage, at the apogee of our oscillations, even though I am almost in the same orbit as he which must make the manoeu-vre fraught with danger.

He seeks the sanctuary of the clouds, for a second, reverses his turn while he's up there and plunges out of the cloud at a different angle and makes for a dried up 'wadi' creek. I have already antici-pated this as I retract the flaps (Phantom sinks soggily beneath me) and unload the aircraft to accelerate. A glance at the fuel gauge and I calculate I have thirty ... forty-five seconds at the most before I must disengage. When he reappears from the cloud, I am 700 yards behind. He flattens above the hard earth and we are back at 500 knots both mutually conserving fuel by staying out of 'burner. He jinks down one creek, comes to a fork and pulls hard to the left, up and over the small ridge. I am tied to his tail by a piece of string and so wherever he goes, I go, jerkily. The navigator calls out the range from the back seat, for he has managed to get a radar lock. '650 yards!' I switch the Telford gunsight camera on. My little fin-ger holds the reticle stiffness switch forward and the gunsight sits, glowing amber, trembling in anticipation before me. He is in my sights and I am following his random weaves. I ignore the rock wall flashing past my port wing-tip, I ignore the thatched shepherd's cottage that appears from nowhere in the barrenness. I ignore the wood leaning out from the hillside to my right, I ignore the flock of sheep that hurtle past my left intake. I ignore the parked car and the white faces of a family sitting round a picnic table in the mid-dle of nowhere, staring upwards. My finger flexes round the trigger, willing that toy in my gunsight to come closer, for the wing-tips to fill the 25-mil circle in my glowing gunsight. 'What's the fuel?' the navigator calls. I ignore him. I have already exceeded by self-imposed limit by ten seconds, but I have come a long way and now it is so near, but yet so far.

He decides to run for the clouds above and arcs skywards. I close the last hundred yards on the inside of his turn, quick and urgent. The pipper bounces on to his radome, holds stationary for an instant, and then runs steadily stitching through the twin cockpits, across the dorsal spine, wavering left and right across the wing roots, before dropping off the jetpipes. My bullets are photographic pulses. The only destruction that takes place is an electrical one on the coated surface of the 16-millimetre gun camera film. One and a half seconds, with my finger firmly on the trigger and the camera clicking busily away. Then he is through and gone, the angle-off building up as he arcs upwards to the right and then disappears into the cloud. My finger comes off the trigger the instant the pipper leaves his aircraft and the camera immediately clicks to a halt.

I half roll and pull to avoid going into the cloud, roll right way up again, and dive down a shallow creek, getting below the horizon line, weaving and ducking as I look behind me for his wingman who must surely be here by now. But all I see is a Phantom reappearing from the cloud and heading off in the opposite direction, my opponent no doubt going off to look for less troublesome prey.

The combat has lasted three and a half minutes. I can hear the Jaguars regrouping after their ground attack. Dave calls up that he has swept the area and there are no Lightnings in sight. Apparently they got mixed up with a four-ship of Buccaneers and they have all returned home as their tanker is long gone.

My fuel 'low level' light is on as I break into the circuit behind the Jaguars. I pray that none of them bursts a tyre on landing, but all is well as I jump over the charred heap still lying just off the threshold of Runway 09 and put my wheels onto the black asphalt. The sortie has lasted one hour ten minutes and I feel I have earned my pay.

I am rather galled when the cine debriefer refuses to confirm my kill. We measure the ranges on the screen and discover that in fact I opened fire at 550 yards which is fifty yards too much. He gives me a probable. This bugs me so much that, on the next sortie where

I am once more back on Air Defence, I bounce a 'Wild Weasel' and this time I make sure of the kill. The F4's wingtips are supposed to fit the inner, 25-mil circle on the gunsight at 500 yards. This time I have the 'Weasel's' twin jetpipes framed in that circle. ... As for the wingtips, well, they are out of sight. The kill is confirmed.

To be sure, Life goes on, but then so does Death. A few weeks after this chapter is completed our squadron QFI and his navigator, both friends of mine, take-off on an affiliation sortie with the Harriers who are flying from their bushy hides out on some simulated battlefield. Up in the forested hills, somewhere near the East German border, they intercept and the two forces engage.

No-one knows precisely what happens, but the one thing that is definite is the great mushroom of smoke as the Phantom flies into the ground, its pilot with one final desperate effort narrowly avoiding a German village. The lack of serious injury to the citizens on the ground is miraculous indeed, for the whole community is peppered with a shower of blazing engines, hurtling generators and the flying shrapnel of hot metal as the awful process of disintegration takes place. The pilot and navigator perish in the inferno, an instant death, both sudden and unexpected.

We are not to know it straightaway, but almost at the same moment in time, some few miles to the south of that spot, an uncanny and macabre coincidence is taking place as a Canadian major in his F104 also flies – fatally – into the ground. If we are the playthings of the Gods, then Fate has truly had sport this morning.

We cancel all flying for the rest of the day and retire to the bar patio where we sit in a circle and, in accordance with the age-old tradition, laugh, joke and drink toasts to our departed comrades while secretly trying to quell the uneasiness stirring within us.

18

....

Last Glance

Although it is mid-June, ostensibly midsummer, outside the world is dank. Heavy stratus cloaks the countryside and the drops fall from the grey heavens, a steady persistent drizzle that cuts the visibility down to a few thousand metres. I am sitting in the Alert shed, at the end of Wildenrath's runway, my feet propped up on a chair. I leaf through a back copy of *Playboy* magazine, marvelling at the pneumatic creatures therein. It is four in the afternoon and dusk has arrived prematurely, a companion to the sluggish front that is sitting over northern Europe and which has been with us for the past couple of days. Brian is fast asleep in the bedroom next door. All is quiet, apart from the metronomic ticking of the telebrief machine and the soft desultory chatter of the groundcrew playing 'Risk' in their sitting room next door to where I now sit. The whole universe is gripped with this soporific midwinter-in-midsummer gloom. I throw the magazine away, stand up and stretch bored limbs before turning to stare out of the window across the spaces.

On the airfield nothing stirs, for the squadrons have long since put their aircraft to bed for the night. Even the birds are on the ground, shivering miserably in their wet feathered skins. They too cannot believe that we are not in the middle of a December twilight as they huddle, those with no nests to go home to, in little silent groups beneath the dripping branches. The rabbits that normally populate the airfield by the hundred are nowhere to be seen either, as they have wisely burrowed away into their warm, dry homes in the earth, there to await the arrival of better times and finer days.

The world is in suspended animation, at a drowsy peace with itself, the hustle of life slowed for a while now that the fury of the jets has been stilled by Nature herself. I know that down in the Mess, in the bar, the lights will be bright, the chatter loud and the 'frosties' flowing as everyone gets down to the bonus of an early 'Happy Hour' that the weather has presented. But for me, on Battle Flight Alert, the lonely vigil must continue until early tomorrow morning when I can expect to be relieved. And so I am alone with my thoughts.

I open the door of the aircrew quarters and step outside into the damp chill, but only for a few moments as I hurry across the short space between my accommodation and the giant steel doors leading into the HAS. These doors are closed, sealing off another kind of beast that sleeps in its warm lair, isolated from the cold, living world by its concrete cocoon. I let myself into the warmth through an airlock set into the HAS door, clanging it shut behind me and operating the foot-long steel handle to seal myself in with the occupant of the shell.

The silence is even more complete in here, for the only active object at the moment is the INAS heater sitting on the ground beneath the left wing and staring at me with a baleful green eye as it pumps electrons inaudibly through a black lead plugged into a socket in the side of the aircraft, electrons that will find their way through the bowels of the machine and on into the innards of the Inertial Navigator. It is a fussy creature, that Inertial brain, its finely tuned cogs and gyroscopic wheels temperamental and complaining at the slightest hint of chill. Because the mother-machine cannot function efficiently unless the Inertial brain is ready to spring into instant action, so provisions have to be made, and that is why the Inertial sleeps with its eyes open. It is the only part of the mother-machine that does so as the whole body waits for the human touch that will bring it to life out of its nebulous limbo existence, waiting for the scramble to be called.

The Phantom sits squatly before me and we face one another in silent meditation. It is ten long years since that first glance and we have aged together, for better or worse, through thick and thin. Together we have stood on the river bank and watched the currents of time slip by, the winds of change blow as regular as the seasons. But even now as I look at the dark shape, it is as if those years had never passed at all. The feeling within me mirrors exactly those same feelings that ran through my mind when I first encountered this elusive machine at that airshow aeons ago. It is highly debatable whether this Phantom is a thing of beauty, but there is no doubt that it will remain a joy forever, and truly this must be so, for why else do I never tire of gazing at this collection of nuts, rivets and sheet metal? Why else has this spell hung over many Air Force heads throughout the world for so long? Why else is the name full of meaning to both the initiated and the uninitiated in things aeronautical? Why else would I be happy to spend the remainder of my flying life fighting my battles hand-in-hand with this ageing mistress, even when faced with the virgin new breeds that trail their cons across the modern skies?

The answers are as elusive, as ghostly as the name with which the machine has been christened, and as ever I fail to grasp the solution, my finger penetrates through the substance to meet thin air. It is not a question upon which the military mind has cause to dwell. That mind is more interested in the hard facts, hard as the four long, white-finned, pointed Sparrows, clinging remoras that live semi-recessed in the four corners of the broad, grey belly. Hard as the great steel bulk of the SUU 23A gun pod hanging like a limpet mine on the centreline station of that belly. Hard as the four snub-nosed Sidewinders clutched in pairs on the weapons' launch pylons, two on the left wing, two on the right. Hard as the two 375-gallon drop tanks, battleship-grey locked to chalky white carrier pylons, one on the left wing and one on the right. A veritable war load indeed, with festoons of red flags drawing attention to safety pins inserted here, there and everywhere to render temporarily safe warheads, arming circuits, launch pylons, jettison circuits, explosive release units. My military mind takes in chocks and overflow bins, ladders and pitot covers, fire extinguishers, the thick black python that snakes across the HAS floor, an umbilical link between aeroplane and drab green Houchin. I take in the domed vastness of the HAS itself, fluorescent floodlights casting their stark shadows, the winching gear at the far wall, the clamshell doors, hard, hardware all. Facts that the military mind can cling to in its search for reality, in its flight from the intangible questions that flit through the mind, will-o'-the-wisps that threaten to interfere with the hard-headed, rational business of military combat.

But wait. Let me pause for a minute, a second, to cast aside this cold, objective aspect of my nature, this preoccupation with factual description and analysis. Let me allow myself the luxury of subjective assessment, a rare and all too short luxury at times as we rush headlong into battle at supersonic speeds and in gravity-defying turns. So now, as I stand with hands in my flying-suit pockets casting my eyes over the assembled machinery, I can cause the extraneous, military, objects to fade away leaving me with nothing but a pure, clean-winged flying machine in which a man can attempt to find empathy with his aeroplane and thereafter to exist in harmony with his chosen three-dimensional environment, the air, his own body fused with the metallic one surrounding him.

Some people call this empathy in flying 'seat of the pants', but let me tell you what empathy means to me. Empathy means high-level combat manoeuvring and I have forced the F104 attacker to fly through my flight path, far out to my beam, and now I am reversing to press home my advantage for he is already preparing to make good his escape. But my machine is sadly lacking in performance at this instant, the wings clutching at the thin air, the speed bleeding away as the forces of drag take a grip, defeating the efforts of the mighty engines. Yet I dare not take my eyes off that dartlike silhouette of the 104 as it pulls upwards through the high-level cirrus into the sun, painting a dirty white streamer in its wake, a tenuous arrow clinging to the limits of my vision in the haze. I dare not lose sight or my hard work will all have been for naught. I dare not spare one second to look into the cockpit at the instruments to confirm my weakened state.

Empathy means I do not have to attempt any such thing. I can *feel* the state of affairs around me, I can *feel* my speed down to the last few knots, I can *feel* the energy-dissipating buffet and so I can feel my angle of attack down to the last few units. I have no need to look in at all as I push the stick forward to 'unload' my body, plucking it away from the high-drag boundaries, allowing my engines to exert their force to drive me into smoother, tighter air upon which my wings can gratefully seize. And then, in this ultimate moment, I feel my body growing, expanding, the power surging through my veins and muscles as the kinetic energy builds smoothly up to the levels I need to catapult myself upwards with a burst that drives me in a tight parabolic curve, arcing beneath his tail to bring my weapons to bear. Thus I am at one with my machine, at one with Nature, Man–Machine. It is an instinct born of experience.

And therein lies the clue, the solution to the hold this particular machine has on me, the reason why I have been hooked on this flying drug, a junkie riding his needle into space. Only in the F4 Phantom have I had the freedom, the power to indulge in my every Phantasy, the realisation of boyhood dreams, the manifestation of every whim and desire. I only have to think Speed, and I am at 600 knots in seconds. Think Height and I am gazing down from an eight-mile-high perch within one minute. Think Freedom and I am wrested away from a dank, grey world, cloudbase at 300 feet, through a brief shock of cloud to emerge into a golden blue world, another dimension, crystal clear for miles and miles. Think Space and I have this whole world to play in, to do as I wish with the machine at my command. Think Manoeuvre and I can whirl round tightly in a 6-G turn, a dizzy spiral that I can hold till I tire or the fuel expires, and when the esoteric business of pure flying is over, the aerobatic skylarking at an end, then I think Power. The power to wreck a city with a nuclear toss attack, the power to destroy giant airliners from long range, unseen and unheard, the power to lay waste to trains and troop convoys, tanks in the field, ships at sea even.

Yet if I flew Harriers, I could destroy tanks more easily. If I flew Jaguars, I could fly deeper penetrations into enemy territory to lay down my nuclear store more efficiently and accurately on the target. If I were a Lightning pilot, I could zoom to 40,000 feet in a shorter space of time. If I flew F104s, I could accelerate faster to 600 knots to win the low-level race. In my F16, I could pull 8-G and hold it for much longer in the tight-turning world of aerial combat. Flying an F14, I could destroy bombers at far greater ranges. In the F15, I could sustain supersonic speeds for much longer in the military thrust range. In my Jet Provost, I can perform far more satisfying and precise aerobatics. In my Buccaneer, I can fly greater distances at lower levels. Without a doubt, in their respective specialised fields, these are all superior machines.

But in my multi-role, multi-capable aeroplane I find the combination of all these qualities in such a balance as to make it (in my eyes) unbeatable. It is this overall capability to satisfy my will, knowing it is a Jack-of-all-Trades and master of most, that I am sure has attracted and held my attention over the years, even though I am called upon to exploit and practise only a small proportion of those roles and options.

Thus my thoughts return, as ever, to the military realities of life. I am not supposed to be here to have fun. The hooter could sound this instant and within minutes I would be boring off into the cloudy darkness to investigate intruders, attempting intercepts low down near the border, the Soviet SAMs waiting impatiently for me to step over the line as I chase my fleeting, evading target. That is a far cry from playing Sundance games up in the blue on a sunny day. It worries me not. I am paid to take the rough with the smooth. That just about sums up my contract. But ask me to exchange this job of flying for any other in the world and I would return a blank stare of amazement. You see, in my room is a book of verse. I quote:

> Nor law, nor duty bade me fight
> Nor public men, nor cheering crowds
> A lonely impulse of delight
> Drove to this tumult in the clouds.

Famous words indeed, and surely in the heart of every aviator, whether he knows it or not. But my own delight is tinged with a little sadness. In my briefcase lies a letter that spells the coming end to this affair, as is inevitable with all good things. My 'Tourex' date has been nominated and a posting is in the offing within the next few months. I am to leave the Phantom, maybe never to return. New worlds beckon, new horizons, new challenges, new skills of the air all waiting to be mastered. I am philosophical. Memories will linger, and when I leave, the Phantom will still be a mighty force in the inventory. But the ravages of time must surely take their toll, and who can tell what will reign supreme in the next decade. Yet I am assured that history repeats itself so I will look on with interest to see what will capture the airborne imagination of the next generation, to see what strange machines will prove unbendingly fascinating to my growing son. The King is dead, Long live the King …

I have grown cold in the silent HAS, lost in my thoughts. The brief attack of melancholy fades quickly as I stir myself and climb up the long ladder to peer into the cockpit, making sure the ground-crew have not changed the position of the straps and switches during their periodic servicing. All is normal. I reposition my helmet, balancing it on top of the ejection seat, and climb back down to check that my harness is still laid out strategically at the foot of the ladder ready for a rapid 'scramble'. I hear from rumour control that we are soon to lose this Houdini contraption in favour of a return to conventional seat straps, and that is welcome news.

I check the INAS heater to make sure it is delivering the correct amps and then I stroll round the bulk of the Phantom searching for any mysterious leaks that may have developed. I see nothing. A clean aeroplane, this particular one, not even the usual drops of hydraulic oil weeping from joints. Even the paintwork is glossy and shiny, the canopies spotlessly free from scratches and blemishes. I suddenly recall – this was the static display aeroplane for the Queen's Jubilee Review. No wonder.

I pause at the airlock door and look back at the aircraft, a slight smile on my lips. A mean, nasty-looking aeroplane to some, but not to me. To me, a tiger on a leash, the both of us wary friends with mutual, guarded respect, a partnership.

My navigator is awake and outside, calling to me that the dinner wagon has arrived. I climb through the door, back out into the chill, rain-filled darkness, and I operate the handle to seal the Phantom in the warmth inside.

Glossary

Other abbreviations and technical terms are explained in the text

AOA	Angle of attack
AB	Afterburner – a method of injecting fuel directly into the hot exhaust gases and igniting the whole to provide greatly improved thrust. Also known as 'reheats'
ACM	Air Combat Manoeuvres
ADIZ	Air Defence Identification Zone
DH	Direct Hit
GCI	Ground Controlled Interception
HAS	Hardened Aircraft Shelter
INAS	Inertial Navigation and Attack System – a method of employing finely balanced gyroscopes and accelerometers to provide attitude, navigational and ground attack information
IAF	Intercept Alert Force, also known as Battle Flight. The Nuclear Strike equivalent is QRA – Quick Reaction Alert
IFF	Identification Friend or Foe. The ground radar station 'interrogates' the IFF transponder equipment carried in the aircraft, and if the correct modes are being 'squawked' an identifying 'reply' is received
IP	Instructor Pilot
IRE	Instrument Rating Examiner (bane of our lives!)
JP	Junior Pilot – the nickname given to all new, inexperienced pilots on the Squadron
'Judy'	Transmitted by the fighter crew to the ground radar station, signifying that the crew has taken control of the intercept
MAD	Magnetic Anomaly Detector – a detection device used by maritime types in sub-hunting
MEZ	Missile Engagement Zone. Indicates the area on the

	ground defended by SAMs
Military thrust	The 'cold' power of engine operations, as opposed to afterburner thrust
NRL	Nav Rad Leader – the senior navigation officer on the Squadron
OCA	Officer Commanding A Flight – for administrative purposes the Squadron is split into two flights, A and B
PIO	Pilot Induced Oscillation – an aerodynamic porpoising phenomenon, dangerous if allowed to develop
PSP/PEC	Personal Survival Pack/Personal Equipment Connector
PWR	Passive Warning Receiver – special equipment carried on board the aircraft that enables the crew to detect hostile aircraft, mostly useful in guarding the tail and beam sectors where visibility is poorest. Also known as RWR – Radar Warning Receiver
Rad Alt	Radio Altimeter (as opposed to pressure or barometric altimeter) especially useful for low-level, high-speed work
RV	Rendezvous point – usually with tankers
SAM	Surface-to-Air Missile system
SCT	Staff Continuation Training
SOP	Standard Operating Procedures
STI	Special Technical Instruction – referring to modifications to the aircraft
TAPS	Terminal Approach Procedures – letdown charts
TCA	Track Crossing Angle (between fighter and target) – usually in reference to intercept manoeuvres
TCIC	'Thank Christ I'm covered' – not to be confused with TGIF – 'Thank God it's Friday'
TGT	Turbine Gas Temperature. Sometimes called JPT – Jet-pipe Temperature – although this measures different parameters
UHF	Ultra High Frequency radio
'Wire'	Hookwire or RHAG – Rotary Hydraulic Arrester Gear – a land version of the system employed on aircraft carriers

First glance—afterburners lit, a Phantom takes off at evening.

Phantoms in close formation over the Forth railway bridge.

'Fighting-Cock'.

A Phantom of 6 Squadron with some of its stores.

High level—a Russian 'Bear' turboprop reconnaissance/bomber intercepted by a 43 Squadron Phantom.

Low level—'A Tale of Two Buccs'. Buccaneers 'on the deck' off Beachy Head.

Formation flying—eight Phantoms at dawn.

Air-to-air refuelling—Phantoms hooked up to a Victor tanker.

Phantoms of 43 Squadron in formation over the sea.

By contrast, three Lightnings over the sea.

'Somewhere in Germany'—a Harrier returns to its camouflaged base.

Lead and wingman—Phantoms of 92 Squadron.

A Harrier strikes the dam.

A Jaguar at low level in the Highlands.

Phantom escort—two Phantoms (foreground) flanking two Jaguars.

Last glance—a Phantom at rest.

Printed in November 2023
by Rotomail Italia S.p.A., Vignate (MI) - Italy